To
Joan,

Enjoy the thrill that is
traveling.

Lynne Bodey Shuman

Travels with Time Share

EXTRAORDINARY ADVENTURES BY ORDINARY PEOPLE

Lynne Bodry Shuman

authorHOUSE®

AuthorHouse™
1663 Liberty Drive
Bloomington, IN 47403
www. authorhouse. com
Phone: 1-800-839-8640

First published by AuthorHouse   12/9/2011

ISBN: 978-1-4670-7632-6 (sc)
ISBN: 978-1-4670-7631-9 (hc)
ISBN: 978-1-4670-7630-2 (e)

Library of Congress Control Number: 2011960078

Printed in the United States of America

Any people depicted in stock imagery provided by Thinkstock are models,
and such images are being used for illustrative purposes only.
Certain stock imagery © Thinkstock.

This book is printed on acid-free paper.

Dedication

To my family and friends who inspired me to write this book.
You are my universe.

Contents

Foreword

The book you are about to read is really a love story. It is full of passion, action, delight and disappointment, happiness and heartache, angst and intrigue. It is the unfolding of a life of unforeseen adventures that started out to be simple, routine vacations, but turned into the stuff of which great memories are made.

In 1985, I was bequeathed a reasonable amount of unexpected money. At the time, I thought it was a fortune. I had just experienced a stunning divorce that had left me emotionally paralyzed and financially crippled. Although in married life I had been an elementary school teacher, I now took a menial job for minimum wage while I studied for a new degree that would, hopefully, take my life in a new direction. My freshly graduated high school son had chosen to enlist in the military instead of pursuing a long-planned college education. My daughter, still in high school, was struggling with the impact of the broken family situation as much as I.

The money should have gone into some sort of sensible account. Instead, I bought two weeks of time share. Ridiculous? Irresponsible? Short-sighted? Perhaps. I reasoned that this money would most likely be frittered away for underwear and grass seed, OR it could ensure me that no matter what life put before me for obstacles or opportunities, I and my children would always have a vacation. AND, being deeded weeks, my children would have an automatic inheritance. The thought was comforting and the prospect was exciting.

It was a couple of years before a vacation became a reality, but once I saw how easy it was to create, and how much difference it made in my ability to function productively, it began to happen with some regularity.

Since I had the choice to keep returning to the delightful destination where I had bought it, or exchanging it for something more exotic and unknown, I opted for the latter. In 1988, our journey began. I invite you to come along.

Cape Cod, Massachusetts-- 1988

I was sitting at my desk at work in Indiana when the phone call came. (By now, I had a real job as Executive Director of a not-for-profit art organization; my son was married, a new father and stationed in Berlin, Germany; and my daughter was off to her second year at university... so many changes in three years.) The call was from RCI.

An enthusiastic young man said, "It is time for you to have a vacation!"

My immediate reaction was, "Who are you and how did you know that?"

He was just doing his job. He could see by my record that I had not yet used my time share. The weeks were piling up in storage and I would lose them if I did not make plans.

RCI (Resort Condominiums International) is an association that holds time share weeks in storage, much as a bank holds deposits, and allows an owner to exchange their stored week for someone else's stored week at a different location.

Young man and I talked a bit about the possibilities... he wanted me to go to the Canary Islands... and, although they sounded intriguing, I knew I could not do that this year. This year I would have to go somewhere more financially feasible. Hmmmm.

I was raised in New England. My mom died of Alzheimers in '86. My dad was home in Connecticut, by himself. I wagered he would like a trip, too. What was available in the New England area? After much discussion, we settled on a townhouse on Cape Cod, in Falmouth, Mass. How cool is that? So I made the arrangements, called my dad to see how all this fit into his life, and finished the day feeling there really was a pot of gold at the end of the rainbow. Actually, he was quite excited at the prospect of my coming east and our having a week away from all that stressed us.

1

On Friday nights several of us met at Henry's, a local, historic, watering hole to wrap the week with a glass of white wine and maybe a tasty nosh. This Friday night I had something to talk about. My friend, Margaret, appeared soon and joined the rest of us. (Margaret was going through her divorce at the same time I was.) She looked frazzled.

"Long week?" I asked as she slid in next to me.

"Oh yeah! I sure could use a break."

"How would you like to go to the beach?" I asked. The look I received indicated she thought I had said the moon.

"No, really. I am going to New England for a vacation on Cape Cod. I am flying into Hartford. My dad is meeting me and we are spending a week at the beach. The townhouse sleeps six... there's plenty of room." I gave her the particulars. We had dinner and one by one people left for other assorted amusements.

Our lives were busy enough that we didn't communicate during the week, but Friday night came and once again several friends were gathered at the same favorite pub enjoying a glass of wine. Margaret was a little later this week. Soon, she was sitting with the assembled.

"How was your week?" I asked.

"Long." She answered.

"Did you give any thought to Cape Cod?" I inquired.

"I have the seat on the plane right next to you." She broke into a huge, happy grin. YAHOO! And so began a tradition of traveling together.

And what a glorious week it was. The weather was beautiful. The accommodations were superb! We did all the touristy things... saw the stately lighthouses, the weathered windmills, the indigenous cranberry bogs, ate great fried whole clams, climbed to the monument to the Pilgrims, strolled the shell-strewn beaches. We had a glorious day at Martha's Vineyard. Had lunch right on the beach at the Black Dog... best clam chowder in the world! Walked among the colorful Gingerbread Houses at the Methodist Campground. Got a little sunburned. Enjoyed the breezy ferry ride.

One day we drove through Camp Edwards -- my dad had been stationed there during WWII as a young Army Captain about to go overseas. Most of the post was gone by now. As we drove, he pointed out where this building had been and that building had been. I gave him my camera to take some photos. (He had photo albums from those days full of black and white pictures of a much younger family.) He was understandably pensive on the drive back to the condo.

One evening we had dinner at the Coonamessett Inn. Great atmosphere! Great food! And a dance floor... and a pianist who played wonderful melodies from the '40s during dinner. Between courses, my dad and I danced to the music of his early adult life... Arlen, Warren, Mercer, Porter, Carmichael.

Nostalgia just couldn't let music like that go to waste. In fact, I remember as a very young child watching my parents dance to this same music at the Officer's Club on post... my dad looking dashing in his smart dress uniform with the shiny brass buttons and my mom looking elegant in a white jersey dress with shoulder pads, a sweetheart neckline and an overall pattern of huge deep red and royal blue roses... gliding blissfully over the dance floor.

But, the highlight of the week, at least for me, was the whale watch. We had called almost daily to see if the boats would be going out on the ocean. Being May, the weather had been marginal for the open sea. By the end of the week, the weather had cleared. We checked in at Hyannis. They were sailing, but by the time we got there the wind had shifted and they had changed their plan. Now they were not going to go out on the turbulent ocean. They called the Whale Watch company in Provincetown to see if the conditions were any better out there... they were. They would be having their whale watch today. We had to go all the way out to Provincetown, though -- a 75 minute drive on a two-lane road. We hoped we would make it in time... and wouldn't get a speeding ticket on the way. After finding our way to the end of the cape and a place to park, we were able to buy our tickets and board the Portuguese Princess. The 100 foot boat seemed quite large enough until we were right next to a humpback whale!

It was the most exciting thing! On board with us were members of the Center for Coastal Studies, a whale study group. They had just returned from studying Humpbacks in Hawaii. As we began to see whale activity, they gave us a running tutorial of what we were seeing... bubble net feeding, sounding, fluke flipping, flipper slapping... what a day! A few miles out, the boat secured anchor and the curious, playful whales came to investigate. For their enormous size, they are amazingly graceful animals.

At one point there was a very small white speck deep in the water, off the side of the boat. (We all moved closer to the rail.) A Coastal Study person said, "Watch that." So I did. The speck proceeded to get larger... And larger... AND LARGER ... and then WHOOSH! Right in front of us the whale leaped straight up, right out of the water. The white spot we had been tracking had been his underside as he rose from the bottom of the ocean to breach, almost within touching distance. We were all splashed with salty sea water and wondered how the whale had judged the distance from the side of the boat and why we were not all capsized... he had come from such a depth at such a speed and surfaced so amazingly close.

"How long can one watch a whale?" You ask. We had been told at the onset that these were wild animals and not predictable. That, in fact, the chances were high that we would not see any whales, but then, one never knows. So, when we saw more than one, and sometimes many whales cavorting with the grace and agility of Dolphins, the answer, for me, was "All day."

The whales played beside us long into our time to go home. The 3 ½ hour tour had to be extended until they became bored with us and moved on. The Captain could not start the motors and the rotors with the whales this close. The final number was three, but over the course of the day we had seen at least eight different Humpback Whales and calves. I want you to know... that was extraordinary! Even the study group was impressed.

We had a fantastic Atlantic shore dinner of seafood and salad in Provincetown in a restaurant poised on a pier extended into the harbor, and then started the long trip back to Falmouth. It had been worth every mile.

It was hard to say good-by to Falmouth and Cape Cod, but vacations do come to an end. We hugged my dad goodbye in Connecticut and Margaret and I flew back to the Midwest having had a FANTASTIC first timeshare vacation.

Europe –1989

A nother divorce in the family... just when we thought life was moving forward. My married son was still stationed in Berlin, Germany. My daughter, a recent college graduate, was home with me, again. One summer evening a knock at the front door revealed my daughter-in-law and 17 month old grandson, Morgan, born in Berlin. She announced she could not tolerate any more military existence and had come home to file for divorce.

Such conflicting emotions! The joy of finally meeting my only grandchild and the anguish of my son's grief. The next day, I phoned my son in Germany and asked if he wanted me to come? He was still in a daze. We decided it would be good for us to be together and weather this new storm.

I was about to finish the second semester of summer school and would have three weeks off before fall semester began. We implored my ex-husband to fund our daughter's trip so my children and I could all be together – for the first time in six years. He complied.

Another Friday night at our favorite watering hole found me sharing the plan with Margaret. Why didn't we make it a party and couldn't she come along, too. While she said she couldn't be gone for three weeks, she might be able to get away for two. And so it was.

My daughter, Amy, and I flew Pan American Airlines from Chicago through JFK, to Berlin, Germany, for a week with my son before we all left for two weeks in Europe. One of those weeks we would spend in the Swiss Alps in a timeshare accommodation.

The flight was long, with a layover and plane change in New York. At J. F. K. my daughter entertained three small, restless children by juggling hacky sacks and working sock puppets while their frazzled mother tended to her fussing infant. The children were delighted. The mother was grateful. I was proud.

My son, Jay, met us at the Tegel Airport in Berlin. Customs was a simple process for us – our bags made it. We had coffee in the airport café before driving through Berlin on the autobahn to his apartment in the American Sector on Lloyd G. Wells in Zehlendorf District where we would spend the week. He still had to marshal the paperwork needed for him to take leave for two weeks.

Berlin was delightful. Although a walled city (and the wall was right around the corner from Jay's apartment ... shiver) we had full freedom to take the u-bahn (underground train), s-bahn (surface train) and buses wherever we wanted to go within West Berlin.

When World War II ended in 1945, the city of Berlin, Germany, was divided between the British, French, and United States in the west and the Soviet Union in the East. By 1946, a pass was required for people to travel from East Berlin to West Berlin. By 1948, two separate currencies had been established. By 1957, all travel from East Berlin to West Berlin was prohibited. And by August, 1961, the Soviets were so adamant about their separation, they built a wall isolating their sector from the western allies' sectors ... supposedly to protect their own, but in reality to keep everyone else out.

This nearly twelve foot high concrete wall was 96 miles around the perimeter of West Berlin... 23 miles of it in residential areas. In reality, it was two walls with 110 yards of "no man's land" between them. This corridor included 302 watch towers containing young sentinels with machine guns and was called "The Death Strip." Over the course of its existence 192 people were killed trying to cross into West Berlin and more than 200 were injured. It is said more than 5,000 people attempted to escape over the wall. When we visited in August, 1989, things were relatively quiet, even though two years before President Ronald Reagan had implored Soviet Premier Gorbachev to "tear down this wall."

West Berlin was under the protection of the allied forces. My son was a Military Police Officer who worked with other police officers from Britain, France, and West Germany. Remember that West Berlin was essentially an island of freedom within the borders of communist East Germany, a good seventy miles away from West Germany.

While Jay worked, Amy and I toured the city. We discovered the Museumdorf Duppel, a reconstructed 13th century village much akin to our Sturbridge Village... only older, much older. Our only drawback was the language barrier. All signs and brochures were in German and even with three years of high school German, Amy's vocabulary didn't include much about ancient villages. After our visit, Amy and I walked to nearby Potsdamer Strasse to the Sparrow's Nest Restaurant for dinner. We had a raw herring salad, which was delicious… and, of course, a Weissen. (We learned early that German food portions are generous enough to share and Weissen is the beer of local choice.)

Another day, we found the famous Berlin zoo… an absolute delight. Right downtown off of the Kurfurstendamm (Ku'damm for short… a main thoroughfare). We had a grand afternoon searching for the Ibis and the Ibex… couldn't remember which was which, off hand… and watching the baby elephants play. Now, that was especially fun for us. Although they were in a large open enclosure with their mothers, the much smaller replicas rolled around on the ground like kittens and enjoyed blowing dust on themselves and each other. They were very Disneyesque. So cute.

Nearby was a small group of observers with distinctively posh English accents. We were close enough to overhear their conversation.

"Ah yes, baby elephants." Said one. "Charlie… you remember Charlie… Charlie was killed by baby elephants." And, with that, they walked on with no further explanation.

Amy and I couldn't help reacting to the incongruity… SO British.

We went on to the Tigers in their open environment – glad for the man-made separation from them. They were huge… and loud… and beautiful.

The Berlin Zoo also has a Giant Panda named Bao Bao. He was the first Panda I had seen in real life. It was really quite large… a magnificent animal, but far from an active animal. Unlike the frolicking baby elephants, he seemed content to park his paunch in the shade and strip his bamboo shoots for a tasty chew. (He faintly reminded me of great uncle Bill.) Another majestic animal was the Eastern Lowland gorilla with a stately silver back… not someone you want to mess with.

For lunch we had Currywurst and Wiessen at a food stand under the shade of an umbrella, then moved on in search of the Ibex. We finally found it. It is a goat… a lovely, graceful goat. The Berlin Zoo is the home of Siberian Ibex… not a species one sees every day. (We also found the Ibis… a bird… a lovely, long-legged, white bird.)

In the middle of the week, we ran errands with Jay. He had to go to Clay Compound (former Luftwaffe Headquarters) on more travel business. The Kaserne was very imposing grand and austere with very high ceilings, majestic marble columns, huge public areas, and cold granite surfaces. However, no photos were allowed here since it is a former SS complex. Jay signed us up for the Duty Train… our transportation out of Berlin to the western part of Germany. From there he took us to Andrews Barracks, his company's headquarters in Berlin. It was quite different from Clay Compound... friendlier. We then went on to Truman Plaza, the American Army's PX complex where we took time for a quick schnitzel und bier... gut bier, but not the best schnitzel in Germany.

Just about every town in Germany has its own brewery... mostly for local consumption. One of the popular beers is a weissen or wheat beer. Berlin has its own style of weissen, Berliner Weissen, which is served with grenadine. Remember the cardboard coasters with the company logos that are so collectable and are served with most beers? Well, in Berlin they, in fact, have a dual purpose. Besides being intended to go under the weeping glass, they are also to be put on top of the glass to keep out the bees. The red or green (rot oder grun) grenadine used to sweeten the lemony Weissen attracts tiny bees... which, if bitten or swallowed, are not a pleasant sensation.

That evening we drove to The Havel River near the Wannsee for dinner at the Wirtshaus. The setting was outside of a very Bavarian looking building... upper floor of ornately carved wood, with wooden balcony full of colorful flower boxes, lower floor of white stucco. The area was like a large park with tables and chairs and umbrellas. Local residents came with families and well-behaved dogs. (We saw this throughout Europe.) Amy and I had pork and kraut casseroles with bacon und potatoes... Delicious! Unlike any pork and kraut I have ever had – even my German mother-in-law's. Jay had a wonderful schnitzel and more good weissen. For dessert we had ein case kuchen und drei gobble (one cheese cake and three forks). The waiter seemed to not understand that we needed that many forks. Apparently, sharing dessert in Berlin is a rare occurrence.

After dinner, we walked along the edge of the Wannsee and saw Peacock Island. The Wannsee is an area in the westernmost Steglitz-Zehlendorf district of Berlin. It is basically an island itself, bordered by two lakes... the greater Wannsee and the lesser Wannsee... and the river Havel.

"Peacock Island" or Pfaueninsel is a separate island in the River Havel. In the late 17th century this island was called Kaninchenwerder, or "Rabbit Island", after a rabbit breeding station was set up by Elector Frederick William I of Brandenburg. In 1793, the Prussian king Frederick William II acquired the island for the Hohenzollern dynasty and had the Pfaueninsel castle built for him and his mistress Wilhelmine Enke. Today the island is the home of several colorful, free-ranging peacocks that can be readily seen from shore.

From there we drove to see the Glienicke Bridge, or the Freedom Bridge where, after WWII, prisoners were exchanged. It had linked Berlin and Potsdam, but in 1989 Potsdam was beyond the wall in East Germany and travel there was not allowed. The bridge was a bit haunting.

We walked up a path to a shrine from which we could see the Pfaueninsel castle on the south tip of the island. The Castle is not large, but its 4-story tall, white twin towers lend a stately appearance. The castle is now a museum of 18th century art and artifacts.

Back in the car, we drove to nearby Steinstucken… a postage stamp sized community of huge homes just beyond the wall. The buildings could almost be touched from where we were, you can get that close. When the wall was built, the community of Steinstucken was outside of the wall – in East Berlin-- but the children went to school inside the wall in West Berlin. A train track ran through the area. The children could walk along the track opening in the wall into West Berlin, catch their school bus and go to school. In 1972 a corridor was built to allow the school buses to enter the community to safely gather the children so they could attend school.

On Friday, we went downtown to see about Jay's Eurail Pass. A Eurail pass offers a passenger largely unlimited ability to travel on nearly all continental European railroads and some shipping lines at a fixed price per day of travel or travel within a certain number of days. The passes are available only to non-Europeans and the best prices are offered before you get to Europe. Amy and I had bought ours in the states at AAA. Although Jay had his own car in Berlin, we had decided rail would be the best way to get around Europe. We loved the idea of selecting a train, having it show up on time, deliver us to our next destination on time, and our not having to worry about traffic or parking.

From downtown we drove to the Tegel district where we enjoyed walking around Tegel Park. Berlin is full of green spaces – well maintained, well designed, well appointed parks.

Then, it was on to Lubars (the last surviving farm village) where we saw a young girl walking her dog along the village street. Not especially noteworthy… except, the dog had the handle end of the leash in his mouth. (I will walk myself, thank you very much.) It seemed to work for them.

Lubars was interestingly laid out. As you traveled along the street, you could see the fronts of the homes with small, well-kept yards. Behind the homes were not back yards, as we know them, but the farm acreage that belonged to the house. The acreage stretched out, long and narrow, back to either woods or river. The areas were individually fenced. Some fields held livestock, some looked as if they were planted with crops. Each house on the street was, in reality, its own mini-farm.

Leaving Lubars, we drove downtown to the Liberty Statue, Checkpoint Charlie and the wall, and Anhalter Bahnhoff... all memorable things to see. We did see the Brandenburg gate, but, of course, could not get close because of the wall. It was actually sandwiched between the East Berlin and West Berlin walls in the "Death Strip". Constructed in the 1780s, it was once a main entrance to the city of Berlin... its handsome boulevard leading to the palace of the Prussian kings. But now, it was not accessible to either tourists or residents.

That night we attended a local Volksfest in Steglitz district, near Jay's house, where we enjoyed brats, beer, music, and fun. This may be a wall defined city, but they know how to make the most of it.

Sunday was a special day for me. I was to go, all by myself, to the airport to meet Margaret. I first caught the bus at Jay's corner, then, at Mexico Platz, I caught the U-Bahn to downtown. (Mexico Platz is a public square – or in this case a semicircle-- where most of life happens... subways and buses provide transportation, markets provide groceries, brewhouses provide a meeting place for friends, refreshment and rest between buses... it is a busy place. Throughout the city there are several such squares.) On the Ku'damm (short for Kurfurstendamm Strasse ... remember the Zoo?), I caught another bus to the airport. The bus driver was very helpful. We conversed in his limited English and my, even more limited, German, but, in the end, I was duly deposited at the correct airline.

I eagerly awaited Margaret's plane. She was flying out of Chicago, with her second leg coming from Frankfurt. The plane finally landed. I kept watching for her to come through the doors... and watched, and watched... no Margaret. Hmmmm. Nearby, in the airport, was a USO office. I must have looked very needy upon entering... several people came to my rescue. They were all very helpful... giving me coffee while they tracked Margaret's movement on the computer. They learned that her original flight had been cancelled in Chicago. She never made it to Frankfurt. She had been put up in Chicago for the night and was scheduled to fly the next day. They gave me her new ETA info. I thanked them and reversed my itinerary on buses and U-bahns back to Jay's house... disappointed and just a bit concerned for Margaret's sake.

Monday, Amy went with me back to the airport to meet Margaret. She was to land in the early afternoon. We visited the Charlottenburg Schloss (that's German for castle) in the morning and learned that, just as in the

States, museums are closed on Monday. But, we were able to have lunch in the garden. Amy's grasp of the menu language did us well. We had a darling, young waiter about Amy's age. She tried her best German on him. He smiled appreciatively, but seemed less impressed than planned for. When she apologized by saying in German, "My German isn't very good." He readily agreed.

On to the airport. Margaret's plane was postponed three times. She finally arrived at 3:30PM ... without luggage. She and Amy stood in line for the allotted time at the appointed counter to give the proper information and Jay's address for its ultimate delivery. (Amy's German served them well in this endeavor.) About that time, Jay showed up... wondering just where we were and what was taking so long. We all piled into his little car and he whisked us off to his unit's softball game.

After the game, we had dinner in a casual restaurant in Steglitz district, near Jay's house. Jay had Cordon Bleu. Amy had a triple plate (a sampling of favorite German dishes). Margaret had schnitzel. I helped with bites from each. The portions were way more than generous.

When we arrived home, Margaret's bags were in the entrance to Jay's building. HURRAY! We only had one more day before we were to leave Berlin altogether. ... that was close. (Our best guess was that her luggage actually preceded her arriving in Berlin.)

On Tuesday, we all took the u-bahn downtown. Our first stop was the Europa Center... spectacular! Located on the Breitscheidplatz, it has a beautiful, cascading fountain (World Fountain) on the outside and a huge water clock several stories high on the inside.

The World Fountain was built in 1983 and is the center of a sunken square directly in front of the Europa Center. Its contemporary hemispherical design of red granite and bronze is an architectural contrast to the nearby blackened historic buildings of prewar Berlin. It is the site of many street artists and entertainers and a favorite meeting place for friends.

The three-story clock inside the Europa Center is called "The Clock of Flowing Time." Its neon green liquid starts at the top story and tumbles downward to fill a small glass sphere every two minutes. When all thirty of the small spheres are full, they flow into a larger glass sphere which denotes an hour. There are twelve hour spheres in the clock. One tells the time by counting the hour spheres and the minute spheres and then determining AM or PM by knowing if it is daylight outside. The building is replete with shops and restaurants, exhibits and events... a bustling building.

Very near the Europa Center is the aged Kaiser Wilhelm Church bombed out ruins from WWII – a grim reminder of the past juxtaposed with the new construction for the future.

We bought caviar and crackers to take on the duty train at the Ka De Wa (Kaufhaus des Westins) pronounced "kah dey vey". This is a huge department store on the Ku'damm. (It is the largest department store on the continent—second in Europe only to Harrods in London.) The entire sixth floor is nothing but food… the largest delicatessen I have ever seen. Jars of caviar were displayed in a barrel… about $1 per jar. We bought several and squirreled them away for the trip. Finally, we took the u-bahn back to Mexico Platz where we had one more Berliner Weissen before returning to Jay's apartment to prepare to leave Berlin.

One more thing before we go, however. We had to take Margaret for a walk around the corner. We walked past the garden plots owned and maintained by people who lived downtown and only had window box gardens. On the weekends, they would come out to their garden plots where it was more open and cooler. They had small buildings – about the size of a garden shed-- where they stored chairs and barbecue grills and gardening tools. (Inside, they may have had cots for spending the weekend. We didn't see that.) They socialized with each other as long time neighbors and waved to passers-by. We waved back.

Around the corner (and it was not seen until you rounded the corner) was the wall. Margaret gave an audible gasp. To the right was a vertical stepway (not quite as severe as a ladder) to an observation platform. From that platform could be seen "No Man's Land" or "The Death Strip" and the boyish faces of the young sentinels with AK-47s in the watch tower. It produced an eerie feeling. It gave us a whole new appreciation of "land of the free and home of the brave."

Jay had arranged for us to leave Berlin by the "Duty Train." The Duty Train was first established in November, 1945, for the transportation of Allied troops to and from West Berlin after the city had been divided. It was used for this purpose until Germany's reunification in 1990.

This was a train like no other. It was painted black and only traveled at night. We arrived at the Berlin-Lichterfelde West depot at the designated time — around four o'clock in the afternoon — and sat in the waiting room with an assortment of travelers. We apprehensively had to surrender our passports and travel papers to the German officials who seemed to be in charge.

About sunset, we boarded the train—being ushered to our sleeper compartments and instructed to remain in them, unless, of course, nature called. We were shown the facilities, but, it was emphatic that we stay in our roomettes. Amy, Margaret, and I were in one. Jay was right next door, rooming with another young soldier. There were no amenities on the train. We had brought our food along (enough for the whole army) and shared it with Jay and his roommate.

The "couchette" was not very large. The couches along each wall were about 6 feet long and above the door, across the top of the cabin, was a loft about 7 feet long. Margaret and I each took a lower bench, Amy took the loft (she is about 6' tall and much younger). Jay is 6 foot 5. I am not sure how he slept that night.

At darkness, the train left the station, passing through an opening in the Berlin wall – quite slowly at first, then gaining some speed when we got out to the open countryside. We had a window, but after leaving the lights of the city, it was difficult to see in the darkness. I slept all night. Margaret did not. She said we were put on sidings several times to allow other trains to pass.

There were other reasons, as well, for our stopping. At one point, the train officials took all the papers and passports in their possession off the train into a station to be reviewed by the Soviets. At another point, the engines were changed on the train. The Soviets allowed only German locomotives to pull the Allied Duty Train across East German (communist) land.

All these delays would explain why it took all night to go from Berlin to Frankfurt on a train... twelve hours to travel a distance of about 300 miles.

The next morning, about daylight, we pulled into the Hauptbahnhof (main train station) in Frankfurt. We were relieved when we were handed back our passports (and Jay his papers) as we left the train. Amy wanted to go on to Bad Muenster for the day for a special event, so she caught a departing train. She would join us later in Garmisch. Jay, Margaret, and I left for the Kasern in Frankfurt. Jay had still more business to do there. We took the u-bahn from the train station and then walked a bit in the outlying residential areas. They were lovely. The tree-lined streets were clean and neat, the morning cool. Recycling bins lined the avenues in an orderly fashion. It was interesting to see. The houses were large and well maintained. Each house seemed to have a fence or shrub wall to give it some privacy from the public street... and an entrance for the car for off-street parking.

Jay accomplished his business and we backtracked to the Hauptbahnhauf. By this time, we were hungry. Would you believe it? There was a Wendy's in the train station... Yup. We had breakfast and checked schedules for trains leaving for Garmisch... our next destination.

When we first arrived at the train station, we had put all of our luggage into lockers. It was now time to retrieve them and prepare to leave. When we arrived so early in the morning, there were luggage carts everywhere… now, not so many. Margaret and I stayed by the lockers, hoping someone would relinquish one. Jay headed out into the train yards proper, thinking there could be some way out at the end of the platforms. While we waited, a little old lady (at least 80) came by using a luggage cart for a walker… no luggage, just a walker.

I said to Margaret, "Have you ever mugged an old lady?"

She replied, "Not yet."

About that time, Jay came around the corner with a luggage cart AND his sister! We were happy to see both. Apparently, when she got to Bad Muenster, the event she had gone to experience had been postponed to another date. So, she took a photo of the town in the rain, got on the next train, and returned to us.

Actually, as a mother, I was relieved. I was not sure about her trekking off by herself in a new country even if she had been here with her German class while in high school.

We boarded the train for Garmisch/Partenkirchen and looked forward to the next leg of our journey. It was 11:20 AM Since we had Eurail passes, we travelled in first class compartments. We did have to check that the car we were in was actually going to arrive in Garmisch. They have a system in Europe whereby cars get switched from train to train… I guess it helps with the efficiency of public transportation. Having purchased wurst brotchen (sausage bread) square, dry, landjaeger sausage and cheese at the depot, we were set for lunch in our compartment. We did buy coffee from the trolley that came by.

The scenery was absolutely breathtaking. We all agreed that this mode of transportation was the way to travel. Everyone was able to sit back and enjoy the gorgeous views.

The train arrived in Garmisch at 5:30 PM By the time we gathered ourselves, and assessed our location, we missed a public shuttle bus from the front of the depot. However, we were able to get a taxi to take us to the Abrams Hotel… a military R&R accommodation. The hotel was originally a WWII hospital. The rooms were large and quite nice, although Spartan… but the washroom was communal and located down the hall. The dining room served American food, but we chose to go exploring into town most evenings. We were within walking distance of downtown Garmisch.

We did have one slight mishap. When we arrived at the hotel, Amy realized that, somehow, she had inadvertently left the envelope with her travelers' checks on the train. She had put them in a pocket and they probably jumped out when she was pulling her Eurail Pass for the conductor. At any rate, we all missed the occurrence. As soon as we were aware of the problem, we called the American Express company. This was our first experience of this kind and, although we had been tutored in how easy it would be to redeem lost checks when we picked up ours, we didn't expect to really need this information. They made it sound as though it happened all the time and the process would be painless. It was after business hours when we called the number provided and they disappointedly were not as lovely as we had anticipated in our stressful hour of need. However, the woman on the phone said she would try to get in touch with the local office and turn the issue over to them. We should be hearing from them soon, but she wasn't sure just when they might be reached. When we hung up, Amy was feeling somewhat less anxious, but not entirely. We shared the situation with the people at the front desk and told them we would be in the dining room having dinner, should the call come soon.

Not only did the call come through fairly quickly, but the local office also gave us amazing service. After determining the problem by phone, an elderly gentleman rode from the local office to the hotel on a bicycle (almost all up hill) and handed Amy DeutschMarks in cash for her loss at a better exchange rate than if we had waited until the office opened the next day. He said it was his pleasure, since we were guests in his country, and it was easier all the way around. We, of course, were delighted. We thanked him profusely in English and in German and would have hugged the man if we thought protocol would have allowed it. Amy found a new location to keep her currency.

Garmisch-Partenkirchen is a delightful mountain resort town in Bavaria, southern Germany.

Garmisch and Partenkirchen were separate towns for many centuries, and still maintain quite separate identities. The villages were located on the historic trade route between Vienna, Austria and Augsburg, Germany. Garmisch and Partenkirchen remained separate communities until their respective mayors were forced by Adolf Hitler to combine the two towns in 1935 in anticipation of the 1936 Winter Olympic games. These games were the first to feature alpine skiing. It is now a center for American Armed Forces to enjoy Relaxation and Recreation.

There are many restaurants in Garmisch with great food. At the foot of the hill from the Abrams Hotel was the Braustuberl. The front was yellow stucco with large windows. Across the front wall was a huge fresco of townspeople enjoying abundant food. Although it had lovely dining rooms inside, it also had a spacious, stone courtyard out front and the best Greek Salad in town.

Further down the street was the Husars Restaurant. Its exterior was gray stucco and the windows had green shutters. Where a real window did not exist architecturally, a faux window was realistically painted on for symmetry. Very convincing fresco work.

One evening, we walked to the Post Hotel. Built in the 1500s, it had been a coach stop and tavern for centuries. Post Hotels were built along the "Post Road", the route the mail traveled from town to town. The front of the three story hotel is a warm buff color with an inviting, sweeping, white, enclosed front porch where one may fine dine at tables with white cloths and linen napkins. We were seated in the alley... a delightful, cozy venue amongst the aged buildings... on rough hewn picnic tables. On the bountiful, Bavarian menu was Kasespaetzle... yup, mac and cheese... but not just any mac and cheese. This one started with carmelized onions, then added crumbled thick sliced bacon, and ended with the tastiest local cheese available. The noodle was akin to a Kluski noodle, and I am sure it was homemade on site. The bubbling, crusty delight was served in a hot cast iron skillet. (This is a dish I now prepare often at home. The cheese that comes closest to taste and texture is Havarti.)

I was impressed with the programs provided for our military and their families while in Garmisch... so much to do and at very affordable costs. (They even had children's programs so the parents could have time for adult interests.) We took advantage of as many as we could.

One day, we took the guided bus tour to Linderhof, King Ludwig II's hunting palace. It was amazing with its pools and formal gardens and ornate Moroccan House and Moorish Kiosk.

The smallest of Ludwig's castles, the exterior is faced with white stone. In front of the palace is a huge manmade pool surrounded by gardens and sculptures and walkways. In the center of the pool is a large sculpture of golden nymphs and maidens.

Throughout the 125 acre park are other buildings representing Ludwig's interests. The Moorish Kiosk, constructed for the 1867 International Exhibition in Paris, was purchased by Ludwig and moved to this site. The exterior of the Moorish Kiosk is decorated with gold leaf. The most lavish piece of furniture inside is the Peacock chair which resembles a luxuriant Moroccan throne.

The Moroccan House was built for the 1873 International Exhibition in Vienna. Again, it was purchased and relocated at Linderhof. Ludwig enjoyed entertaining in this exotic structure.

Ludwig II was a great friend and supporter of composer Richard Wagner. He had a grotto constructed as a tribute to Wagner's opera Tannhauser complete with an underground lake and ornate golden shell-boat. It is a sight well worth the visit.

Back on the motor coach, our journey took us next to Oberammergau, the site of the Passion Play which is performed every ten years. In the years 1632-33 the Bubonic Plague swept through the area claiming as many as twenty people per month. The residents of Oberammergau vowed that if God spared them from the effects of this deadly plague, they would produce a play every ten years thereafter for all time depicting the life and death of Jesus. After making the vow, deaths began to subside until there was only one death in the month of July, 1633. Rehearsals began post haste.

The Passion Play was first performed in 1634. This year (1989) was a year of rehearsals, not performances. However, we were taken on a tour of the theater, full of the hustle and bustle of volunteer townspeople. The next year of a Passion Play performance would be 1990.

The architecture in Oberammergau is stunning. The colorful, stuccoed buildings throughout the town are covered with fresco paintings depicting life from the 14th century. There was also a fast food restaurant in town where we ordered simple hamburgers... well, nearly fast food. They do enjoy a more relaxed pace there. Oh yes, and their own tasty, tangy, tawny catsup.

Our tour took us next to Ettal to the most spectacular Abbey out in the middle of the verdant countryside. It was created as a Benedictine Monastery in 1330 by the first King Ludwig. The interior looked like it was covered in marble, but it was all trompe l'oeil... it was really wood painted to look like marble... spectacular, none-the-less. The monks at the abbey make the most delicious liquor which can be purchased in the gift shop.

Moving on, we had one more stop at a woodcutter's shop (I don't think he knew Red Riding Hood) to see his amazing work of sculptures and intricate cuckoo clocks. Then, it was the scenic route through the rolling Austrian countryside back to Garmisch.

The rivers in this part of the world are remarkable. They come cascading rapidly down the mountainsides and their opaque shade of pale green makes them sparkle. Apparently, the unusual color is a result of local minerals in the water. No one seemed to know just what minerals --- possibly some copper. They were a striking color.

On Friday we took another motor coach tour to the legendary Neuschwanstein Castle in Schwangau near Fussen. How often we have seen pictures of this iconic castle (it is said to be the model for Disney's Sleeping Beauty's Castle and is featured in Ian Fleming's Chitty-Chitty Bang-Bang) but I never thought I would see it in person. Built in the mid 1800s, by King Ludwig II, it was his home only briefly. He moved into the unfinished castle in 1884 and died in 1886. The Gothic Revival castle, built to honor his friend, Richard Wagner, was erected high on a craggy hill... I remember the longgggg climb up to the entrance. It was spectacular. However, for all its homage and dedication to Wagner, the prolific composer never saw this beautiful structure... Wagner died in 1883.

Looking from the castle grounds down into the valley one can see the Schwansee (Swan Lake) and Hohenschwangau... Ludwig's mother's stately residence... far below, near the town of Schwangau.

Our bus took us into the town (past the buildings and grounds of Hohenschwangau) to have lunch at The Park Restaurant... a very American name, but it served very German fare. Amy had the most scrumptious schnitzel yet, Margaret had the hearty goulash soup, Jay had an herbaceous spaghetti Bolognese, and I had the traditional liver soup. We tasted around. All was so delicious! I think this has to go on my wish list of things to do one more time.

At lunch we shared a table with Angelica and Bob. A very interesting couple, she was from Germany, he was from England. They traveled a great deal around Europe and we were able to share many fascinating travel stories. Although Angelica was born in Germany, she was from the northern part of the country and confessed she was having trouble understanding the language in southern Germany... Bavaria, especially.

As the bus winded its way around the Bavarian backroads, I was intrigued by the unusual patterns of the evergreen trees along the hillsides. Seemingly a species indigenous to the area, the trees were quite tall, and full, with long branches angled sharply to the ground. As they stood close together, reminiscent of soldiers in review formation, their intertwining branches created a variegated forest green tapestry of eye-catching, herringbone patterns.

Weekend overbooking brought our stay at the Abrams Hotel to an end, so we found a Guesthouse in town for the remainder of our visit. (Our timeshare in Switzerland did not begin until the next week.)

Making the new arrangements had been fun. We had learned of this guesthouse from Angelica and Bob who were staying there. With their directions, Amy and I knocked on the substantial, reminiscently medieval, wooden door and were met by the proprietor, Frau Aichinger. She was the epitome of a tourist-related business owner... friendly and informative, but, all the while, just the tiniest bit wary of these unannounced Americans on her doorstep. Employing Amy's best German, we told her of our plight. Smiling, yet reserved, she said she had two rooms available for the time we needed them. (We must have passed the muster.) We prepaid her in Deutschmarks for two nights and two breakfasts and returned to share our good news with Jay and Margaret.

At 8:00 AM Saturday morning, we moved into Frau Aichinger's Guesthouse at 35 Fruhling Strasse (Spring Street) ... a delightful, Bavarian home with a wooden balcony full of flower boxes across the front, wooden top story above and stucco beneath. At 8:40 AM we caught the train for Augsburg. We let the Frau know we would be gone all day and back fairly late that evening.

Augsburg was a bonus. Having Eurail passes allowed us the freedom to make spontaneous choices. This was to be one of them. I am not sure we normally would have chosen to spend time in Augsburg, Germany's third oldest town, but, it turned out to be a joy.

Located on the convergence of the Lech and Wertach rivers, Augsburg was part of the Roman Empire for 400 years and later evolved as a center of commerce on the major trade route of the Middle Ages. Declared an Imperial Free City in 1276, Augsburg came to produce large quantities of woven goods for the trade market. In more modern times, the industrial revolution further developed Augsburg's textile industry.

The wonderful thing about traveling by train in Europe is the "i". At every train depot there is an information building with a big blue "i" on top. Since it can be readily seen as the train arrives, we looked for it each time. This is where one gets lists of lodging, restaurants, transportation information, shopping directions, event schedules, etc., and it is manned by lovely people, eager to be helpful. It is very valuable to the traveler.

After stopping at the "I" to get information about Augsburg, as well as a map of the town, we decided to walk the alt stadt (old town) within the ancient Roman walls to visit the Kaiser Wilhelm Museum. This museum, and the church in downtown Berlin, are dedicated to the first Kaiser Wilhelm. As King of Prussia, he became the first Kaiser (or Emperor) of a United Germany, reigning from 1871 – 1888.

The second Kaiser Wilhelm (grandson of Queen Victoria) was emperor from 1888-1918. He abdicated the throne at the end of World War I. The name Kaiser Wilhelm is associated with many buildings and monuments throughout Germany.

The museum, not hidden, yet not easy to find, was on a very narrow, winding, cobblestone street that we in America would mistake for a walking mall. It was a regular street with traffic to dodge... no sidewalks, here. (If you closed your eyes, you could readily imagine a coach and four rumbling'round the bend.) The entrance doors opened right onto the street.

We went inside. Now, I am a museum professional. By that I mean, I am a not-for-profit administrator who, sometimes, manages a museum. But, being a museum professional may be more of a burden than a blessing. In my case, as we walked through the rooms which held artifacts from the 11th century, I had such appreciation for the workmanship and the working conditions of the artisans that I could not absorb very much. The hand-hammered wrought iron work on exhibit was as delicate as fine silk lace. By the third room, I had hit an emotional wall. My mental receptors had shut down. My feet would not move. Now, this museum had four floors of display space built around a central courtyard. It was extensive. I'm not sure just how many exhibit rooms there were to be seen, but I knew I could go no further.

OK. Now, a severe talking-to was in order. If I was going to be able to enjoy one more artifact, I was going to have to separate the physical item from all that I knew about its provenance. I was only going to be able to look at it and say, "Isn't it pretty? Isn't it nice"... no more and keep moving. And thus, I was able to continue the tour and see some of the most outstanding examples of china, glassware, tapestries, furniture, and ironwork from the early artisans of the area. The laborers did not live in the same conditions or have the same means as those who would own these beautiful items, yet, they produced wares of incomparable quality. They did not have the tools or technology we have access to today, yet their work was finer and has lasted longer. Hmmmm.

After the Kaiser Wilhelm Museum we moved on to visit St. Anne's Church (Carmelite Monastery built in 1321) with its amazing frescoes and Martin Luther museum. In 1518, Martin Luther stayed at this monastery before his excommunication from the Catholic Church. Originally Roman Catholic, St. Anne's has been a Lutheran church since 1545.

All too soon, the day was disappearing and we said "Good Bye" to Augsburg, went back to the hauptbahnhof and caught the next train for Munich.

What can I tell you about Munich? You must go there. I can tell you that we did not leave enough time in the schedule to thoroughly enjoy this city. It has to go back on the wish list.

We were informed at the "i" that the Glockenspiel in Marianplatz sounded at 11:00 AM and noon (We had missed that!) and at 5:00 PM (We would make a point to see that one.) So we set our schedule and headed for the U-Bahn to see as much as we could in the few hours we had. Our first stop was the Lowenbrauhaus... one of the noted bier gartens in town. It was everything the stories say... Frauleins in dirndls carrying several steins of beer in each hand, wonderful architecture, rousing music. And, it was cool inside.

Refreshed, we walked to Mozart's home and stood in awe. (Mozart made many trips to Munich and lived here while in town.) All of the architecture in these German towns is spectacular. Again, the thought of the tools available and the amount of labor needed in centuries gone by... structures often took decades to build... it boggles the mind.

Tempus was fugiting, so we worked our way back to Marienplatz. While we ate our vendor food, we sat on the platz pavement (along with dozens of other tourists) and listened to the street performers playing an assortment of musical instruments. It was delightful. At 5:00 sharp, the Glockenspiel went into motion.

Picture a five story Gothic building with a 260 foot Gothic tower. On the front of the tower is a two story protruding, bowed, open balcony. The center-seamed doors on the left side of the balcony open concurrently and two levels of life-sized figures dance out and about to the tunes of the carillon and then disappear on the right side. As part of the construction of the new Rathaus in 1908, each level of the mechanical Glockenspiel now simultaneously tells two entirely different stories from the history of Munich's 16th century. The Glockenspiel consists of 43 carillon bells and 32 life size figures. It even has a joust with horses! Now, that's a clock!

I don't remember how long it played... 10 to 15 minutes... it didn't seem long enough. But, it was sensational! As it played, the world on and near Marienplatz came to a standstill.

Completely in an awed stupor, we worked our way back to the hauptbahnhof and caught the evening train for Garmisch.

Our late arrival found keys in an envelope at the front door. Everyone else had retired. We let ourselves in. The entry door opened on the central hallway and it was dark inside. Our rooms were on the second floor. We found our way to the light switch and started up the stairs. Ooops. The light was on a timer. We couldn't get all the way up the stairs before the light went out... SO. one of us stayed at the bottom and manned the light switch until all could get to the second floor and into their rooms. That was new and exciting. (The next morning, we found the hot water in the shower was also on a timer.) Oh well, small price to pay for otherwise comfortable accommodations. The beds were covered with Eiderdown quilts. Now, that is comfort! (Note to self-- Must get one of these for home.)

Sunday is truly a day of rest in Garmisch – no shopping today, all shops are closed. We started the day in the Fruhstuck Zimmer – a charming breakfast room with hand carved furniture, a colorful, glaze-tiled corner stove, and much morning sunlight coming through the shiny rustic windows. To our delight, Bob and Angelica were seated at our table for breakfast. We had brot, medium boiled eggs under a quilted cozy, Quark (a German cream cheese with an attitude... delicious), jellies, jams, butter, wurst in a tin, kaffee... so delectable!

Our egg allotment was one per person. The men seemed unaware of that and had eaten two, leaving us short for the late arrivals. We had animated discussion about how to receive delivery of more eggs. It was reasoned that since she had expected each of us to eat only one egg, perhaps we should ask for only one more egg. It was then cavalierly suggested that I be the person to go to the kitchen and request them from the Frau. Hoping I would be excused from such a task, I pleaded ignorance of the German language (and our hostess did not speak English). However, my begging fell on deaf ears. Between Amy and Angelica, I was tutored in the correct sentence structure for our request. Apprehensively, but with a sense of adventure, I found my way to the kitchen and faced the Frau.

"Noch ein mal ei, bitte." I said with all courage, grace, humility, and sense of pride. She gave me that look of disbelief...

"Ein mal ei?" She repeated. I felt the confidence escaping... perhaps they had come from the golden goose.

"Ja, bitte." I replied.

She turned to the big black stove and I returned to the breakfast room. We chatted with uncertainty while we waited to see what would be delivered. A few minutes later, she appeared bearing one more egg. Our last arrival gobbled it up.

I was now close to giddy. I had actually ordered one more egg in German and it had actually been delivered to the table. O. K., so I had group help, but my sense of achievement was becoming dangerous. Perhaps, with more tutoring, I could be even more helpful. With much more convivial conversation, breakfast lasted until noon.

In the afternoon, Amy napped, Jay read, Margaret and I went to the Kure Park for Schwartzwald Torte und Kaffee und music by Strauss. The park was the site of an afternoon live concert by local musicians. People came with their families, their blankets, their picnic baskets, and their pets. They spread out on the spacious grounds and enjoyed the leisure of a summer afternoon. Margaret and I, having none of the above, chose a table and chairs on the deck of the nearby Kaffeehaus. The music was fantastic (what could be different with all those strings?) The food, eaten slowly and savored lingeringly, was equally as good. After the concert we enjoyed the scenic walk back to Fruhling Strasse.

In the evening, we realized that we could not decide on one last place to have dinner, so we fashioned a progressive dinner throughout the town. We started at the Braustuburl with that wonderful Greek Salad. We ate it out on the front stone courtyard. As we ate, we were aware of the sounds of cowbells... really? ? ?... and they are getting closer.??? Street traffic took on the air of being just a bit frantic. As we watched, an entire random gathering of wandering cows came into view. They were alone... no one herding them – no humans, no dogs. At this time each day, they come down from the mountain meadows on their own to find their way down the middle of the busy city streets and one by one, peel off into the driveways of their own properties. Truly! They know which barn is theirs. (The houses along the streets have their own barns on the property... not out in the country, right in town.) In the morning, after milking, the owner slaps them on the rump to send them back to the pasture with their bovine buddies. Local traffic, even buses, respectfully negotiate and share the streets with them.

Well, we can now truthfully say, "We will be yours, 'til the cows come home." Who knew?

For the next course, we moved on to the Post Hotel for the scrumptious Kase Spaetzle, and, of course, ein bier. From there we walked to The Alpspitz for the most elegant Mushroom Soup and Trout. Bob and Angelica came in to join us for the rest of the evening.

When the trout came, it had been baked whole... yup, head and eyes and everything. We knew this was a culinary coup for a kitchen, but we weren't quite sure just how to approach its consumption. Jay was assigned the task of carving. He deftly severed the head and set it aside. Angelica asked if he was going to retrieve the cheeks. We collectively looked her way for further comment. "They are the most delicate and delicious part of the fish." She volunteered. So, not to be seen as completely obtuse, Jay searched for and surgically separated the cheeks from the head. Now, they were not very large… tenderloins about the size of a penny… so it wasn't feasible for everyone to have a taste. We collectively agreed that since Jay had done the work, so Jay should get the prize. He said they were very tasty. (In the face of the circumstances, could he say anything else?)

We finished dinner with a curled ribbon of white daikon radish. As the hour grew later, groups of men appeared wearing Lederhosen, colorful suspenders, and Alpine hats. They were the music ensembles who had been playing at the upscale restaurants around town and were now returning to enjoy their own dinners at their favorite spots. (We know how to pick restaurants.) It was quite an enjoyable evening.

Monday, August 21, 1989

I was appointed to call for a taxi at 5:45 AM (I had been scripted by Sunday's breakfast group on how to do this.) The issue, of course, was that I conveyed the time correctly and that the taxi came in the morning and not in the evening. We learned, however, that Garmisch lived by the military 24 hour clock, so the risk was slim… but still.

So, on the success of getting one more egg delivered to the breakfast table, I ordered a taxi to come to funfunddreisig Fruhling Strasse at funf und funfundvierzig in den morgen fur vierpersonen bis zum Bahnhof gehen. Bitte.

We waited outside in front of the guesthouse in the brisk predawn air, but left the front door ajar, just in case we had to return to make another phone call. The taxi came on time to 35 Spring Street at 5:45 in the morning to take four people to the train station… a Mercedes Benz sedan… into which we stuffed four strapping adults (two of which were over 6 feet tall) and all our luggage… oh yes, and my plentiful pride. The taxi actually did come… and, it actually took us to the train station.

(Footnote – after all that, the taxi driver spoke English… and, yes, we remembered to close and secure the front door of the guesthouse.)

We left Garmisch and headed for Switzerland (via Munich, Zurich, and Lausanne) at 6:30 AM In Munich, we purchased breakfast pastries and sandwiches for lunch in the Hauptbahnhof before catching our connection south to Switzerland.

For the first time traveling, we were separated on the train. I went into a compartment with room for only one more. I think Amy and Margaret were able to be together, and I saw Jay in the aisleway leaning against the window for awhile. Not sure where he ended up.

It was August, holiday time in Europe. The train was more than crowded. It surprised us that more cars were not added on to accommodate the increased number of travelers. As we crossed the border of each country, border guards entered the train to walk the aisles and randomly enter compartments to check passes and papers. As we crossed the border from Austria into Lichtenstein, the compartment I was in was chosen to be searched. I was singled out by a border guard. He issued a directive to me in German. Not knowing much German, I gave him my Eurail Pass. He did not seem happy about the gift. In the corner by the window sat a young woman. She had been reading a book whose cover title was in Italian. She was conversing with the man across from her in what sounded to be Polish or a Slavic tongue. Now, she said to me in perfect English, "They want to see your passport." I quickly dug down into my bosom and pulled up the small, zippered, soft cloth packet that hung around my neck and held my passport. Quickly retrieving it, I obediently handed it to the guard. He seemed pensive for a minute or two, gave me a long, searching gaze, mumbled something to the other German guard, and then handed it back to me without comment. I bewilderedly thanked him in English and also thanked the woman at the window. (With all those languages, she had to be from Switzerland.) Still wondering about the incident, I returned the document to its secret sachet and reinstated it securely in its hiding place.

The train was boarded one last time as we crossed from Lichtenstein into Switzerland, but our compartment was bypassed.

By the time we entered Switzerland, there were many questions arising as to why we were so closely scrutinized at every border crossing. We finally arrived at Lausanne where we changed trains. Consulting the time tables on the platform, we waited for a train which would take us around Lake Geneva (The Swiss Riviera) past Montreaux, Vevey, and Aigle to Bex (Bay). At Bex, we bought tickets for $5. 40 in Swiss Francs for the cog railway which took us straight up a craggy alp to the resort village of Villars-Sur-Ollon. I say "we." It was actually I who bought the tickets. We were in the French-speaking area of Switzerland, now, and I was the only one in our group who spoke any French – and it was rusty high-school French, at that. However, it seemed to work and in a spectacular climb, up and around and up and around and up (I swear I saw Heidi and her goats in the meadow on the far alp) in a rather rickety wooden train car, we clackity-clacked our way through the clouds to Villars.

There were no taxis readily available so I went into a shop to get directions to The Hotel Panorama where our timeshare accommodations would be. Again, in my best high school French I asked for information and I repeated and translated what I was told. They kept nodding their heads, "oui" affirming that I was getting it right.

"Cinq minutes?(I held up five fingers) Sous?(Unbelieving, I pointed down) Sous? A pied? (I pointed at my shoes) Oui, Merci. Au Revoir."

I went back outside and told the others, "We are a five minute walk to the hotel, but we have to go down."

We looked around to ascertain how we would accomplish that and saw a wooden stairway descending to a lower level street. That must be it. There was no one in sight to ask for confirmation, so we shouldered our luggage and confronted the flight of stairs. About five minutes down the street, we came to our hotel. Villars is built literally on the side of an alp. Our hotel lobby was on the lower level, but our fourth floor unit was on the level with the next street up. Interesting. Great for emergency exits.

As soon as we got into our rooms, we ran to turn on the television set. For the first time in two weeks, we were able to watch an English speaking TV channel. We wanted to find out about all the border guards at all the crossings. We were astounded to learn that the first, massive wave of emigrants was moving from the communist block behind the iron curtain in Czechoslovakia, down through Austria and back up into the freedom of West Germany. Each train passing through any of those or its bordering countries was being searched for defectors... and worse, yet, I was thought to be one. It was a time to be concerned. In the spring, Tiananmen Square had been a devastating example of what could happen when communism and democracy danced out of tune.

I reasoned that Margaret, Amy, and I could fly out of Geneva if we had to, but Jay still had to get back to Berlin in East Germany. All we could do was watch and assess and plan. We settled in and went to the dining room in the hotel for supper – mountain trout... without the head, local wine, and scrumptious desserts.

Villars is a ski resort area in the Bernese Alps. It is quintessentially Switzerland with its chalet style buildings overlooking the lush, green meadows and steep, craggy hillsides. Although it was August, Les Diablerets (the name of the mountain above us) was a glacier and still had snow...

people were still skiing. There were also several golf courses on our level for those who played golf. The village was full of shops, bakeries, galleries, and restaurants. And by taking the train, or bus, one could take day trips with ease to nearby towns and attractions.

In the morning, we had a big breakfast at the hotel. Our unit had a kitchenette… small, but large enough for our needs. Outside our alp-side glass door was a patio and a bit of lawn with a panoramic view of the stunningly picturesque Alps. (The hotel was truly aptly named.) The sight was breathtakingly spectacular. The air was crisp and cool. It was truly an idyllic place for morning coffee.

After breakfast we went 'splorin' to see just what this town had to offer. We cashed some traveller's checques at the Banque on the corner and admired a beautiful, white, Great Pyranees dog. We resisted the temptation to pet him, though. He looked affable enough, but his keeper—not so sure.

Early in my adult life, I had vowed that, if ever I was able to visit Switzerland, I would treat myself to a Swiss watch. Here was my opportunity. On the next corner was a jewelry store with the most attractive watches in the window. The prices? Not so much. I went in anyway. Inside the intimate shop the full selection of watch prices was more reasonable.

Chatting amiably (remember – high school French and this part of Switzerland has its own dialect) with the salesperson, we finally agreed that I should purchase the watch with the large face and readable numerals and the green alligator band. He rattled on about the warranty (I guess he thought I understood) and how much I was going to enjoy this precision timepiece. I smiled dutifully, handed him my VISA card and put the watch on my wrist. I was pleased.

When I got outside, I proudly showed my new purchase to my daughter. She said, "Mom, you can buy a Swatch at any corner drug store in the states."

Undaunted, I replied, "Oh yes, but I bought mine in Switzerland."

Nothing could bring me down from that. (By the way, I still wear the watch. It is on its fourth wrist band… which is not green – I never could get another green one – but it is still leather. I love it.)

From noon until two in the afternoon, Switzerland shuts down. It is nap time. School children go home for a long lunch, shops close. It gets a little dicey to get lunch until later. We left Villars on the bus for Montreaux, Lake Geneva, and the Chateau de Chillon.

The rock on which the Chateau e Chillon stands was a defense point for men of the Bronze Age and later by the Romans. The innermost structure dates back to the 11th century. It was added to, periodically, through the Bernese Period… roughly the late 16th century. From 1798, it has been under some mode of renovation and restoration. It is truly an amazing structure. They do offer tours in English to groups, if reserved ahead of time.

In Montreaux, we experienced our first dual sectioned buses… yup, almost a land train. We had boarded the bus as we would have boarded the bus at home… thinking we would pay the fare as we got on. Not so in Switzerland. Apparently, we should have purchased tickets ahead of time. The driver waved us on to the back… we would take care of the fare when we departed. As we discussed the situation among ourselves, an elderly man with white hair… a rather distinguished looking, well dressed gentleman… spoke up. He explained to us how the system worked. We asked what he thought would be the best way to rectify our error. He thought for a moment then reached into his pocket and pulled out his own multi-ride bus pass. He said there were enough rides left on this pass for all four of us to pay for this ride and at least one other. He was willing to relinquish his pass to us to make the transition easier. He could purchase another pass at any time. Feeling surprise and grateful relief we thanked him and paid him the correct amount for the ticket's remaining value just as we approached his stop. As he was leaving the bus, he identified himself as the former Swiss Ambassador from the United States under President Eisenhower.

I believe "speechless" is the word I am looking for.

We retraced our steps to Villars by bus this time. Traveling by bus gives a completely different view of the countryside than by cograil train. In Bex, we passed Salzbergwerk, a working salt mine where the public is allowed to take tours. We put it on our list of things to do.

That evening, we had dinner at Le Sporting, the restaurant on the street above and behind our hotel. Amy, a six foot tall, college graduate, was served Coca Cola in a Care-Bears glass. Not sure why, but we all had a good laugh. We met a lovely couple from Belgium who owned a chalet in Villars for the summer and wintered in Florida. (I wondered if they would like to adopt us.) Luckily, they spoke very good English and suffered my very marginal French.

On Wednesday morning, we shopped, bought food at the local market and patisserie. (My French was OK there… actually, they loved it when I would repeat their pronunciation… we got good service.) Then, we took the bus to Aigle to see another castle. From the bus station, we walked along the Rue de Jerusalem, a 13th century street to the Chateau D'Aigle. A stronghold in the 13th century, from 1798 until 1972 it was owned by the city and used as a prison. Restoration began in 1973 and is ongoing. It was incredible with its turrets and courtyards and huge wine cellar. We spent the rest of the afternoon within its aged walls.

It was our desire to be back in Villars before sunset… just because we were newcomers. We took the bus from Aigle up the winding roads to Villars enjoying every turn and vista. As we departed the bus and watched it pull away, Jay became aware that he was missing his wallet. Now, his wallet not only contained his currency for the remainder of his vacation, but also the formal documents that would readmit him to West Berlin.

We were momentarily immobilized trying to sort out our options. My thought was to enter the bus station and ask the stationmaster for help. We dashed into the station and approached the window. Now, remember that my French vocabulary is from the American high school class room. It obviously did not include too many words about emergencies in the Swiss Alps. The station master was not the most tolerant about listening to our plight.

Gratefully, also in the station were people who were. They graciously asked if they could be of assistance. We explained in English what the problem was. They translated to the station master our need for information about the bus. He then told them that the bus was through with its run for the day and was on its way back to the busbarn.

As soon as Jay heard that news, he bolted out the front door and began running down the street in the direction of the departing bus… now long out of sight.

We stayed to thank the interpreters for their help and discussed what to do next. It was decided that Amy and Margaret should go to the restaurant, Le Sporting, which would be on the route of Jay's return to town and sit at one of the outside tables. I would go to the hotel registration desk and see if we could get any assistance from that quarter. Remember, the year was 1989. None of us had cell phones, then.

The people at the hotel front desk were not anxious about the situation. When I asked if we should contact the local police department, they were quite negative. "No, no, no. This is not a matter for the police. There is only one bus. And they are only papers. Papers can be replaced."

I listened in disbelief. Did these people not know what was going on in the world nearby?

Dissatisfied and a bit disheartened, I took the elevator up to the fourth floor, exited out the back door of the hotel, climbed the short path up to the next street and headed for Le Sporting restaurant.

What a surprise when I arrived! There was Jay sitting on the patio with Margaret and Amy. AND he had his wallet. However, his right hand was red and swollen and he was cradling it for the pain.

I tried to ask our waitress for some ice cubes in a napkin, but, again... insufficient vocabulary.

Some people at a nearby table came to our rescue... glacons... ice cubes. The waitress disappeared to the kitchen and returned quickly with an entire pitcher of ice cubes and four napkins... serviettes. We wrapped Jay's hand with the icy compress and listened to his adventure.

He had chased the bus as far as the edge of town, but to no avail. In defeat and frustration, he had doubled up his fist and punched a wooden sign on the roadside that told of construction. Hoping that the pain did not indicate any broken bones, he stepped beyond the sign and there, parked by the side of a small roadside café, was the bus. The bus driver had stopped for a bit of day's-end refreshment before heading to the barn.

Jay approached the bus to assess all possibilities and found the door to be open. He simply boarded the bus, went straight to the back bench seat where he had been travelling and there, on the seat, in full view and unharmed, was his wallet.

He retrieved it, retraced his steps to town and was thankful to hear his name called from the friendly restaurant patio where a tall, cold beer could be obtained. And that we did... we all did.

That evening, after the swelling in Jay's hand had diminished, we had dinner at Alpe Fleurie – a restaurant that cooked its entrees on an open wood fire AND served Raclette. Margaret and I both had wanted to try Raclette. Traditionally Swiss, Raclette is a large chunk of cheese, similar to gruyere, that is allowed to sit quite close to the fire and melt. It is served with small, new, boiled potatoes and sour gherkins (or cornichons). It tasted a bit like fondue, but it was the adventure of scraping melted cheese off a block and onto a potato that was intriguing. My son called it, "cheese on a radiator."

We began the meal with Portwine soup with jellied consommé. Amy and Jay both ordered veal chops. Their dinners came quickly... ours, not so much. They were each served two of the largest veal chops I had ever seen. Margaret and I were getting a bit hungry, so they shared the veal with us. It was wood-smoked delicious! We were all reaching satisfaction when the Raclette came. It was delightful, but a small portion. We enjoyed it, but were secretly glad we had eaten the veal. When finished, the waiter whisked away the empty dishes and brought more. We smiled and thanked him and ate some more... sharing this portion. When it was gone, we thought we had done quite well, but then – he brought another plate. He seemed quite disappointed when we said we just could not eat another bite. We were also disappointed. If we ever get back to Villars, we will know the proper way to eat Raclette: all evening.

Even good things must come to an end, and so was our stay in Villars. We left very early in the morning, while the alp was still above the clouds, and departed gorgeous Switzerland. We traveled by train through Biel, Basel, up the Rhine River to Mainz, Germany. This time no border guards came to inquire. All behavior had been civilized during the weeklong emigration.

Originally, we had thought we would stay in Frankfurt, but the city was hosting an international garden show and there were no available rooms. When we got off the train in Mainz, we went directly to the "i" to get accommodation information. Amy took the list and headed for the public telephone. She found rooms at the Hotel Stadt Coblenz, on the Rhine. We went to see if it was where we wanted to stay. (In Europe you check out the room before you register.) It couldn't have been more convenient. It was right across from the Rhine River public park. The 40 DM included fruhstuck. If we split the rooms, it would cost each of us about $10 per night with breakfast. How good is that?

We had dinner at the most extraordinary Yugoslavian restaurant just around the corner which served such delicious food and such large quantities. They served a wild mushroom soup that is still unsurpassed. (And loving mushroom soup, I have it often.) Perhaps it was the paprika, perhaps it was the butter, perhaps it was the sour cream… or maybe they just have tastier mushrooms growing in their forests. It was dark and rich and full of woodsy flavor! I can still taste it.

The next morning, we decided to take a cruise on the Rhine. It was included in our Eurail passes and the day looked lovely. We could travel by boat as far as Koblenz and return by train – all in the same day.

We packed some food and a bottle of wine and boarded the river-sized cruise ship. It had several levels, but we went right to the top deck and staked out our spot. On the side railing of the boat were small tables that folded down, so we pulled one up, gathered our deck chairs around it and prepared for a scenic cruise on the romantic Rhine River.

And scenic it was. It was a mixture of ancient castles, tiny towns, narrow passages, and commercial towboats pushing their barges of goods up and down the river. Every turn was a new vista.

About an hour out, the weather turned inclement. At first, we thought it was to be a short summer storm and would pass on. But, mistaken, we were soon uncomfortable – cold, wet, irritable. So we closed down the top deck observation post and went below.

The boat had restaurants on every level. We checked each one to see if it would be our choice. Passing the one with the white tablecloths and settled in to one much less formal. We took a table by the window. Now, everyone on the ship's staff was accepting of the fact that no one wanted to be out in the rain, but after a while it became clear that it would be proper of us to purchase some food. We asked for menus. The young waiter smiled and brought one for each of us. Amy was elected to do the ordering. A bowl of hot soup that would go well with the sandwiches we had in our packs as well as warm our shivering bodies sounded really inviting.

When the hot, fragrant broth came, we began to rally. Next, we brought out the wine and the paper cups. (What? We're traveling!) The Swiss Army knife I had bought at the Berlin Airport, just for this occasion, came out of my bag. From the shiny red penknife with the Swiss emblem on the side, I selected the cork screw and set to work. Lo, and behold! The compact cork screw was too short to do the job. Amy summoned the waiter (he was about her age). We aren't sure just what she said to him in his native tongue, but he reappeared with a proper corkscrew AND stemware for the wine. We made a mental note to leave him a BIG tip.

There are about twenty medieval castles between Mainz and Koblenz. Each has a story. Some are B & Bs, most give tours. Two are privately owned and Stahleck Castle has a youth hostel. All are imposing. We only saw them from the boat and heard their stories over the sound system. Another trip to this area will find me on shore exploring these segments of history.

The Castle Klopp is in Bingen. It is said to have been built on Roman ruins. The Castle Klopp, the Mausturm and the castle ruins Ehrenfels were all toll gates. Although on different banks and a few miles apart, they worked the river together.

If the island in the middle of the river is small, so be it. It will hold a castle anyway. What better place to collect tolls? In 1327, Ludwig of Bavaria (the first King Ludwig) built just such a castle on Pfalzgrafenstein Island. It was used to collect tolls until 1866. An imposing building with its turrets and towers and pointed end, on approach it resembles a large ship. A chain across the river to the nearby town of Kaub forced ships to comply, and uncooperative captains could be kept in the dungeon until a ransom was delivered.

The river gets narrow near St. Goars and the massive Lorelei Rock looms overhead. According to German folklore, there was once a beautiful young maiden, named Lorelei, who threw herself headlong into the river in despair over a faithless lover. Upon her death she was transformed into a siren and could from that time on be heard singing on a rock high above the Rhine River, near St. Goar. Her hypnotic music lured unsuspecting sailors to their death. We listened intently, but did not hear her song. It is, nevertheless, an awesome passage with rapids and reefs abundant. Ours was a modern, sturdy, steel-clad ship. We tried to imagine being on a smaller, wooden boat propelled by sails and oars, and lured into oblivion by Lorelei... had some trouble with that.

Along this stretch of the river are Castle Katz, Castle Maus, and the ruins of Rheinfels a stronghold built in 1370 by the powerful counts of Katzenelnbogen.

Marksburg is one of the most imposing castles. It sits high on a hill above Braubach and intimidates the surrounding area. I am sure its owners ruled the river and protected the countryside for many generations. It was built in the early 12th century and was purchased by Count Eberhard of Katzenelnbogen in 1283. It is the only remaining, fully intact castle on the river.

Almost to Koblenz, on the west side of the river is the Schloss Stolzenfels, another imposing structure. It was built in 1242 as a fortress. Through the centuries, disrepair reigned. Restoration began in the mid 1800s, enhancing its crenellated towers and Gothic architecture. The décor today reflects the taste of the Hohenzollerns who lived there in the late 1800s.

By the time we reached Koblenz, the rain had subsided, but we never left the restaurant.

Koblenz is a fascinating city. Again, it has fantastic old world architecture. Not only do you appreciate the character of the city, but you feel transported to an earlier century. The town supposedly was named by The Romans. Its name means Castle at the Confluence of Two Rivers. The rivers are the Rhine and the Moselle. It is the very heart of wine country. Indigenous wines are available here that are not exported to any other part of the world. And they are delicious.

There wasn't much time for us to visit. We had to get to the train station to return to Mainz. We did walk through a city park close to the Rhine. It had public bathrooms... a rarity. Margaret, Amy and I stood in line with many other women. (From overhearing conversations, I would say they were visiting from all over the world.)

Using a restroom in Europe is its own experience. There is very little modesty here. When it was my turn to enter a stall, I was a bit surprised that the attendant was a man. He smiled broadly, held up his hand to indicate I should wait while he rushed in and gave the commode a quick washdown... and a double flush. He then indicated I could enter. I thanked him in my best German, secured the door and tried to be nonchalant about my business. Now, I suppose I should have tipped him, but I was not aware of how much to tip for a double flush. As I left, he was busy with other stalls and customers. I did not see anyone else hand him a tip. I will never know the protocol for this.

We walked through the alt stadt... across one of the beautiful platzs, full of shops and restaurants. Concerned that it would resume raining, I popped into one of the small shops and purchased an umbrella. It was sweet... a lovely light teal color with blond bamboo shaft. It would be my memento of Koblenz... and, it would keep us dry.

The train ride back to Mainz took us through many of the lovely river towns we had seen from the boat. The tracks ran between the river and the road. Beyond the road lay Inns and restaurants and attractions. I really must return.

Back in Mainz, we prepared for the next day's departure from this three-week escapade in Europe.

After fruhstuck, we took the train from Mainz directly to the airport in Frankfurt. Margaret, Amy, and I would head back to the States, Jay would be meeting friends for another week along the Rhine before returning to Berlin.

Jay had just begun the long healing process of divorce, but this week was just the break he had needed. And I had enjoyed having the family together, again.

Yes, Jay would have no trouble getting home. All had gone well with the freedom movement. The Germans and the Russians had behaved very differently from the Chinese. By Christmas, the Berlin Wall was down, checkpoint Charlie was out of a job. New Year's Eve, Jay was at the Brandenburg Gate. January 15, 1990, he was home – bringing souvenir pounds of the wall home with him. We had all experienced history first hand, this year.

Year Of Change -- 1990

This was a year of change. A time share vacation was not on the schedule. The weeks were put into storage for later use.

In 1990, my dad entered the hospital in very poor health. The final diagnosis was Emphysema. From the hospital, he entered a rehabilitation center. When he was allowed to return home, he called me to see what my future plans were. I had some large decisions to make.

In May, I earned a new degree in Business Management. My second time around the college experience had come to fruition. In August, I packed all my belongings in the largest Ryder truck, hooked a dolley on the back for my '79 Corolla, picked up my daughter who was now at Kent State University and headed east for a new life. I was 50 years old.

It was quite a year.

Quebec--1991

In 1991, Margaret came east again. She and I drove to Canada for a week. (My dad was doing much better, but opted not to go.) There are many choices for timeshare in Canada. Over the next decade, we had four trips to our neighbor to the north. This one took us to Magog... a small resort area just over the border from Vermont. It shares Memphremagog, a thirty mile long, glacial, freshwater lake with Newport. (The name Memphremagog comes from the Abenaki vocabulary for "large expanse of water.") There are strong rumors of its own "Nessie" in residence, but try as we might, we missed seeing her this week. The condo was lovely – two bedrooms, (one up, one down) cozy living room with a fireplace for the cool evenings. It was located midway between Quebec and Montreal. Great for day trips.

Magog, although small, is interesting on its own. In its early history, it was a haven for rest for the Abenaki hunting parties making their way to the St. Lawrence. In 1776, Loyalists from south of the border, disagreeing with the revolution, fled the colonies and settled here. They were soon followed by the Irish escaping from political upheaval in their homeland and, of course, the French expanding west from Quebec City.

Soon, mills of every useful kind were built along the Magog river to precipitate and support the building of a community. Originally known as The Outlet of Lake Memphremagog, the area became a lucrative trading post. Its name was soon shortened to The Outlet and could be reached by a stagecoach line from the nearby town of Sherbrooke or the village of Stanstead. In 1855, the name was changed again... this time to just plain Magog.

By the end of the 19th century, the railroad had replaced the stagecoach and the trading post had become a vacation destination for guests from Quebec, Montreal, and the United States. More industries and commercial

38

businesses as well as recreational navigation developed upon the long, scenic lake. A tiny steamship, "The Jenny Lind" traveled the thirty miles from Magog on the north shore to Newport, Vermont, on the south shore, stopping often to deliver visitors, goods, and services along the way.

The original trading post building expanded to include the first post office and that building still stands today. It is now occupied by the Bank of Montreal.

On the western coast of Lake Memphremagog along the Chemin des Peres, stands a Benedictine Monastery, le Saint-Benoît-du-Lac Abbey. The manicured grounds are open to the public for meditation and silence. Retreats may be held there by reservation. The monks have a small shop where they sell their own cheese, cider, and fudge. Now, I am not a big fan of fudge – so sugary – but this was delicious! They make the fudge in several flavors and sell it as one of their fundraisers for the abbey. Yes, we bought some. No, it didn't make it home.

Taking out the map of Quebec Province, we discussed the many points of interest that we thought we would like to visit during the stay. There were way too many to accomplish in only one week, so we selected the high points… just in case this would be our only trip to this area.

We had a wonderful day in Old Quebec. It was a bit of a drive, but we arrived in time to have lunch in the shadow of the Chateau Frontenac Hotel in a tiny, rustic restaurant with white stuccoed walls and a bright red roof. On the outside, near the door, was posted the menu du jour printed both in English and in French. Inside, the atmosphere emitted the essence and warmth of a country cottage. The food was delightful -- urban yet hearty.

Now, when we say "Old Quebec City", we are talking 1608 old. Settled by the French, in the name of the king, under the guidance of Samuel de Champlain, this majestic, walled city is perched on the top of 200 foot bluffs overlooking the narrows of the St. Lawrence River. In fact, the name Quebec is said to mean "where the river narrows" in the language of the first tribal inhabitants of the region.

The city stayed under the control of the French until 1759 when they succumbed to the British in the battle of the Plaines of Abraham. However, The British, in true gracious form, allowed the French to keep their native language and religion, and thus their culture, intact. French is still the first language here, although most of the younger residents are, at least, bilingual.

We walked the beautiful grounds of the colossally grand Hotel Frontenac, and shopped (or at least, window shopped) the many small stores on the periphery. Then, we made our way down the steep, winding walkway from the Upper Town (Haute-Ville) to the Lower Town (Basse-ville) where Champlain first set foot on this land. The age-old stone buildings, once homes and offices, are now boutiques and art galleries. In one shop, I found a striking painting of a black cat in a red frame. The yellow eyes were hauntingly reminiscent of my own black cat, Emily. The painting found its way home with me.

There is a funicular (inclined railcar) that climbs the 200 foot cliff from the lower city to the upper city. When it was time to return, we enjoyed its convenience – and the view. The ride was not nearly as long as the cog railway in Switzerland, but it was quite reminiscent.

One day we went 'splorin' again. (Roughly translated, 'Splorin' means wandering around the area just to discover what is offered on the by-ways. It always turns into something interesting.)

One of the interesting things we found in Quebec was that many of the towns have both English and French names. If the name appears on the map in French, it was originally settled by the French and, chances are, French is the spoken language. But, the town may also have an English name. If the name appears in English, it was settled by the English and English is the spoken language.

I tried to use my High School French here – remember it had been so useful in Switzerland – but Canadian French is quite different. They, most often, chose to converse in English, of which I was most grateful. Their English was much better than my French, in this case. (Most people who interact with tourists speak English… and, I suspect several other languages as well. Canada is a country that is frequented by people from all over the world. Toronto, especially, is quite the International city.)

On this day, we ended up in Brome or Knowlton, a small village near Lac Brome. We had a delicious lunch at the local café and then enjoyed the many charming small shops. In one Antique Shop I found a lovely wing-back wicker chair with an upholstered seat. It sat high. Just the thing my dad needed for his sun porch. He had been having trouble getting up and down from his age-old porch chairs. Although stylish, they sat lower with a more relaxed sitting angle. I bought the chair and had it shipped. It would take a while to be delivered, ensuring that I would be back home in Connecticut by the time it arrived.

We had a great week of resting and 'splorin'. One afternoon, out in the middle of a beautiful scenic byway, we had lunch at a small Mom and Pop restaurant. It was here that I was introduced to Putine. It doesn't sound exciting, but it tastes divine. The dish is made up of French Fries with thick beef gravy and white cheese curds. At this restaurant, the fries were crisply fried, the gravy was rich, and the curds squeaked when you bit into them. What a flavor combination. The curds really make the difference. I have tried it at home with mozzarella cheese sticks and it just isn't the same. We had many outstanding meals in Canada, but this simple dish remains one of my favorites!

Being a skier, The Laurentians have always been on my wish list of destinations. We were now close enough to bring this wish to fruition. Margaret is not a skier, but she is plucky and agreed that this would be an interesting day.

We drove to Montreal and then headed north to Mt. Tremblant. What a delight. It was May, so there was not a flake of snow to be seen, yet the ski area looked every bit as European as winter in the Alps. The chair lift was in operation for the purpose of taking people to the crest of the mountain to have lunch in the lodge and enjoy the view from the top of the world. Margaret had never been on a chairlift before, but she was game to try and couldn't resist the idea of getting a new perspective on Mother Earth. So, up we went.

Now, I cannot tell you how many times, or in how many places, I have ridden a ski lift, but, I have to say, this was the first time without skis... or poles... to steady by. I spent a bit of the trip up that long, steep, high mountain thinking about how to get off... with skis on it takes no thought at all... but without skis... hmmmm. Luckily, we must have looked like greenhorns, or extremely apprehensive, because the attendant stopped the lift when it was our time to land... no jumping off and assuredly gliding away this time. To my peace of mind, we simply stood up and walked away toward the lodge with all of our dignity and nerves intact. I was a bit shy about looking at Margaret's face, lest she see my relief. We entered the Chalet, found a table by the expansive front window and ordered lunch as if this was what we did every day. (We're so Foxy.)

Our visit up there enjoying the spectacular view lasted about an hour, but acknowledging time constraints, we headed back down. Now, there is another first... for all those trips up the mountain on ski lifts, normally found me skiing down... not riding down the hill on the chair facing the descent. It was a lot like crossing a deep ravine on a creaky rope bridge... DON'T LOOK DOWN!

Fortunately, riding on the four-seater chair with us was a ski instructor who had taught or skied at many of the same places that I had enjoyed.

He kept us talking and listening and not looking down. It was a beautiful ride, but, when we reached bottom and, again, the lift was stopped for our departure, I was grateful. As innocent as it turned out, and as confident as I had behaved, I mentally noted that from that point forward, all chairlifts will involve snow and ski equipment.

Margaret admitted that she, too, was proud of her personal courage about this adventure. With renewed conviction and satisfaction that we had, indeed, accomplished a feat of bravery in the face of challenge, we headed back to Magog.

Realizing that Montreal was really quite close, and far less intimidating than Mt. Tremblant, we set out the next day for the city. Montreal is actually on an island in the St. Laurence River. It gets its name from Mount Royal, a large hill in the center of the city. Although its primary and official language is French, much more English is spoken here on the street than in Quebec City. Laid out rather geometrically, it is an easy city to navigate.

In 1535, French trapper and trader, Jacques Cartier visited the Native First Nation residents. By 1611, Champlain had built a trading post here. The growing area became a base for further exploration of the northern regions. In 1832, Montreal was established as a city. Today, it is the second largest city in Canada.

We parked our car and headed for the Underground City… a complete megalopolis of shops, services and metro stations underground… the largest of its kind in the world. Once inside, the daily weather – which can be brutal in the winter—is of no consequence. One is able to pursue any interest from shopping to eating to museum hopping to watching a sports event to working to living or simply enjoying hotel accommodations in this 20 miles of tunnel connections. There are even Universities accessed from here through several of its 120 entrances.

We tried our hardest to do it all, but failed miserably. We did have Putine again at a fast food stand, but it paled in comparison with our first taste in the countryside. When our feet began to let us know it was time to rest, we took the Metro to Old Montreal, the historic area. More walking took us past so many interesting shops and museums that we had to make choices and vow to return on another trip. We chose to visit the Notre Dame Basilica. A smaller version of the Notre Dame in Paris, this grand Gothic Revival edifice was begun in 1824 and finally finished in 1879. A separate chapel and offices were constructed and in use by 1888. To extend proper homage to this building, one should plan to spend an entire day.

Alas, we could not. Time dictated that we retrace our steps to retrieve the car and head for home. The conversation about all that we had seen continued from Montreal to Magog.

At the end of the week, we headed back to Connecticut and Margaret flew back to Indiana. We were already discussing where our next trip would take us.

However, in October, my Dad's health took a turn for the worse. He died October 30. Everyone came home... my sister and her family from San Francisco, my son from Virginia, my daughter from Ohio. It was good to all be together again, but it was a very sad time.

Great Britain -- 1994

In 1993, I moved to New Hampshire to start a new job managing an historic house museum.

In 1994, Amy was an exchange student in England. She would be at BESG (British and European Study Group) at Cambridge working on her certification in Shakespearian Stage Combat. When she made the announcement in August of '93, Ole mom started saving her pennies and counting on a healthy IRS return.

In February, Amy sent her spring break schedule – March 11 to April 15 – and Mom made phone calls for travel arrangements. We had first talked about B&B and BritRail to be footloose and fancy free. (Time Share exchange seldom seems to work in Britain. Although they have many, they always seem to be in use. People who own timeshare weeks in Britain, use their timeshare weeks in Britain. Can you blame them?) We could bop around the UK at will – probably wouldn't get to Scotland because of the distance, but would not rule it out. Would like to see Wales. Did not want to be burdened with a car--wrong side of the road, narrow passages, expensive gas, roundabouts, all that sort of rot. Arrive sometime in Late March to ensure good weather and flowers.

Heh, heh, heh. The first call I made was to RCI, just to see, and behold they had timeshare to exchange – two in Wales and two in Scotland to choose from. I could not have been more surprised. I chose Kenmore Club, Kenmore, Loch Tay, Perthshire, Scotland. Next hitch: it was only accessible by car. I called Amy and said, "Remember all those things we weren't going to do? Well, guess what we're doing."

The next call was to get airline reservations. The agent spent 20 minutes working at the computer checking all the airlines before she said the best arrangements would be BritAir arriving Heathrow on March 11, leaving

March 22. A little sooner and a little longer than I had originally hoped, but, oh well, I will survive.

Now, for a car. Alamo, $135 per week for a small 4-door similar to the Ford Escort we had had once before. Good.

Last detail – how to get to Boston. Taxi to the bus station, bus to Logan Airport. O. K. The ducks are all lined up, the exchange rate is under $1. 50, the travelers checks are in British pounds. Cool. I am on my way to Great Britain.

The trip to the Boston airport was routine. Arriving with no fuss (and with a bit of extra time) I was soon comfortably situated in seat 51D, no smoking. We were almost an hour late departing, but, we were assured, with the jet stream at our backs, we should soon make it up. Drinks were welcomed. Dinner was delicious (no joke). And I was sitting next to a woman from New Hampshire who worked for BritAir and knew of the museum which I managed. Small world. We shared light patter until time for lights out and sleep.

March 11, 1994. Ping, the lights came on again. It was morning where we were and time for breakfast ('though in reality it was only midnight and dinner was not digested yet). Wake up, stretch, be bright, be hungry, be sociable, even though your teeth feel like wet wool and your brain is full of thick brown fur. Where *is* that coffee?

When breakfast trays were collected and we were beginning to think about the day ahead, the Captain's silky, professional, baritone voice came over the intercom. "Well, Ladies and Gentlemen (those English – always so proper), we didn't want to unnecessarily concern you through the night, but we have been told that the IRA has, once again, lobbed mortars on to the runway at Heathrow."

Hello!!! Fur is gone! I'm awake! Mortars? Runways? My airport? What is next? We were told that, for the time being until further decisions, we would be diverted to Stansted airport. Actually, that was closer to Cambridge for me, but what of all those making other connections. We all donned our stoic attitudes and busily engaged in polite conversation with our neighbors to hide our uneasiness. The Captain announced that he was going to reinstate smoking (normally, this close to landing the no smoking light would be on) in the rear of the plane – which suddenly included my row. The entire tail section looked like a Glasgow pub. I went forward to visit another section for awhile.

We landed at Stansted right on our scheduled arrival time, but stayed on board. No news. The Captain announced that we would use the time to refuel – at least 45 minutes – and as soon as he heard anything he would let us know. About 30 smoke-filled minutes later, the same smooth, steady voice told us that we would not be deplaning at Standsted. The airport did not have the staff or custom facilities to handle so many unexpected guests. Heathrow had been secured, terminal 4 (the international terminal) had been reopened and one runway had been cleared for traffic. As soon as we had a flight time, we would take off for Heathrow.

Two hours later, I was pulling my luggage through terminal 4 and it was unquestionably clear that all airport personnel were intent on whisking us through and out of the building. With a brief stop at the Alamo desk for directions, I was quickly standing on the curb waiting for the shuttle to take me to the Alamo car rental. Another couple with two very small children and carts full of luggage joined me. They had been diverted to Birmingham.

During the shuttle ride, the driver pointed out all the closed roads and runways and gave us a rundown on the mortar attack which had occurred two days earlier. The IRA was fashioning mortar launchers out of stolen automobiles, parking them on the street or hotel parking lots as any other car would park, then, after getting safely away, would detonate the mortars by remote control. (Irony of Ironies, this morning's mortar had been lobbed right over the neighborhood police station.) None of the mortars had exploded as yet, but the message was loud and clear that there was great potential for massive damage.

To disguise our discomfort, we chattered about the daffodils in bloom and the budding trees until we arrived at the rental car agency. I accepted an upgraded auto and started off to Cambridge, fifty miles away.

The route was direct and plainly marked. Travelling with the traffic up to 95 MPH, I arrived in Cambridge in forty minutes. (Not bad for right hand driving on the left side of the road.) With little trouble, I reached the correct address and quickly parked as close as I could. I found Amy in the common room at her house waiting patiently (along with several roommates who also were anxious since they, too, had people coming and going at Heathrow.)

We reparked the car, regrouped the luggage, and started off to restore the day's schedule. Cambridge is a walking town full of students with bookbags, professionals with briefcases, and residents with shopping bags. We know it, of course as one of the most prestigious university towns in England (maybe in the world) with more than 22,000 students attending its many colleges. More time would be spent here after our week in Scotland. But right now we were focused on getting away.

Amy took us to her favorite local sit-down restaurant (most of them are "take-away") The Raj Belash, a tandoori with a scrumptious menu, and ordered Chicken Mowgli as well as a la carte items -- enough for a substantial lunch. Then, we got out the maps and chatted and planned and ate and felt better.

From the restaurant, we walked to the Royal Bank of Scotland to cash some travelers checks. It was the Royal Bank of Scotland, right? Someone should know how far it was to Edinborough. Actually, it was a customer who said it was about 7 or 8 hours to drive. Exchanging looks of instant comprehension, it was agreed that we should start off immediately.

We were away from Cambridge just before four. About an hour out, upon impulse, we made the decision to spend the night in Nottingham, so we left the four-lane A-1 and headed 'cross the fens.

Many tourist–related services in England do not open until April 1, but, with the help of the local Information Bureau, we found The Forest Hills Hotel, a B&B in Nottingham that also served dinner. It was not the highlight of the trip, but the accommodations were pleasant and within our budget.

The building was very typical of English homes-now-B+Bs... tall, narrow, deep with non-assuming facades. They are often two rooms wide with a center entrance, rather deep, and at least four floors high. This one was not quite as grand as Fawlty Towers.

Our room was on the second floor, front, and we had our own en suite WC. (I think it actually was once the closet.) We settled in for the night. I, at least, being thankful that the day was done; I was in England, and I was not at Heathrow, since they had had another bombing later in the afternoon – four mortars in all today. After watching the news and the commentaries on the day's events, we concluded we were hungry after all and would inquire about the glorious aromas wafting up the staircase.

At the foot of the stairs, we were presented with two options – to the left were two dining rooms, set properly for dinner – to the right were a bar and a lounge, or clubroom, outfitted with dark green leather-covered wingback chairs and occasional tables placed in a random arc in front of a small Victorian fireplace with metal railing. It looked cozy. We went in.

We ordered drinks and discussed the evening's menu with the same man who had shown us our room (obviously the owner, doorman, concierge, waiter, and cook depending on which hat he had on) then sat leisurely in the clubroom before the fire, sipping our aperitifs and enjoying catching up on each other's news while our dinner was being prepared.

Although he had said it would take five minutes, we waited fifteen before we went in to the dining room. There, we had another round of cider and waited another thirty minutes before dinner arrived. It was delicious... well worth the wait. We went to bed satisfied and tired from the day's unexpected activities.

In the morning, we ate an early, hearty British breakfast sitting at the same table as supper. Now, an English breakfast is its own experience. Lovingly known as an"English fry up" it consists of baked beans, rashers of back bacon, bangers (sausages), two eggs, black or white pudding, and a fried slice (bread fried in the bacon drippings). The plate is then garnished with cooked tomato halves for color. It was more than a substantial meal to start the day. Eating should not again be necessary for a week.

We paid our bill, packed up the car, and, since it was so early, headed for The Tales of Robin Hood – a Disney-style presentation of Robin Hood and Sherwood Forest in downtown Nottingham. It was very similar to the Viking presentation in York – cars on a track moving you through tableaux of history complete with sounds and smells. A fun day. We tarried some in the gift shop, then left to walk the block from Nottingham Castle, past the Lace Museum and the Costume Museum to the oldest Inn in England for a quick pint of ale.

The tavern's name is Ye Olde Trip to Jerusalem. It was constructed in 1240. Its address is 1 Brewhouse Yard, Nottingham. The building is four stories high with white stuccoed walls and a thatched roof. Its wavy glass windows are a bit off square and from the number of chimneys, each room is individually heated by its own fireplace. Although one enters at the side front, the rear of the Inn is built into the cliff under the castle. Inside, the rustic rooms were small and on the dark side with massive beams in its low ceilings. Very Medieval. One expected Robin Hood and his band of merrie men to be in the next room enjoying a stout. (Although Little John's physical comfort might be questionable.)

By noon we were on our way north. It was a beautiful drive. The sun was shining. The flowers were not in bloom yet this far north, but the grass was green and the view was lovely. Every time we saw a castle ruin we oohed and aahed and tried to find some information about it. We said "hi" to all the sheep (that took some time) and tried to mentally store all the vistas before dark. It was turning dusk as we approached Edinborough. Amy found a by-pass – ring road – around the city that took us directly to the Firth of Forth bridge. At 7 o'clock, we were past Edinborough, but not close to Kenmore. At Perth, we left the highway to call for a late arrival and explicit directions.

We stopped at a large supermarket/filling station complex called the Wm Low. A call to Kenmore assured us we were expected, the key would be at the pavilion, but we were still about an hour away. We bought some groceries for the weekend and some Chicken Olives -- hot deli food -- which we ate for supper at tables conveniently provided at the grocery. (Chicken Olives are the MOST delicious dish! Chicken breasts are pounded thin and wrapped around an assortment of scrumptious fillings. The baked morsels are moist, tender, flavorful, and satisfying.)

Our stop took less than an hour. We filled the car with petrol and continued on. It had started to rain in Perth and as we came nearer to Kenmore the rain turned to snow.

We made good time on the A-9 and we were sure we would arrive before the allotted hour was up. At Ballinluig, we turned onto the 827 toward Aberfeldy. The night became darker, the road became narrower, the hedges grew higher, and the snow came down heavier. As we twisted through the village of Aberfeldy, the solitary sign of life was the lighted tavern sign that jutted out from the entrance of the corner pub offering McEwen Ale. (This was an especially good omen... we are McEwan's by lineage... it seemed almost a personal welcome.)

Once through the tiny town, again, darkness and snow. A few miles further on we turned a lonely corner into a teacup size village of white stucco buildings. On our right was a stunning medieval gate looming through the snowstorm. Ahead was a hotel, behind was a post office/grocery, and on our left was a church. A sign read, "Kenmore Club across the bridge." We inched through the tiny center, crossed the bridge, (one of those picturesque arched stone bridges so characteristic of Scotland), and turned into the entrance of Kenmore Club. (Drat, I wish I could see better.)

The woman with the key was waiting for us. She met me half-way down the path in her eagerness to go home for the night. It was close to nine o'clock. She said we could drive to the cottage to unload, but should drive the car back outside the wall to park. Wall? What sort of a wall? Where's the wall? We drove on in the darkness, the snow was wet, cold, and coming straight at us.

We found the atmospheric opening in the tunnel of bad weather that led to our cottage, unloaded food and luggage, and then I took the car back to "the other side." As I walked the murky route back to the cottage, I could vaguely see the outline of another huge gate to my left... but the swirling snow and the lack of light hindered greatly any positive identification. When I got inside the cottage, I said to Amy, "Come daylight, we have some exploring to do. This is no ordinary wall!"

Now, the Scottish cottage: From the outside, it was a typical white stucco cottage with a loft window tucked into its dark thatched roof. When we entered, we quickly found that the designer had a delicious sense of humor, taste, and comfort. As provincial as the outside was, the inside was urbane.

The ground floor of the cottage held two spacious bedrooms, two comfortable baths, a utility room and a center hall with a staircase which led to the upper floor. Climbing the stairs, we caught our breath as we were greeted by beautiful silk flower arrangements, comfortable contemporary furniture, an inviting fireplace and an open floor plan. The stairs arrived in the living room which was one half of the cottage. The end of the room at the head of the stairs was all glass with a door which led to a large wooden deck. The opposite end of the room elled into a dining area which shared the other half of the house with a kitchen. The kitchen was well appointed, well planned, and well equipped with any utensil or appliance needed for any cuisine.

Into the dark, snowy night, we stepped out on the deck to be haunted by the sound of water lapping and again, that faint outline of the enormous gate looming ever closer to us. Tomorrow!

Bone weary, we figured out the electric heat in one bedroom and one bath and decided to make all other decisions in the morning.

Morning found us moving rather slowly; some because we were having trouble shaking the sleep from our shoulders; some because it was Sunday and we had no real plans; but mostly because each step through the house was one of exploration and discovery.

Each room had its own radiator and thermostat. The bathroom was even blessed with a heater for the towels, a heater for the room, and a heater for the Jacuzzi. Good thing, too, since the entire room was finished in cold ceramic tile. All of the thermostats for the bathroom were in the hall. The utility room had a door to the outside, a washer/dryer (all one machine) and a separate hanging area with heat and thermostat. We had to explore that room more later in the week. The bedroom windows and rear entrance on the ground floor all faced the back yard and an old stone wall. Hmmmm.

The other bedroom and bath were mirror images of the rooms we had used the night before. Now, for the stairway. Outside it was still snowing and blowing, but bright. We ascended to the upper floor with a sense of expectation and went directly to the end of the living room which was glass.

The view was spectacular! From the deck we could look above the wall directly out onto the loch. The water's surface was choppy and rippling, raising the question as to whether it was a tidal loch. We could see across the loch to buildings in the foreground and hills behind. It appeared to be some sort of resort.

Looking to the right, we saw the rock wall extending almost to infinity – and when we looked to the left we caught our breath and felt ever so weak in the knees. There, almost close enough to touch, was the most magnificent stone gate which had to date at least to the 1300s or 1400s.

Where were we? This was not a stage prop nor a resort developer's marketing strategy. This was medieval and it was real. Somewhere out there were the answers, we had to go find them, even if it took all week.

Today was "Mothering Sunday" (Britain's Mother's Day). Amy and I ate a light breakfast and made plans to go to the main pavilion mid-afternoon for dinner and conversation with the staff and residents to fill in all the gaps in the information about Kenmore Club.

The weather was quixotic. One minute the sun was shining, the next minute it was snowing. Diehard sailors were wrestling with their light sailboats in the loch. As one capsized for the third time, we thought it best to alert the troops. Amy called the pavilion only to be told others had also been watching them and help was already on its way. So satisfied that they were in good hands, we turned our attentions elsewhere and totally missed the rescue.

About 2:00 we walked to the pavilion for dinner. It actually was more like a clubhouse, but the food and drink were lovely. The vista was spectacular as we could see down the loch to the right and over the arched stone bridge to the left. Although the sun had been out as we walked over, a very dark cloud threatened bodily harm as we left. The jog back to the cottage was more of a survival tactic than a fitness activity.

We spent the remainder of the day warming up and drying out in front of the fireplace. We once again went to bed early and rested well.

In spite of (or maybe because of) my time lag, I was the first to arise. I made coffee with one of their wonderful electric pots which must be turned on at the pot *AND* at the receptacle on the wall, turned on the BBC, and got out the maps. When Amy came upstairs a while later, we sorted through all of the wonders in the 'fridge, cooked breakfast, and planned the day's excursion.

It quickly became apparent that the unpredictable weather was going to be a significant factor in our plans for the week. We made a list of all the things we wanted to do (far too many for just one week), plotted them on the map, and then decided that wherever the sun was shining that day is where we would plan to go. On Monday, March 14, the sun was shining on the east coast… the west coast was enveloped in winter squalls and freezing temps.

St. Andrews was on the east coast and was on the list. They had the neatest shops there, as well as ancient ruins, and who knows – a golf celebrity may be about.

We arrived at St. Andrews late morning only to find that the shops were closed because of a local holiday (some of the townspeople didn't even know which one). However, we were able to shop for Christmas gifts at the Old Tom Morris Golf Shop, so all was not lost.

Being golfers, a visit to St. Andrews is the equivalent of a pilgrimage. The Old Tom Morris Golf Shop is immediately across from the 18th green of The Old Course. The Old Course is said to be the oldest golf course in the world. Written records date from 1552, but King James IV is noted to have purchased golf clubs there in 1506. The area of land covered by the course was community ground where the public could "play at golf, futball, schuteing... with all other manner of pastimes." Originally the course boasted 22 holes, but somewhere around 1863, Old Tom Morris modified the course to the standard 18 holes that are played today.

In 1895, Old Tom created a second course adjacent to the existing links. It is called The New Course. Although they are both public courses, the Old Course is the ultimate quest for any golfer and it may be extremely difficult to secure a tee time. The New Course is equally as challenging and satisfying to the soul… and is, after all, still St. Andrews.

We spent a bit of time watching the players finishing their rounds on The Old Course and mentally promised to return some day to actually play golf here.

From there we walked past the Royal and Ancient Clubhouse to the Seaquarium on the North Sea (not as far as it sounds) where we had a delightful time poking among the exhibits, petting the rays, and watching the seals play in their outdoor pools. Another Christmas gift or two and we decided to have lunch at the Oyster Shack nearby. Lunch was nothing spectacular – sandwich and tea – but we sat at a table by the window overlooking the North Sea – very picturesque.

After lunch, we went back to the car with the plan to find the center of town. Somewhere, we made a wrong turn, or as it turned out, a right turn and ended up on the street which led to the cathedral and the castle ruins. OOOH, OOOH.

The St. Andrews Cathedral was built in the 12th century. There isn't much left standing. The West end was blown down in the 1270s. The east gable remains, as does part of the priory. There is also a museum to be visited. According to the museum guidebook, "St. Andrews, in the Middle Ages, was Scotland's premier cathedral city and a major pilgrimage place. Its great cathedral was the largest church in the land, and its encircling precinct wall the most impressive… The Scottish Reformation of 1560 brought an end to the medieval church. The day when John Knox's supporters broke into the cathedral and tore down the rich medieval furnishings effectively marked its demise."

Around the corner and a short walk along the high coast brings one to the ruins of the castle. This rocky promontory structure was the home of wealthy and powerful archbishops and at least three Scottish Kings. Built circa 1189, its notable features include a 'bottle dungeon' and mine and counter-mine tunneled during the siege that followed the murder of Cardinal Beaton in 1546.

During the turmoil of the Scottish reformation in the early 1500s, Protestant preacher George Wishart was imprisoned in the bottle dungeon. Cardinal David Beaton had him burnt at the stake in front of the castle. Followers of Wishart gained access to the castle disguised as stonemasons, overpowered the garrison and executed Beaton... hanging his body from his window in the front of the castle. The Protestants then took possession of the castle.

The Scottish Regent, the Earl of Arran ordered a siege of the castle and began digging a mine through the solid rock beneath the castle walls in an attempt to force an entry. The defenders of the castle were digging a counter-mine from the inside to forestall the attempt. This formidable tunnel was rediscovered in 1879 when a basement was being dug for a house across the street. These siege works are the finest of their kind in Europe. They are quite extraordinary to investigate. Amy explored further along inside the tunnel than I... almost crawling on her knees, it is that small.

The Sea Tower was largely a prison accommodation. People were held in different types of prison accommodations depending on their standing in society and the nature of their supposed crimes. The infamous 'bottle dungeon' is in the cellar of the Sea Tower.

A new visitor's center nearby has great exhibits and much more interesting information on the castle's history... oh, yes, and restrooms.

On the way home from St. Andrews, we stopped in Perth to shop... they were not celebrating the same holiday, apparently. We discovered the Edinburgh Woolen Mill Store as well as the McEwan's department store. (Who knew?) After much fun admiring the woolens in the mill store, and wondering how we must be related to these McEwans, we stopped at the Wm Low market and shopped for groceries before heading back to our cottage in Kenmore.

When we awoke on the morning of March 15, it looked like it was going to be a decent day. While eating Scotch Eggs for breakfast, we watched the telly which confirmed that it was going to be bright and sunny in the north. Amy had wanted to go to Glenfiddich distillery and it looked like today was the day. We dressed warmly, packed boots and mittens just in case, threw in some easy food and started north. It was glorious driving through the Grampians.

For the most part, the trip was solitary. Little villages were spaced far apart. We kept busy watching the lovely scenery and reading the map. When we got to Glenfiddich, we took the routine tourist photos... standing next to signs to prove you had been there, etc. Since it was off season, not all the shops were open, but we went on to the main buildings and took the very interesting tour illustrating how single malt Scotch is made. At the end, we were treated to a wee dram of the golden, peaty, elixir. Mmmmm Ggooood.

Just up the hill from the distillery was Castle Balvenie, a castle of enclosure first owned by the Comyns with a rare curtain wall from the 13th century. It was added to and updated in the 15th and 16th centuries. The difference in construction style is very visible. Judging by the stonework, I would guess that our own stone wall at Kenmore was 13th century construction. Twenty year old Mary Queen of Scots was a guest here in 1562 after her return from France. The imposing castle continued to be a residence until the 1700s when it became obsolete as a genteel dwelling.

Now ready for a bit o' nourishment we drove into nearby Dufftown for lunch. We ate on the short main street in a tiny restaurant with only about 6 tables. They had the MOST delicious hunter stew and smoked salmon plate. We had to share each other's food, everything was so tasty.

After lunch, we drove to Culloden, unfortunately arriving just as it was closing. We walked the moors awhile and then headed into Inverness where we shopped a bit and took more pictures. We took a photo of the striking Inverness Castle, but it is not the original castle. Apparently, the original castle was destroyed after the Battle of Culloden. The current building was built in the mid-1800s to look like a Norman Castle. Impressive, nonetheless.

At 5:00 PM, the town emptied and the shops closed up. Concerned about returning home in the dark, we retraced the route we had come. By so doing, we totally missed Loch Ness. Bummer. I have just put returning there on my wish list, just to travel that one stretch.

It was a bit of a trek back to Kenmore, but on the way we saw the most amazing sight. Nestled in the lap of the nearby gloaming was a charming Scottish Cottage– white stucco with black roof, like ours – but it sat under a brilliantly colored, double rainbow. When there is mist in the air (which is much of the time) the rainbows are just over your shoulder (and nearby cottages). Ireland does not have exclusivity on rainbows.

That night we went to bed tired, but content.

On March 16, the weather was not good anywhere. We decided to stay close. We shopped a bit in the nearby village of Aberfeldy and went on to Perth for more woolens. (I tried my best to shore up the international economy.

Besides, the sales were terrific and, now that I lived in New Hampshire, I needed woolens badly.) From Perth we went on to the Stirling Castle.

This Castle is commanding from its position atop a high hill above the town. It overlooks some of the most important battlefields of Scotland's past including Stirling Bridge, the site of Braveheart William Wallace's victory over the English in 1297, and Bannockburn where Robert the Bruce defeated the same foe in the summer of 1314.

In spite of the inclement weather, we enjoyed the museum and the castle. They were doing massive renovations in the Chapel and the Great Hall. The home of James IV, his infant granddaughter, Mary Queen of Scots, was crowned in the Chapel in 1543. And the Great Hall is the largest medieval banquet hall ever built in Scotland. One can also visit the huge kitchens that serviced those sumptuous banquets. In time, the Queen's chambers in the new section will also be restored. (The plan was to have an accurate depiction of the Castle's era ready by 2005.)

In addition to the royal residence, the castle houses the regimental museum of the Argyll & Sutherland Highlanders. This group has been associated with the castle for almost a century.

We bought some books and souvenirs in the bountiful gift shop and headed home the long way round – up A84 to the west end of Loch Tay. The scenery along the lake was so gorgeous, we vowed another trip on a better day so we could stop and take more pictures. Today, we actually drove through some snow drifts and wondered if we would have to go back.

The next morning when we turned on the telly, we got really excited – it was going to be partly sunny to the west on the Cowal peninsula! Today was the day we would trod the sod. (We are McEwans and their castle ruins are on the Cowal peninsula.) We gobbled down a hearty Scotch breakfast and packed a light lunch not knowing what the weather would be like when we got there, or what facilities we would find.

Full of enthusiasm, we headed out westward to Killin and then on. However, as we approached Killin we knew we had to take a few moments to get some photos of this picturesque town. We took many photographs of our own, but just to make sure we captured the essence, we also purchased professional postcards. (This was way before digital cameras.) The River Dochart is one of the best known scenic attractions in the Scottish highlands. And Dochart Falls and Bridge at Killin are unbelievably magnificent! Even now as I look at the photos of them, I can't believe they are real.

We travelled south along Loch Lomond to the Arrochar turnoff. As we approached the road B-8000 which sported a sign saying "Otter Ferry"

(McEwan land), we could see a snow storm off to our left. If we turned, we would drive right into it, so instead we decided to drive on to Inveraray on the west coast of Loch Fyne hoping the weather would clear.

Note about roads: An "A" road is a well-maintained two lane road, easily traveled. A "B" road, such as the one to Otter Ferry, can be two lanes, but more often is just a bit wider than one lane with "lay-bys" to pull into to let an approaching car go by.

Inveraray is almost a two hour drive from Glasgow with travel connections to Oban and Fort William making it a natural stop for tourist buses. It is the ancestral home of the Duke of Argyle (yup, the socks) who demolished the original ancient castle and spent forty years rebuilding a more modern Classic Georgian style grand residence in the mid 1700s.

In addition to the castle, the town also offers the Argyll Folk Museum, The Inverary Maritime Heritage Museum, and the The Georgian Inveraray Jail to its tourists.

We visited a few charming shops and then the jail. The 1813 building plans called for three jails... one for men, one for women, and one for debtors, but finances only allowed the construction of one. The courthouse and prison, located at the end of the main street, opened in 1820. It depicts a basic, no-nonsense approach to 19th century punishment.

While we were in the jail, the snow squall from Otters Ferry crossed Loch Fyne and was blowing snow sideways past the jail windows. We took our time. After the gift shop, where we bought some wicked good whole grain mustard from the Isle of Arran, and some shortbread for travelling, we decided to head for the nearest pub, have some stout Scotch soup and wait out the storm. However, when we left the gift shop, the sun was shining, with nary a snowflake to be seen. "Hit the car, we're traveling!"

We headed back around Loch Fyne and turned right at the sign that said "Otter Ferry." Standing at the corner was a man with a pack begging a ride. As I drove past, Amy said, "We may be the only car he sees today." So, I turned around, picked him up and had colorful company as we neared the land of McEwan. He was a farrier whose truck had broken down. If he could make it home, his wife could take him and his new parts back to repair his vehicle, yet today. He had been walking most of the morning. We let him off just before we turned onto the single track road that led to the ancestral weal

The road followed the banks of Loch Fyne. Off to the right we could see a castle out on a spit of land. We turned into the parking lot of a restaurant to get a better look. It wasn't Castle McEwan or Otter Ferry. It was Castle Lachlan.

Castle Lachlan must surely be one of the most picturesque castles in Scotland. Not a large castle by castle standards, it was at one time the headquarters of Clan Lachlan, where the clan chief, Ian of MacLachlan, held court. It lies, needless to say, in the parish of Strathlachlan, near where the Lachland waters run into Lachlan Bay!

Who were these Lachlans? The name derives from the Lochlann, which was the surname for the Norse invaders and settlers who ruled the Hebrides from 800 AD until they were finally defeated by Somerled in the 1150s. They descended from Lachlan Mor (Lachlan the Great), active in the middle of the 13th century. By the 15th century they were allied by marriage with both the Lamonts and the Campbells, so they had a foot in both camps as these two clans fought for supremacy on the Cowal peninsula.

Now, who were the McEwans? Briefly, the clan takes its name from Ewen of the Otter (area) and flourished in the early 13th century. In 1432, Swene, the 9th and last in the Otter line, ceded all McEwan lands to Duncan Campbell (now that's another long, interesting, and well- disputed story). When the McEwan Clan was fractured, it was absorbed by the neighboring MacLachlans. The McEwans were then scattered over a fairly large area of the highlands. Many becoming scribes or bards to the Campbells.

We took some pictures of the Castle Lachlan ruin, the nearby Inver Cottage (a restaurant, but it was closed), and also of the new Castle Lachlan where the current chief of clan lives today. Then we moved on.

At last! Otter Ferry! And the weather had turned again. All was not lost, though. We went into the Oystercatcher Pub and Restaurant and had oysters right out of Loch Fyne! Elegant! We tried to order McEwen's Ale --- being McEwan land and all – but they didn't carry it. So we had tea. And good it was, too.

By the time we left, the weather had cleared enough to get a few good pictures of Otter Ferry. Parts of the pier still exist. We did not go roaming through the gloaming to the McEwan ruin. It was now on private property and we did not know where to get permission... we also were not wearing "Wellies." There is another unknown... the McEwan Castle is known to have been a ruin in 1740... does any of it still exist at all? That will have to wait for another visit. Instead, we headed across the peninsula on the narrow B roads to see as much as we could before the light failed. When we encountered a herd of highland cows, we had to stop for a moment and talk to them...

they are SO furry and cute! Several curious calves came up to the fence and enjoyed having their topnotch scratched. ... calves will be calves.

When we got home, we felt very good about what we had been able to see, but there were still too many haunting holes in our understanding of the McEwan saga.

March 18. Ah Friday! What a day! In the morning, we went into Aberfeldy to shop and poke and gather whatever last minute information we could. All week we had driven through Aberfeldy on the way to or from a destination and deadline. Today, we took our time to explore the lovely little village bustling with shoppers and visitors.

A visit to the information center rekindled our enthusiasm of the area; the gate and wall; and the castle we could see en route.

The Castle Menzies lies a few hundred yards west of Weem (another tea cup tiny picturesque village). It was built to replace a mansion house, "The Place of Weem", which had been pillaged and burned in 1502. This Castle was built before 1577, when it was known that the dormers and pediments on the second floor were added.

Bonnie Prince Charlie stayed here for two nights en route from Stirling to Inverness, prior to the Battle of Culloden in 1746. Four days later the castle was occupied by Cumberland's troops under the command of Lt. Col. Leighton. A west wing was added in 1940 and is being renovated by the Clan Menzies Society who are the current Keepers of the Castle.

But, the overflowing excitement came with the information about Taymouth Castle.

Remember that very first medieval gate on the right as we entered the village of Kenmore the very first snowy night? Well, it is the entrance gate to Taymouth Castle. In the gateway are five heraldic stone panels taken from Taymouth's predecessor, Balloch Castle, built Circa 1550 and demolished in 1806 to make way for this grand Victorian structure. The Castle throughout is built of local stone, mainly from Kenmore Hill, and represents the work of many Scottish architects, but the greatest story lies in the family.

The 15th century Colin Campbell of Glenorchy built the keep of Kilchurn Castle in Argyll in 1440. (Remember, Argyle is west... Loch Fyne area. This castle is central, in Kenmore... Loch Tay area.) His great-grandson built Balloch Castle, here in Kenmore, in the 16th century. The McEwans ceded their lands on the Cowal Peninsula in Argyll to the Campbells in 1432 and become bards, or shaunessies, to that clan.

The gorgeous, enigmatic, medieval stone wall outside our cottage originally surrounded the garden that belonged to Balloch Castle. We were actually staying in a medieval garden that belonged to a castle that, in all probability, had housed McEwans!!!! We were excited! Talk about providence!

The Taymouth Castle is not open to the public, else we would have gotten a much closer look.

We returned home to clean out the fridge as best we could and then headed west to Fearnan to go pony trekking. Amy had talked all week about seeing this splendid countryside from the back of a horse. Mother, of course (it is a mother's duty) resisted. The last time Mother had been trail riding was in Tennessee the year I bought the timeshare. I couldn't walk without pain for a week.

But, here we are going pony trekking in the Tay Forest as if we did it every day. We pulled into the stables, said hello to all the horses and set off to find our fearless leader.

We were outfitted with crash helmets, asked our weight in stones, and instructed on the Scottish seat (stirrup straps not quite Jockey length). My old muscles, which, when placed on the back of a horse, immediately revert to 1950s English show seat, would have no part of it. I had to have my leathers lengthened to a longer, more comfortable position before we started off. (The length of my arm.)

The sun was bright at 2:00 PM as we walked single-file down the road to a side trail which would take us up and up and up along the edge of the forest. On occasion, the ponies (actually, full sized, strapping horses) would break into a trot, lope, or gallop without any suggestion from us. (They had done this before.) I, heroically, hung on, trying for all the world to look as if I were calmly glued to the saddle when my thighs, calves, and ankles were all screaming, "You fool, you fool, you middle-aged, over-weight, out–of–shape fool!"

On occasion, a sheep or two would bound up onto the path from out of nowhere, be equally surprised by our being there, ponder us a moment before deciding we weren't worth too much of their time and go bounding on up the next hillside. Thank goodness the horses were not impressed.

After about an hour climbing and talking and smiling while we clung to these thrill seeking beasts, we came to a wide flat spot in the trail and turned around. I had been aware of the beauty of Loch Tay below us, but when we turned to face the west with the late afternoon sun streaming its bright golden rays through the menacing dark gray clouds and illuminating the silver water, the view was breathtaking. It had been worth every muscle-cramping mile to be in that spot at that moment. Every penny spent and every adversity overcome was atoned for. If I never am able to travel again, I have been fulfilled.

We stayed a few moments to etch this spectacular view on our memories, then started back to whence we came. The clouds were carrying snow, 'though we knew by now that in another moment the sun could be shining again. Could we make it back in time? It was all downhill (as they say). We mostly walked to assure safe footing. (A good thing, too. By now, I wasn't sure there was any feeling or control in either leg from the thigh down.) I had kicked free of the stirrups to let my leg muscles recover somewhat.

We made it back by 4:00 PM. The storm held off. With mustered dignity we dismounted in the straw strewn barn. (I didn't fall down, 'though there really wasn't any feeling in my ankles.) I walked a bit until the pins and needles came and went and my feet felt like two alien clods of mud at the end of my weary legs. I cannot remember which of us drove back to Kenmore.

The garden and gate were a welcome sight. As soon as we were inside the cottage, we filled both tubs with steaming water, turned on the whirlpools, and simultaneously languished in our separate Jacuzzis challenging each other to get out first.

Supper was wonderful that night. I don't remember who cooked it, but I do remember that it was delicious and diverse... lots of leftovers, including the haggis we bought at Wm Low. We left just enough for breakfast and nibbles for the road and ate every other last bite of food in the refrigerator.

The next morning we said, "Good-bye" to the Scottish cottage, the medieval stone gate, the American football stadium-sized village of Kenmore (one goalpost was the gate to Taymouth Castle, the other was the kirk) and traveled through the braes and burns to the city of Edinburgh.

March 19--Edinburgh is a fascinating city with its 16th century old town and 18th century new town, its lower city and upper city. We drove straightaway to the castle, found a place to park fairly close and looked for a place (pub) to eat lunch. While walking the Royal Mile, we found a sign announcing a restaurant with an arrow down a cozy close (we would call this an alley). Our sense of adventure led us through the lengthy, narrow walkway into a courtyard arrangement of several aged, stone buildings. (We dropped breadcrumbs so we could find our way back to the Royal Mile.) If my memory serves me correctly, the name of the restaurant was the John Knox. It was quite rustic with a medieval flair, the menu was Scottish fare, and the prices were good. It looked very much like a local lunch spot. We were delighted with our discovery. With a ploughman's and a pint we prepared for the afternoon.

When I called the B&B where we had once stayed on a former trip, we were told that the city was full of soccer players and fans in town for an international competition and there was not a room to be had. We went on to the castle anyway. We could drive south a ways later that evening to spend the night, if we had to.

I will not spend pages and pages describing Edinburgh Castle. It is something that one must experience for themselves. It, like Stirling, sits on a bluff high above the city and dominates the skyline. The oldest part, St. Margaret's Chapel, is Norman. Mons Meg (the enormous 300 year-old siege cannon), the Crown Jewels of Scotland, the Great Hall built by James IV, the Scottish National War Memorial and the Scottish United Services Museum are here. The architecture is amazing. If you are there at 1:00 PM, you will witness the firing of the noon cannon… one shot is more frugal than twelve. There is something for everyone to enjoy and we enjoyed it all. Then, we left to terrorize the shops along the Royal Mile on Lawn Market.

As we purchased a wax jacket for Amy and a tartan cape and tam for me, we chatted with the sales people about accommodations. They were very helpful, giving us the names of streets and sections of town where they were familiar and just that morning still had vacancies.

We bought more Christmas gifts and headed for the car. Amy had wanted to see a particular museum and I was concerned about lodging, so I dropped her off at the museum entrance, promising to return at 5:00 PM and went hunting for a room.

I found one in the northeast part of the city on a quiet side street lined with B&Bs (mostly full). I felt lucky. I carried a few things up to the third floor and went back to pick up Amy.

She had a perfectly glorious time finding just the information she had hoped for. We drove back to the B&B, emptied the car of every valuable treasure and started thinking about supper. There were several good restaurants within walking distance, so off we trudged.

We settled on The New Bamboo, a nearby oriental restaurant, had a wonderful buffet meal and were back and in bed at an early hour. It was March, the weather was raw and unpredictable. We had planned for warm clothing, but we weren't prepared for a room with no heat! Apparently, in the wee cold hours of the morning, the proprietor shuts off the furnace. It wasn't just cold, it was crazy cold. We piled on coats and sweaters and blankets to ward off the chill, but it was an uncomfortable night. In the morning, the heat returned and all was normal. I wondered if anyone else thought anything about it… I was miffed.

For breakfast we were seated at a table for four in the bay window. Around us people began to appear. (I didn't hear anyone mention the heat – but then, we were surrounded by the sounds of French, Italian, German, everything but English. – oh, yes, the soccer games.) As we were ready to leave, a couple from America was seated at our table -- apparently, the only other English speaking visitors, it was thought we would enjoy each other. Enjoy each other, we did. They were from Woodstock NY, a sculptress and a retired teacher now a painter. We talked for two more hours instead of getting our early start. But, it was indeed a worthwhile two hours. By the time we left, everyone else was well on their way.

We packed the car and started our journey out of Scotland through the borders towards Hadrian's Wall... the one thing I was determined to visit on this trip. The late start meant no extra stops, so we ate fruit and snacks in the car, caught quick glances at the list of ruins we had wanted to explore, and kept heading south.

We still had a stash of Scottish food and a good thing, too. We wanted to get to Hadrian's Wall in good weather. Nibbling our shortbread cookies, we drove through rolling but uninspired territory. At Corbridge, we turned to follow signs directing us to National Trust sites where visitors can experience this magnificent Roman Wall which stretches nearly 74 miles from Wallsend to Bowness. It was built 122-126 AD to defend the Roman frontier from the ancient northern tribes – the Celts, Scots, and Picts (who painted their faces, therefore must have been satanic). The wall was about 8 feet wide (or one chariot width). The forts were strategically placed every 3K (a bit less than 2 miles) with blockhouses midway.

Our first stop was at Chester's Fort, but it didn't seem to be the most inclusive presentation, so we bought some postcards and kept searching. It turns out that Chester's Fort is the best preserved example of a Roman cavalry fort in Britain. Built after Hadrian's Wall was completed, it stands beside the line of Hadrian's Wall and includes the famous bath house on the bank of the river North Tyne. But, time was short so we traveled on to Housesteads, the next recommended visitor site for the wall. The weather was turning ugly with rain and mud and cold, but we were here, it was incredible, and we were going to see it.

The terrain is unbelievable. The wall and fort sat on top of a rise (understatement) with defense trenches dug on either side. To reach the fort one first climbed down from the carpark/gift shop site level across an open space and then began to climb up. There was a path, but it was slippery with mud. Even with boots on, it was miserable.

We made it to the museum level, then had to pay to get into the fort. I was so thrilled to be standing on the site of a fort built by the Romans in 124 AD and so annoyed that it was so much trouble to see. We paid for our tickets and made our muddy way up to another level, yet.

The site was spectacular! Once we reached the top, we could see miles of rolling countryside in each direction. It was easy to understand how this area was chosen for a defensive fort. The Fort itself covers about five acres, and, in its day, housed about one-thousand infantry men.

The remains of the foundations and partial walls map out many buildings. The headquarters building was located in the center of the property. To its south stood the Commanding Officer's house--with heated bath--constructed around a courtyard. (Rank has its privileges.)

The grounds also included a hospital, a granary, two barracks, and – quite foreign to us 20th century prudes – a rather large, communal latrine. The latrine was fascinating. Placed at the lowest point of the property, it was situated and designed to collect water which flowed through stone channels and created a constant and fluent flush.

After two hours of walking among the stoneworks, we retraced our steps down the slippery embankment, across the plain, up the steps to the car park and started on our way again, planning to spend one more night on the road. We had dinner in Darrington at an interesting hotel and restaurant with tasty food. Out on the open road and a tad isolated, we imagined we were approaching this half timbered Inn in a coach and four. (Part of its charm.)

After a fairly quick dinner, we proceeded to the A1 (major highway) and headed south. We stopped for petrol outside of York. If we had gone into York to spend the night, we knew that the next day we would want to stay. Since time did not allow such a luxury, we pushed on and on until we reached Cambridge. We all slept well that night at Amy's house.

March 21 -- The day was bright and sunny, but chilly. The first order was to move the car from the street in front of Amy's house to the train station for long-term parking. From there, we didn't go punting on the Cam, but, we did take the Guide Friday bus tour of the city – always a pleasant trip.

Cambridge is literally as old as dirt... the remains of a 3,500-year-old farmstead was discovered at the site of Fitzwilliam College. There is further archaeological evidence of settlement on Castle Hill in the 1st century BC. We know it more for Cambridge University which was first formed in 1209. Peterhouse, the first college that still exists was established in 1284. King's College Chapel, one of the most recognizable structures in town, was begun in 1446 and finished in 1515. I would consider that to be old.

World famous 1940s big band leader Glenn Miller's name is posted on the 'Wall of Missing' at the Cambridge American Cemetery and Memorial located on the outskirts of town. Miller was flying from Bedfordshire to Paris in December, 1944, when his single engine plane was lost over the English Channel. No remains of people on board or plane were ever found. Glenn Miller is still listed as missing in action.

We didn't ride the tour bus all the way back to the depot. Getting off at the Cam, we walked past shops and pubs and other interesting places, until we were hungry enough for lunch. A local pub with true Elizabethan qualities lured us for a pint and a ploughman.

Amy took me to shop at the open-air market. What a hoot! I bought a colorful silk shirt for eight pounds, a subdued linen shirt for five pounds, and a pair of black knitted tights for one pound fifty which I love and wish I had bought more. Then it was on to Oxfam for a pair of wool slacks for eight pounds. No loose change to take back home for me!

We enjoyed supper at a little restaurant nearby and walked home. That night, we went to bed early, tuckered out from all the fresh air.

March 22 – Time to leave merrie olde England. Amy walked to the train station to get the car. I packed the luggage, squeezing and tugging until everything fit. I did have to leave a few things for Amy to wear 'til the end of the semester and threw away a pair of slacks that I had literally worn the ... seat out of.

Amy drove with me to Heathrow. I had not thought about the mortar attacks for an entire week, but now they were creeping into my consciousness. We had no trouble finding our way through traffic to the airport. We filled the car with petrol and returned it to Alamo, took the shuttle to the airport and checked in. I had purchased so many articles of clothing that I had to declare my purchases. Going through the process was very interesting. I was asked several times where I had been, how long I had stayed there, and had I been to Ireland.

We had lunch and window shopped for awhile, enjoying our last moments together. Then, Amy took the tube from Heathrow into London and I found a comfortable seat to curl up in and read until flight time.

Customs in Boston was a bit slow, but not too bad considering all my foreign purchases. It had been a delightful trip. Amy and I had a wonderful time exploring every wonder. We were especially pleased about the McEwan discoveries. It turned out to be much more than we had expected. One more trip may uncover the rest, but that trip will have to be planned in the future.

Germany -- 1995

Ah yes, it is vacation time again! This year it was in April and I spent three weeks with Jay in Germany and environs. We had a glorious time. Jay was in the middle of a two year tour stationed at Kaiserslautern, Germany. What better time to revisit a country full of history, culture, scenic beauty and adventure.

A friend came to the house every day to feed and attend to Emily, the cat. He had dropped me at the bus station in Concord and kept the car just for that purpose. SO, to travel by car to Storrs Street, by bus to Boston, by Continental shuttle to Newark, and then by Continental DC10 to Frankfurt to meet Jay on April 11 was the start of my itinerary.

I tried to sleep on the plane (really, I did), but it was a short night. Jay met me at the right gate at the right time even though he didn't have the correct flight number and didn't know I was coming from Newark. (Full information was not disclosed on the travel plans this time.) But there he was looking very dapper in his uniform. We drove the hour-long route from the airport to Kaiserslautern getting caught up on schtuff and avoiding Staus (traffic backups).

It was Wednesday morning, April 12, in Germany. We arrived at Jay's quarters around noon after doing some errands. Jay lived at Sembach – a mini base in the much larger Kaiserslautern complex which makes up Ram Stein Air Base. His building sat on a hill overlooking the wonderful, rolling German countryside. He had two fairly large (motel size) rooms joined end to end by a full bath. One room was set up as his kitchen/dining/living room and the other as his bedroom. Very comfortable, I, of course, got the living room.

The first evening, Jay's friend Kat, Nikki and her boy friend, Brian, fixed dinner and we ate in. We enjoyed drinking local wine and getting acquainted, but it was an early evening since they all had to work the next day, and I was in jet lag.

Thursday and Friday, Jay worked and I rested trying to get my inner clock synchronized.

Jay was off at noon on Friday. We packed, got money exchanged, and ran errands until Kat got off work at 5:00. By 7:00 we were on our way to PARIS!!!! Oui, oui, we were. April in Paris. Off for the weekend. C'est si bon! Toujour l'amour. Toulouse-Lautrec. Mmmmmmoi!!! It was indeed Good Friday.

The drive to Paris took 5 hours. The countryside was pretty, very open and rolling. After dark, I tried to keep my eyes open so I wouldn't be up all night, but it was hard to do. Kat didn't try to fight it… she slept. I talked with Jay, found change for the many tolls and recorded the information so we could be better prepared for the return trip. We stopped at one rest stop to get a sandwich and a cup of coffee and another to get Mobil gas.

Paris rises straight up out of the flat darkness. First, you see a halo of light, then the multi-lane highways begin. Then, without much notice, you are turning left, crossing the Seine and traveling along the left bank of the city.

We arrived after midnight. The traffic was light, but there was traffic. The city was lighted everywhere. (How do people sleep?) As we traveled along Tolblac toward our hotel, we were able to absorb some of the ambience of the city that for the next two days would be one continuous wonder.

On an island in the middle of the river Seine stood the Cathedral of Notre Dame. We approached it from the back. The famous flying buttresses were ablaze in light. The structure seemed to fairly glow against the midnight sky. It was the best introduction to Paris and the best view we were to be given of Notre Dame. Unfortunately, I didn't get a midnight photo.

Jay was right at home driving on the narrow streets and reading the small, sometimes obscure street signs. We followed the river to the Alma Bridge without hitting curb, cab, or pedestrian. Once across the Seine, we proceeded straight on George V Avenue to the Champs-Elysees and turned toward the Arc de Triomphe.

What a grand approach. The Arch was also bathed in light – as pretty as any postcard shot. We circled the Arch looking for MacMahon Street. We found it on the first circle – no easy task with traffic, small streets, and smaller street signs. But with the help of a good map and quick reflexes, we turned right on to MacMahon, then began hunting for Neil Avenue and Rue des Renauds.

The Rue des Renauds is not the smallest street I have been on in a car, but at 12:45 at night in an unfamiliar city, it was the most sinister. Dark, dank, narrow, and flanked by huge stone buildings, we were wondering if at any moment the phantom of the opera (or his clone) might appear in front of the car, halting any passage. Our imaginations in check, we scoured the buildings for street signs to give us our bearing. There it is! Poncelet Street! Arretez! Stop! There's our hotel! Only its west on a one-way street going east. It's GOING THE WRONG WAY! – But, not when you put the car in reverse and back up to it.

The street was extremely narrow. Jay's tiny Mitsubishi Eclipse was almost too big. He turned tightly and properly left, then backed up the street right into a parking space in front of the hotel. It was 1 o'clock in the morning. We rang the bell near the hotel entrance. The concierge welcomed us, registered us, and gave us directions to our accommodations. Our luggage, which fit so well in Jay's small car, seemed too large to carry up the tiny spiral staircase, but we made it to the premier etage, (first floor) unlocked our doors and guardedly entered our rooms.

Our rooms, across the hall from each other, were very plain (understatement) and on the small side (gross understatement), but clean and comfortable. My room held a single bed, a tiny round table, a small wooden closet, a normal sized straight chair, a large French window (which faced the alley rooftops and wouldn't lock) a small sink, and a bidet. (The last two behind a curtain.) Oh yes, and room to turn around.

Jay's room held a double bed, a larger closet, a chair, a sink, a shower, and a bidet. (The last three in a square carved out of one corner of the room.) His window (which faced the street) locked.

I went to bed wondering if we were the only people in the hotel and if there were any Orangutans in the neighborhood.

Saturday morning, Jay knocked on my door saying he was going down to breakfast. I met him soon after. He had gotten up early to look after the car. (It might get a ticket parked in front of the hotel.) When he inquired as to parking charges in a garage, he decided to take his chances on a ticket.

Breakfast was a croissant, a brioche, assorted jams, and the most wonderful coffee. Kat chose to sleep a little extra and forego breakfast. Jay ate his and hers, too.

By 9:30 AM we were walking down Rue Poncelet toward MacMahon to find the metro. Poncelet was abustle with people making choices for their carte du jour. In the early morning, Rue Poncelet was a marketplace. It was delightful seeing the wares of the vendors – scallops with the coral on, fresh meat, whole lambs (moving on quickly), fresh produce, cheeses, knick-knacks.

We found our metro station close by at Ternes (another etoile or traffic circle), bought our tickets and set off for the USO to change some marks to francs and to gather information.

Many of the buildings in Paris open, not onto the city streets, but onto side passageways which are located behind doors or solid gates with no identification which face the public sidewalks and hide a separate community. The USO is in one of these. We found the address, but no entrance. Then, the unmarked passage door opened and an American military couple magically emerged. Jay asked them about the USO. They pointed through the enigmatic opening. Feeling like Alice and the Looking Glass, we cautiously entered. Inside, there was a cobblestone street which went through to a courtyard or atrium. Along the cobblestone street were several doors leading into smaller buildings. We found the USO, asked millions of questions, were given trillions of answers (there were two French attendants never agreeing) and planned our stay in Paris.

Feeling informed and fortified, we changed money, bought cartes muse (tickets for the museums), multiple metro passes, and headed for the Tour Eiffel. (How many people are there in the world? They were all at the Eiffel Tower.) We decided to buy our guidebus tickets and ride around the city rather than spend precious hours waiting our turn to go to the top of the Tower.

There is more to see in Paris than one can manage in a week-end or a week of week-ends. But, we gave it the old college try.

On the bus, we passed the Invalides. Actually, Les Invalides is a vast complex of buildings which include the Hotel des Invalides, the Dome, and the church of St. Louis. Ordered by Louis XIV, it was designed as a refuge for old and invalid soldiers who were often forced to beg for a living. The Dome, considered a masterpiece, covers the entrance to the crypt which contains Napoleon's tomb. It's a symmetrical building braced by long buildings with mansard roofs which are divided into apartments. As we passed by on the bus, a gray tiger cat stepped out of one of the open upper windows, tippy-toed along the narrow ledge of the roof and went for his daily walk.

Further on we passed Le Petit Palais which was built for the 1900 World's Fair. This museum now houses the Tuck and Dutuit collections.

We left the guide bus at the Louvre and walked a bit along the Seine. Still undergoing its massive refurbishing, The Louvre was nevertheless a well attended attraction. All the people in the world not at the Eiffel Tower were at The Louvre. The Square Courtyard and Clock Tower were once the enclosure of the early castle. It was now one of the routes to the main entrance – the pyramid.

The pyramid is awesome. A great contrast to the rounded ornamented older buildings of the palace, it is smaller than I had imagined, but very imposing. The clean lines and plain glass are less obstructive than a solid building would have been. Its grace comes from its simplicity of design and its attending fountains.

The great thing about having pre-purchased our museum passes, (Cartes Musee) we didn't have to spend time standing in lines, but could proceed directly to the entrance and the exhibits.

Once inside the glass pyramid, one descends a spiral staircase to the lower level where tickets, information, rest rooms, coat rooms, and pack-stashing rooms are located. From that point one can choose which part of the museum to visit and proceed in any direction. We had a great time searching for the Mona Lisa, the Winged Victory, other works of Leonardo da Vinci, delicate marble sculptures, ancient Egyptian artifacts... and on and on and on. It finally became clear that if we were to see anything else in our visit to Paris, we would have to leave the Louvre.

The guide bus took us next to Le Musee D'Orsay. Originally a railway station, it was opened for the 1900 World's Fair. It now houses exquisite pieces of art and sculpture by impressionist and post impressionist artists. It currently housed the Whistler exhibit. Unfortunately, this exhibit was not included on the Cartes Musee and was much too extensive to see the same day. (We did entertain returning on Sunday, but that day did not have enough hours in it either.) We got back on the bus and headed for the Arc de Triomphe and food.

When we arrived at The Arc, we were faced with a tough decision. The Arch or the stomach? We decided that we really wouldn't appreciate any more buildings or their vistas on an empty stomach so we strolled the Champs-Elysees until we found a little restaurant to suit our taste. We chose the Bistro Romain. (It was located right next door to a Burger King... go figure. Something for every taste.) We had a wonderful evening of good food (not great food, but really good food), good wine, good service, and good fun.

Since I was the only one in our party who spoke French (remember Switzerland?) I read the menu and discussed its contents with the others. When we were certain of our choices, I relayed them to our waitress. Now, my American French had bought us metro tickets and museum tickets in

Paris with great success, but I was not at all sure about dinner. When the food came it bore no resemblance to what we thought we had ordered. It was very good, but not what we had expected. I had this nagging skeptical impression that when the waitress got to the kitchen, she simply said (in her authentic Parisian French) "I have a table of Americans, give me a 1. a 2. and a 3." Did she have the last laugh? No, we had a delightful dinner. But, years later, we still wonder... and laugh about it.

We spent more than two hours eating dinner, but it was early enough to beat the ever-growing dining crowd and we still had an evening to see more of Paris.

We returned to the hotel to regroup. Kat and Jay dressed more warmly and headed back to the Eiffel Tower. I begged off and went to my monastic cell to get some extra sleep. (My inner clock still had not adjusted well and tomorrow was Easter in Paris.)

In the morning we, once more, had croissants and brioches and incredible coffee for breakfast. Once more, we started off for the City of Lights and all its secrets. Only today we headed straight for the Metro and Notre Dame. Because it was Sunday, we knew there would be crowds. Because it was Easter Sunday, we did not know the full extent of those crowds.

The Metro was swift and sure. We surfaced near the flower and bird market and got our bearings. To the right was the Palais de Justice and Sainte Chapelle. As beautiful as it was, we passed it by to get to Notre Dame.

The front of Notre Dame was beautiful, but not as dramatic as the back. Most of the front was covered with scaffolding for cleaning, so our view was obstructed. The entire courtyard was filled with people lined up to get into the cathedral. As much as we would like to have seen the interior, it was enough for us to even be there, so we absorbed for awhile, took a few pictures and waited for the tour bus.

If I ever return to Paris, I will go to Notre Dame on a quiet day (if one exists) and see everything.

Back on the guide bus, we sat back and enjoyed the views. The trip was relaxing and informative. We passed La Conceirgerie, dating from Philip the Fair, and Le Place St. Michel.

Built in 1665 as a college for 60 students, the Institute of France is linked to the Louvre by the Pont des Arts.

The Palais Bourbon was originally built in 1722 for the Duchess of Bourbon, the daughter of Louis XIV. It has undergone several changes and embellishments through the centuries.

The Opera is the largest theater for lyric opera in the world. Gorgeous from the outside, there is a cutaway model of it at the Musee D'Orsay showing the equally interesting interior.

Next on the itinerary, The Grand Palais was built for the 1900 World's Fair. It is now used for contemporary exhibitions and conventions.

We were soon passing The Pont Alexander. Named for Alexander III of Russia when it was built in 1896, it celebrated the alliance between the Russians and the French. The bridge joins the Esplanade des Invalides to the Champs-Elysees.

The majestic Egyptian obelisk stands in the center of the Place de la Concorde. It dates back to Rameses II and was donated to Louis Phillippe in 1831. The Place de la Concorde stands between the Louvre and the Arc de Triomphe at the beginning of the Champs-Elysees. This is the site of the infamous guillotine during the French Revolution.

Standing in the center of La Place Vendome is the monument in honor of Napoleon I. Along the periphery is the Hotel Ritz where Chopin died in 1849. It is not just the labeled or public buildings that are magnificent… all buildings in Paris have magnificent architecture. It is an aesthetic joy just to drive past them and see their beauty.

We finally made our way to visit the Arc De Triomphe. However, it was now Sunday, and it was closed. It is impressive, to say the least.

I had worked hard on my French for the two days we were in Paris and thought I was doing fairly well at understanding and being understood. I had successfully purchased museum tickets and metro passes, and had ordered delicious meals. As we left the tour bus in front of the Louvre, we browsed for awhile at a souvenir stall along the Seine looking at the wonderful art and books, etc. Realizing that in two days we had not see the Moulin Rouge, I asked the attendant, in my very best French,

"Ou est le Moulin Rouge, s'il vous plait?"
He answered me in plain-spoken, Midwest American English, "Do you have a map?"

It was time to head home. From here we would walk through the Louvre, through the Tuilleries Gardens to the Place de la Concorde. There we would catch the Metro to Ternes, walk to our hotel and prepare to leave the City of Lights. But, first we would have lunch.

Now, we had been very proud of making our franc stretch and still receive memorable value – especially when it came to food. We entered the jammed café and were escorted to a small table. Jay and I ordered sandwiches, (I had a croquet monsieur, I don't remember what Jay had, but it looked delicious) and coffee. Kat, who was on a fat-free diet, said she would wait and eat in the car, but would drink a coke. Le garcon asked if she would like a large coke. She said she would.

Our food was wonderful, the coffee was tastefully strong and was served in double-handled cups. The coke was a coke—a large coke, but a coke. When the bill came, we nearly fell off our chairs. Kat's coke was 80 francs, or $16. We had to take a picture of such a valuable drink. It was to be one for the scrapbooks.

Oh well, we were leaving town anyway. We had enough francs for tolls and left almost the balance of our wallets on the table for lunch... just one more amusing memory of our weekend in Paris.

The trip home to K'town was uneventful. Since it was daylight most of the way, we were able to see the French countryside we had missed in the dark. And there is A LOT of French countryside.

Tired, but happy about the weekend, we arrived back at Jay's about 9 PM, unloaded the car and collapsed into bed.

On the morning of Monday, April 17, Jay and I prepared the car to leave for Garmisch. We ran some errands, had lunch at Ramstein, and finally were underway in the early afternoon. The weather was a bit overcast, but not bad. We talked and watched the scenery all the way to Munich.

We stopped at a Brauhaus on the outskirts of Munich for supper. We each had a schnitzel and a local weissen. Jay like the beer steins so much, he bought two of them.

After dinner, we continued on to Garmisch. It was dark by the time we arrived. We traveled as far as was familiar, then stopped at thememorable Post Hotel to ask directions. (The Post Hotel was where we had had that scrumptious Kaese spaetzle on our last trip in '89. Remember, we ate on picnic tables in a narrow alley at the side of the building.)

We weren't far from our destination of the General George Patton Hotel and were shortly getting settled in our room. The room was considerably smaller than the rooms we had had at the Abram's, but we did have our own en suite bath this time – no parading the halls in our skivvies.

After a bit, Jay and I walked back to Marien Platz. We tried to find a restaurant in which we had eaten twice in 1989. We must not have ventured far enough on our first attempt, or the place had closed. Planning to return in the daylight to tour the winding streets and try again, we found our way to a local watering hole where we watched the singles and the wannabees play their games and dance their dances while we had a couple of tasty brews.

Tired from the trip, yet eager for the morrow, we walked back to the hotel and tumbled into our eider down beds.

Tuesday morning we awoke with great eagerness to re-explore Bavaria. There were several things we wanted to redo in Garmisch and many new things we wanted to discover in the surrounding areas. In 1989, we could see the highest alp in Germany, The Zugspitz, from our guesthouse, but there hadn't been enough time to go there. I really wanted to see what a Bavarian Glacier was all about.

The morning weather was overcast and damp, but our spirits were high. We had a very American military breakfast of thick sliced bacon, over-easy eggs, crisp hash browns, buttered wheat toast and copious cups of coffee in the hotel dining room and then went to the tour office to collect information.

The direct telephone line to the Zugspitz said the winds were high and the visibility low, so the glacier would not be open today. We turned our focus instead to Mittenwald, a small Alpine village a few miles away. Outfitting the car with gear for the day, we headed southeast among the mountains.

Mittenwald is a climatic health resort and winter sport center nestled amidst forest, meadows, alpine lakes (sees) and the Kranzberg and Karwendel mountain ranges. Its altitude is 7,087 feet. On the edge of town is the Karwendelbahnhof (depot). It houses the cable car which takes skiers and sightseers to the top of the Viererspitze.

Mittenwald lies between Garmisch and Innsbruck and was once the crossroads on the medieval trade route between Venice and Augsburg.

We found a place to park and read the large glass-encased community map to get our bearings.

Bavaria loves its frescoed buildings and Mittenwald is no exception. For a small village, Mittenwald has many interesting streets and buildings. The date on the St. Peter and St. Paul Baroque parish church is 1746.

Browsing a bit in quaint shops and neighborhood groceries, the streets led us to the violin museum. In 1684, Matthias Klotz returned to Mittenwald from his years as an apprentice in Italy and brought the industry of Violin making to town. It is now known for its internationally recognized violin-making school. This history has been documented in its museum and, in its workshop, you can watch a master violin maker while he is creating a new, delicate, velvet-throated violin from the 100 year-old stack of wood outside the door.

We spent a delightful morning in Mittenwald. Would hope to be able to return there another time. On the way back to Garmisch, we detoured a bit just to enjoy the Bavarian countryside. It is idyllicly splendid.

The weather was clearing, now, and I was still hoping to get to see the

Zugspitz. The AFRC (Armed Forces Recreation Center) tour of Innsbruck was tomorrow and Jay wanted to move on the next day, so today seemed to be the only opportunity. We decided to try. We checked with the hotel and were told the winds had subsided and the Zugspitz was now accessible. A train from the Garmisch Bahnhof would take us there.

Well, we missed the train at Garmisch, so we drove out through the meadows to the tiny village of Grainau where everyone transfers from the first-leg normal train to the second leg cog-rail train and joined the excursion there.

The cog-rail climb to the top of the glacier was awesome. At times, we looked straight down to treetops or lovely lakes. The track was so narrow that the ascending train moved to a siding long enough to let the descending train go by … passing so close to each other you could read the title of the book in the hands of the other train's passenger. Less than 1/3 of the way up the mountain, the train entered a tunnel which ran inside the mountain up to the point of departure. The tunnel was lighted occasionally so that you could see the construction of this engineering miracle.

Where the train arrives at the summit, there is a building which houses rest rooms, a restaurant, and facilities for the skiers who come year-round to the glacier. These people are tourists like us who have come for the adventure.

Nearby is a small chapel dedicated to those who have lost their lives on the Zugspitz.

Jay and I had a light lunch at this level before braving the absolute peak of the highest alp in Germany. From the building where the train arrives, one must still take another gondola to get to the very top of the alp. We squeezed in with a regiment of skiers and their gear and looked upward toward the building in which we would safely step very soon. To look down was very daunting.

Once inside the building, we read the history of the building of the railroad and even watched a short movie documenting its construction. Then we climbed more stairs (inside) to yet another level. This level was only a landing which exited to the narrow, upper level of the alp. Going out huge glass doors onto the deck, we looked up once again to see the gold cross implanted on the ragged peak of the frozen alp. In good weather, one can climb that high. Looking down was not for the faint of heart.

From the deck on the alp peak in Germany to the opposite alp peak in Austria was a narrow walkway. Feeling quite bold, we maneuvered the snow-covered catwalk across the border into Austria and into their buildings. We didn't want to stay outside too long since the wind was still howling and we were dressed in trench coats and street shoes. (No gloves or hats for us.)

Inside the Austrian building was a restaurant – quite nice—will have to eat here next time. Again, we looked around enjoying their pictures and history. We had checked the time for the last departure of the gondola for Germany (our tickets were not good for Austria) and finally decided it was time to return to the German building. We walked back across the catwalk and approached the glass doors to enter the building. They were stuck. We pulled harder. No... they were locked. We pounded, thinking someone might hear us – but not for long. What if we were also locked out of the Austrian side? We tore across the catwalk and ran into the building, out of breath. It took us a minute or two before we found anyone to talk to. Those minutes seemed like hours. What if everyone was gone?

We finally found two men who obviously seemed to be closing the building. We tried to tell them of our plight – they tried to tell us that we had to go back to the other building. We said it was geschlossen. They said, "Nein, es ist nie geschlossen." (No, it is never locked.)

I crossed my arms across my chest and pumped one arm like the barrier at a railroad crossing. "Das ist geschlossen!" They finally looked at each other, talked among themselves and seemed to be enjoying our misadventure.

One man went to check the German building. When he returned, he confirmed. "Ja, das ist geschlossen." (Yup, it is locked.)

Perhaps it was the terror in my eyes that led them to finally decide to allow us to ride in their gondola down to Ehrwald, Austria at no charge. They took us around the gate and we joined the others who had planned to be on the last gondola going down on the Austrian side of the Zugspitz.

When we arrived at the bottom, the same helpful attendant told us to follow the signs and walk to the village where we would find a train to Garmisch. What he failed to mention was that the village of Ehrwald was four miles away.

We stoutheartedly started off. Of course the others on the gondola drove by in their cars thinking that we knew what we were doing and had chosen to walk that far (natives do it all the time in that part of the world).

We enjoyed the first couple of miles – the trek was nothing for Jay, trooper that he is – but old Mom was grossly out of shape and at one point turned her ankle on the beveled road edge carving up her knee in grand style.

When we arrived at the train station, we must have been a sight. We tried our best to converse with the station master in this tiny village in the midst of alpine isolation. As soon as he knew we spoke English, he switched to our language. Actually, he was from Innsbruck and eager to speak with someone else from the outside world. He turned out to be delightful as well as helpful. We stumbled through currency and found that we had enough Deutchmarks to buy train tickets to Garmisch (they were only 6 marks but a helluva lot of Austrian shillings). He told us where we might find a beirstuberl so we could wait for the next train in some semblance of comfort. (Of course, we had just missed the previous train.)

So, we started off to find the pub/gas station at the foot of the hill. By now, my feet were numb clear up to my quadriceps (or the reverse... it was hard to tell). And, of course, the place was closed. Jay asked if a beer sounded good enough to walk further into town to find out if the grocery was open. I looked in the direction of town and looked back up the hill in the direction of the station and decided it probably was the most sensible decision to use whatever strength I had left in my body to climb the hill to the train station. That way, if I died, I would be closer to the train and Jay wouldn't have so far to drag me.

We waited on the platform. The station master responded gallantly when Jay asked him for a band-aid for my knee. He appeared with a first-aid kit the size of a carpenter's tool box. The two of them consulted like brain surgeons on which antiseptic to use, what width gauze would work best, and how long to cut the rolled bandage. If it hadn't been that it was my bloody leg they were oohing and aahing over, I might have thought it tender.

When the triage was over, I thanked them both profusely, (actually, it did feel a great deal better) and pulled my pantleg down over my tattered hosiery and World War I wrapping.

Jay garnered what daylight was left and took home videos of our unscheduled destination. "Let's go to the Zugspitz, she says."

The train ride from Ehrwald to Garmisch (this line didn't go through Grainau) took about 20 minutes. I'm sure the scenery would have been spectacular, but we had just run out of daylight. When we arrived in Garmisch, we were faced with two decisions: how to get to the hotel, and how to get Jay's car. I was sure a fellow serviceman would be happy to help us out... (Right after they quit laughing.)

So, we WALKED (ooh, aaah) several blocks to the Military Police station to see what we could find. The best the young soldier behind the desk could do was call for a taxi (shoot, we could have done that from the depot -- oops, do I sound grumpy?) With the cutbacks, he had no one on the road and he could not leave his post.

So, we took a cab to the hotel, paid the fare, and then, from the back seat Jay asks, "How long would it take to drive to Grainau?"

"Now" asks the driver with a ring of anxiety in his voice. (I guess Jay didn't want the extra exercise to walk the bike path which dissects the miles of meadow between the towns of Garmisch and Grainau. And, it was, after all, dinnertime.)

I went up to the room and poured a much needed scotch and waited for Jay's return. Supper that night would have been room service, except it was Italian night in the hotel dining room and I needed some comfort food. That night I could have slept on a bed of nails – hand wrought, finely pointed, torture fashioned nails.

The next morning dawned bright and sunny ('though still windy) and we were bound for Innsbruck on a big, warm, motor coach with soft, cushy seats, and a well informed tour guide. All I had to do was relax, look out the window, and laugh occasionally at his hometown humor. Actually, he was originally from Indiana, but he had been in Bavaria for so long it was hard to notice that about him.

When we arrived at the center of the Historische Altstadt, (historic old town) the bus deposited us at the edge of a park. We were with our tour guide, but for those who aren't, there are a number and variety of horse drawn conveyances for hire. Actually, we were told that, if approached by anyone authoritative in appearance, we were all to say we were with "Uncle David", a man who happened to have a large family and know a lot about Innsbruck. They have their own certified tour guides for hire -- anyone else is illegal.

Following "Uncle David", we walked past the Hofburg (Imperial Palace) which was built 1754 -73 during the reign of Empress Maria Theresa. It stands on the site of an earlier castle that was destroyed by earthquake and fire. It contains splendid ornamentation, ceiling frescoes, pictures, and tapestries. We did not take the time to go in... next time.

The Altstadt is reached through an archway leading to some of the most wonderful buildings. On the corner of the square is one of the most spectacularly ornate buildings I have seen anywhere... even Paris. I am not sure of its significance, but it is gloriously painted white with very baroque gold trim on every window. It is listed in the guide as a "Gothic town residence built in the 15th century." The gold work decoration was added in 1730.

Across the square is a building I do know about. It is called the Goldenes Dachl (Golden Roof). It is a small, three-story, late Gothic balcony of a former palace in stadtplatz, known for its gilded copper roof. The roof sports 2,657 gilded copper tiles. The former royal residence was built by Maximilian I in 1500 as a royal box for watching spectacles in the square below. The area around the square contains several fountains as well as several café's with sidewalk tables. We had a wonderful lunch there. I had sausage, potatoes, and sauerkraut with my beer.

Across the platz, and along the Herzog-Friedrich Strasse, stood many interesting buildings, including a 13th century jail. While we were eating our lunch, a rather professional camera crew kept tracking up and down the platz. They approached Jay, but before any communication took place, Jay explained that we did not speak Austrian and they went away. Three weeks later, Good Morning America was on its European expedition, shooting from this very platz. We wondered if we had encountered their advance crew.

After lunch, we backtracked a bit to visit the Hofkirche (Court Church) and Tiroler Volkskunstmuseum (Museum of Tirolian Folk Art).

The Hofkirche contains the magnificent marble tomb of Maximilian I, which is covered by 24 carved scenes depicting the Emperor's deeds. An impressive figure of the kneeling Emperor is guarded by 28 huge bronze statues of his real and legendary ancestors and relatives.

The Tiroler Volkskunstmuseum was awesome. In its three floors of extensive displays of costumes, furniture, and art there are also rooms of several houses furnished as they would have been in earlier centuries and of the distinctly different areas of the Tyrol. Amazing!

At the other end of the platz (after passing many stores of beautiful Austrian crystal), near the river Inn, stands the Ottoburg. Built next to the town wall, this 15th century Gothic tower has always been an Inn and restaurant.

Along the Inn River are many colorful and newer houses of more modern architecture.

We met at the bus at the designated time and started for the other side of town to visit the Olympic Village. At the top of the spectators' level are the flags of the participating nations and the flame containers from two different years. Below that are the tally board and the stands for the ski jump. To the right is an elevator for the skiers. We were given the option to climb to the top – some people did… somebody else, not me.

In town, below the Olympic Village, in line with the ski jump is a church and a graveyard. "Uncle David" told us it is said that in Garmisch if they miss the ski jump, they land in a hospital. In Innsbruck if they miss, they land in the graveyard. ☺

Although it was April, there was still snow on the ground at the Olympic Village. It must be at an impressively high altitude.

We had a lovely ride home. At the border between Germany and Austria are the remnants of a Roman Wall – still in very good repair.

That evening Jay and I had dinner at the Posthotel in Garmisch. We ate inside after a beer on the terrace. It was too early in the season to eat in the alley, and our favorite, kaesespaetle, was no longer on the menu. But, we ate well. It was the season for Spargel (white asparagus), salmon, wild mushroom soup almost as good as our other favorite place around the corner -- that we never found. No, we didn't dream it.

We returned to the hotel, weary, but content. The next day we would leave this charming little city of Garmisch—Partenkirchen still not having seen it all. (Next time.)

Another scrumptious breakfast in the General George Patton Hotel (they do feed our armed forces well) and then off to pack the car and continue on our way.

We traveled north retracing our steps to the west side of Munich and continued on to Dachau. It was a gray, misty sort of day which seemed to be in keeping with the Dachau experience.

The modern village of Dachau itself is quite charming. We made several passes through it until we became sensitized to the tiny signs which finally directed us to the site of the WWII concentration camp. The office building is now a museum filled with large black and white photographs of the camp and the total movement. They are grim. We then walked the grounds and visited the buildings. I did not feel moved to take any photographs. It is not a destination that I want to preserve that well. I will always have images in my memory. That will be enough.

We left Dachau and continued north along Germany's Romantic Road, an ancient trade route of medieval villages along the western boundary of Bavaria. It runs from Fussen in the south, through Augsburg, to Wurzburg in the north. We joined it near Augsburg. North of the Bavarian Alps, along this part of the route, the countryside is fairly flat and open farmland. We talked and absorbed the ambience of the scenery and noted the dotting of many castles along the horizon

Suddenly, we rounded a bend in the road and there, up high on a very large hill above us was this unbelievable medieval structure which completely dominated the area. The road, in fact, went underneath the castle.

We quickly decided to find access, made some fast turns to follow signs, and found ourselves at its gate. (Or so we thought.) We actually parked on the back side and had to walk almost three quarters of the way around it until we found the actual gate of entry. This gate was huge! ... and SO medieval! The opening was protected by a menacing iron gate which was woven in a grid of black wrought iron cross beams. It was at least twenty feet high and fifteen feet wide and the iron beams were ferociously pointed at the bottom. Of course, to be open, the gate was raised and secured at its full height, but imagine the force it wielded as it came crashing down... don't want to be the attacking marauders here. Once inside we could see several buildings of different time periods – all before 1600. This walled castle complex is an Inn and restaurant and museum.

We wanted to learn more. With every door we opened and every room we explored, we "hallooed" to gain someone's attention. All to no avail. If we had found anyone in, we would have stayed the night. The place was HUGE and, if there were others about, they had plenty of places to be sequestered. We never saw a single soul.

Once we decided not to stay the night, there was not enough time to visit the museum. We did learn that the name of this enigmatic castle was Harburg. We will have to return.

From there we continued north along the Romantic Road noting other medieval villages to visit next time. By now we had determined that our destination would be Rothenburg ob der Tauber.

When we arrived at Rothenburg, it was evident that this was, indeed, the place to be. We circled the walled city until Jay found the gate that was familiar to him from a previous visit and we entered a true fairy tale land. We skirted the outside perimeter inside the wall until we found a rather large parking lot edged with 13th century buildings. At the Hotel Meistertrunk, a guesthouse on Herrngasse that was made up of three separate historic buildings, we chose to spend the night. Our room on the third floor was tucked away under a roof gable and charming – rather small, but charming.

After settling in, we walked across the parking lot to a small gift shop just before closing, bought some trinkets for gifts, and decided to come back the next day to spend more time. That night we had dinner in the guesthouse dining room. The setting was medieval storybook. The food was excellent.

The next morning, we started out early, on foot. There was so much to see. The only other people we saw out and about that early in the morning were the bakers and other sight seers. The market wasn't even completely set up yet in the shadow of the rathaus. The rathaus (town hall) is an imposing building composed of two parts. The Gothic section dates between 1250 and 1400, the front section, in Renaissance style, was built 1572-78. The arches facing the Market Square were added in 1681. A courtyard separates the two buildings.

Rothenburg is a walled town overlooking the valley on the River Tauber with ancient towers and ramparts and old fountains. It covers seven centuries of history as a free imperial city.

Along the walls are ramparts that you can walk upon as well as many towers – pretty and interesting, but no longer used for sentinels. The view from these towers is spectacular.

The city has many gates for entrance. One was especially intriguing. It was a double gate constructed in a figure 8. The road was one lane, but not one way. I don't know how the vehicles sort it out, but they do. We did not try to drive it. Inside the gate, the roads were narrow and the buildings interesting. Some were of daub and wattle, half timber architecture, but did not look anything like those in Britain. As I stood looking at these beautiful buildings, I was sure I heard the pied piper just beyond the bend.

At Whitsuntide, (the week of the seventh Sunday after Easter) the festival of "Master Draught" is held in honor of the old mayor Nusch who, in 1631, is reputed to have quaffed in one draught a 6-pint mug of wine in order to save the town from invader ruin. Mayor Musch is reputed to have taken three days to sleep off the stupor, but suffered no other ill effects.

One of the interesting buildings in town is the horse mill (or Nag's Mill). Although they have a river, the town sits far above it and access to the river and its mills could be tentative at times of hostilities. So, in 1516, the town built its own mill within its walls. The four grinding wheels at this mill were powered by 16 horses walking round and round. The building looks to be about five stories tall with a full row of eyebrow dormered windows on each level. Very picturesque. Today it is a youth hostel.

We visited a toy shop that had wooden soldier nutcrackers taller than lifesize. And separate from the shop they also have an extensive toy and doll museum housing more than 600 German and French dolls representing more than 200 years. It also has doll houses, puppet theaters, railways, farms, virtual toy villages to delight the child in each of us. Fantastic!

We had lunch in a delightful restaurant close by and then visited several more museums (The town has a museum for every interest… even medieval crime) and a few of the many beautiful churches.

About tea time, we bought schneeballs and other sinful baked goods to eat in the car from one of the tiny bakeries whose tantalizing aroma lured us from a block away, and then reluctantly drove away from this medieval wonderland.

Traffic was good. We made it all the way back to K-town where we indulged in schnitzel du jour at the Schnitzel Haus. These people know how to eat! After dinner, we stopped by Ramstein to get supplies for the next leg of our trip – our timeshare week in Rott, Germany.

Jay and I arose early to head for the city of Heidelberg. Kat and two of her friends were planning to meet us in the afternoon at the world renown castle. The magnificent, imposing castle, again, sits high on a hill above the town. It can be seen from every vista.

The tour book says, "The tranquil riverside setting of Heidelberg was an inspiration to several 19th century German writers, including Goethe. The 16th century castle is the most prominent landmark, but the colorful Church of the Holy Spirit and Renaissance buildings associated with the university also are of interest. The Old Bridge and the Philosopher's Walk along the right bank of the River Neckar offer the most romantic views of this town, which is often shrouded in mist."

We drove through the tiny, narrow streets of the city and parked in a multi-leveled parking garage. The hills are steep enough that almost every level of the garage was ground level. Then, we walked the tiny, narrow streets of the city. The architecture is diversified, but beautiful.

There are several gates to the city (typical for the time period). At the gate near the Old Bridge is a statue of a mandible. History says there was a monkey statue at this spot as far back as the 15th century – not sure why. It disappeared at the end of the 17th century. The current bronze sculpture monkey was placed here in 1979.

After lunch in the marvelous Weinkruger restaurant in the center of town, we moved the car a bit further up the hill and then climbed straight up 999 steps (or more) to the castle. Jay left me in the dust, since it was getting close to time to meet the girls and he didn't want to be late. It took me quite a while to get there. I stopped to rest often at the stone seats provided. I must have looked dangerously out of shape since a man and his wife, who were coming down, stopped to express their concerns in caring tones, but they were speaking German far too fast for me to sort it out and breathe at the same time. In my limited vocabulary, I thanked them and assured them I was fine and enjoying the view. (And hoped my nose wasn't growing.)

It took a few more stops, but I finally made it. We waited outside the castle for Kat and the girls. It gave me a chance to recover from my climb and for my purple face to return to its normal pink.

The Heidelberg Castle was built in stages through the centuries. The architecture is reflective of that. The center part of the building is the oldest – probably 13th or 14th century. On the left of center the architecture is French Renaissance, and on the right the architecture is Italian renaissance.

Inside the first building is a large model of the entire castle. Although the tour took about an hour and we saw a great deal, we only saw about one-tenth of the entire complex.

We did see the Heidelberg Tun in the cellar of the castle. The first big keg was built in 1591. The wine growers in the area had to pay their taxes in wine which was stored in this huge barrel. The barrel seen by tourists today was built in 1751 and is even larger. It holds 55,345 gallons of wine. Some party!

We walked the gorgeous gardens and grounds until it was time to leave for Kaiserslautern. The girls went straight back, but Jay wanted to get video of the castle at night, so we stayed a bit longer. We went back to the main street and had scrumptious coffee and dessert outside of an interesting restaurant called the Futterkrippe. Regretfully, we weren't hungry enough for a whole meal. We watched the interesting people walking the promenade for awhile (they were probably all tourists like us). Then, we retrieved the car and drove across the old bridge and waited for dusk.

While waiting, we walked along the riverbank hoping to get a guidebook shot of the castle. It was a lovely last look. Jay was able to get his video. We left having had a wonderful day.

We spent that night at Jay's apartment in K-Town and awoke fairly early, eager to head north. Our journey would take us along the east bank of the Rhine. (In 1989, you remember, we sailed the Rhine from Mainz to Koblenz and returned by train along the west bank. This time, we would actually get to stop in all the little towns we had seen from the boat.)

We drove through Wiesbaden and Eltville to stop in Rudesheim midmorning. The area of Rudesheim was first settled by the Celts and later by the Romans... it is that old. Its first mention in documented history is in the year 1074. Evidenced by archeologically-found glass, the area was already a wine growing region. The modern town of Rudesheim is a wine center and tourist destination second in visitation only to Cologne. Its most famous street is the Drosselgasse, a VERY narrow street lined with cozy wine taverns.

At the far end of the Drosselgasse is the Oberstrasse. On it stands the

Bromser Hof which was built by Heinrich Bromser in 1542. Once a fine residence, it now houses Siegfried's mechanical musical cabinet, a collection of self –playing musical instruments covering three centuries. The music could be heard up and down the entire street.

The Bromserburg wine museum in the Bromserburg Castle exhibits the history of local wine making. Herr Bromser was surely a most prominent citizen.

This tiny historic town also sports a museum of Medieval Torture which illustrates crime and punishment in the Middle Ages. A strong testimony to law abidance.

We rode the gondola car up to the Neiderwald monument. The 132 foot tall Neiderwald monument was erected in 1877-1883 to commemorate the re-establishment of the German Empire. The first tourists to the monument traveled by cog-railway. Today the mode of transportation is a small cable car.

The two-seater gondola car carries one above the acres of vineyards of Reisling grapes. Many of the restaurants have their own homemade wines. On the far horizon could be seen the Rochuskapelle (a pilgrimage chapel to St. Roch). On the edge of the river is the Bromserburg, the oldest and best preserved of Rudesheim's three castles. From the 13th century it served the archbishops of Mainz at times as living quarters and as a refuge. Later it became a hiding place for robber barons. Goethe also stayed here in 1814. Today the castle belongs to the town and houses the Rheingau folk and wine museum with a large collection of drinking vessels.

When we finished our cable car ride, the tiny Drosselgasse was beginning to get crowded and we decided it was time to continue our journey. Up the road a piece is Kaub. In the center of the Rhine, at Kaub, is the five-sided, six story tower of the Pfalzgrafenstein (or Die Pfalz) castle built in about 1325 by King Ludwig of Bavaria as a customs house.

Up on the hill above Kaub is Burg Gutenfels, built around 1200 by the Falkenstein family. In 1326, King Ludwig der Bayer (the Bavarian) resided here and tended to his tax collecting on the river. It is now a hotel. On the hill across the river from Kaub is the majestic, thousand year old Schonburg Castle. The town of Oberwesel sits on the site of an old Celtic settlement (400 BC). The castle is divided into three parts, with two keeps and one tower with living quarters.

As we drove toward St. Goarshausen for lunch, we passed the famous Lorelei Rock, but we were too close to it to get a picture. The view is much better from the center of the river.

The sister towns of St. Goarshausen and St. Goar are across the river from each other and are connected by a car ferry. St. Goar was a hermit who lived in the 6th century. His tomb is in the preserved 8th century church.

A few miles up the Rhine is the magnificent castle, Marksburg, the only knight's castle still standing. The climb from the car park was a hike and a half. But the view was spectacular. Unfortunately, the tours, which were in German, took more than an hour. We were still looking at another 3 hours to drive to get to our chalet near Hamelin, so we terrorized the gift shop for a few minutes and then continued, regretfully, on our way. We stopped to stretch our legs once, but ate a supper snack in the car.

It was still light when we reached Rott, but barely. We found our home at Ferienpark Extertal for the next week and settled in for the evening. The rustic chalet was very comfortable, and very private. From the back, it looked out into the springtime woods full of fragrant blossoms. My bedroom was on the first floor in the front. Jay was in the loft, which actually had two rooms and a balcony, but the stairs were hardly more than a fat ladder. There was a sauna off of my bathroom. (We used it once to dry clothes.) The knotty-pine great room was furnished with comfortable leather furniture and the kitchen faced out to the woods and the blossoms. Between the full travel day and the cool, crisp mountain air, we had no trouble sleeping well that first night.

We had not been to the north of Germany before, so we had no idea what to expect. This first day in the quiet, pastoral splendor of our chalet, we assessed our surroundings to decide on a travel plan. The city of Hamelin (Hameln) was close. Knowing the legend, we decided to see the town. We were already off the beaten track, so we decided to take a side road on the map instead of the highway. The road followed a small river (The Weser) through the rolling countryside. It was idyllic. However, when we arrived, we quickly found that the city was essentially closed for tourists on Monday. So, we did what the natives did – we shopped.

We found that the core of the walled city was, indeed, circular with access only by a few gates. First, we toured the outside, then found a place to park and walked the inside.

Architecture is decidedly different in the north. Not only different from other regions, but also different from each other in different times. The main square of Hameln traces the history of architecture through the ages of this city.

The Leisthaus Museum was built as a home by master builder Cord Tonnies for a local merchant named Gerd Leist in 1585-89. The jagged gable decorated with slender volutes above the attic has a rather bizarre appearance. The wide two storied protruding bay window is integrated with the façade by stone sills. The antique figure of Lucretia was placed on top by the classically educated Gerd Leist, probably as a contrast to the Cardinal Virtues depicted on the frieze between the two stories of the bay window.

The picturesque, timber-framed Stiftsherrenhaus was built for the town councilor Friedrich Poppendiek in 1556-58 and originally had four floors. The façade has, however, been retained in its original design. The carved figures on the timber supports form the principal feature of this building and represent God the Father, Christ, the Apostles, David, Simon, Cain and Abel, and the antique planet Gods. The master builder's choice of these motives are characteristic of the renaissance style and bear witness to Germany's classical heritage. The facade was renovated in 1969.

The Rattenfangerhaus (the Pied Piper's House) gets its name because of an inscription on the side wall concerning the exodus of Hamelin's children. It was actually built in the style of the Weser renaissance in 1602-03 for a local councilor named Herman Arends. The large reception hall and richly decorated front indicate a deliberate show of wealth. The whole façade is decorated with numerous ornamental designs of the late Weser renaissance period. The protruding bay windows resemble those of the Leisthaus and coats of arms have been incorporated into the sills above the windows similar to those of a castle.

The city is dotted throughout with beautiful bronze sculptures integrated into the walkways. As you are admiring the buildings you are reminded to look behind you at the adjacent free-standing sculptures.

A small grocery and a smaller specialty shop lured us to buy interesting meats and garni. We also picked up some literature about the city and decided to return another day. We took our culinary treasures back to our mountain hideaway via yet another scenic trailway enjoying some of our odoriferous cheese, zesty meat sticks, sinful rye bread, and tasty local beer on the way.

After relaxing at the chalet (the weather was still a bit raw to lounge on the deck), we decided to eat supper at The Bogerhof, a little inn we had seen down on the main highway between Rinteln and Rott.

We had great fun trying to pick out the most interesting entrees on the menu, but we seemed to have trouble being understood by the waitress. This led us to wonder if the northern dialect might be beyond our limited grasp of the German language. Two women were dining across from us, near the window that looked out onto an early spring garden. The younger woman came to our rescue with amazingly good English. She helped us with the menu and the waitress, although, she said the waitress was Dutch so we wouldn't have had much luck being understood – even she was having trouble.

The waitress sent the chef to the table to discuss our selections after we seemed to have a mix-up on our order of cocktails. The chef was delightful. Wanting to be helpful, we conversed in German, English, and a little French, but we were confident that we had a better understanding of all that the menu had to offer. We ordered something for two (the meal itself became incidental by this time). The food was good -- not great, but good-- but the conversation with the woman at the next table was terrific. She lived in Rinteln, worked in Hameln, and was married to an Englishman who spent a great deal of time in America. She was delightful and erased all of our feelings of inadequacy and frustration of the day.

On Tuesday, we agreed to get an early start, wind our way through yet another mountain pathway (they were all beautiful) and spend the day in Hameln. We were poking along enjoying the shops and the people and taking more photos in Hameln when Jay said, "Well, look who's here!" I hurried to take my shot of the Pied Piper statue critiquing the passers-by and turned to see the same woman we had met the night before. She was on her lunch hour and would we like to join her at a tiny, out-of-the-way restaurant few tourists ever find. OF COURSE WE WOULD!

She took us past McDonalds to find a delightful restaurant which served only crepes – except they were just a little heavier – filled with the most sinful of goodies. The building dated to the 13th century and held only a few tables. Seated on the second floor, six-foot five, Jay ducked a lot with the low beamed ceilings. Renate helped us order once again and we ate every bite of our chicken, cheese, and mushroom filled crepes. By the time lunch was ended, Renate had invited us to her house for Friday evening. We took directions and phone numbers and parted ways looking forward to the rest of the week knowing that our visit would end on a good note even if the week might be filled with challenges.

The afternoon was spent walking the narrow streets, visiting museums, and watching the restoration of the ancient buildings – each preserved to its original architecture. (We saw this everywhere in Germany.)

A local corn and general merchant named Henning Eichmann had a very attractive house built in 1639 during the 30-years war. From 1900 -1928 it was the property of the Lucking family when it was purchased by the town council. The richly decorated timbers with their carved inscriptions and ornamental designs together with the high portal and recessed entrance are special features of the timber work architecture in Hamelin during the 17th century. It is now called the Luckingsche Haus and is being painstakingly cared for.

Even though badly hit during the Second World War, most restoration in Hamlin is historically authentic and not contemporary. They take great pains and pride in preserving their centuries of history. With narrow streets and limited space, large buildings are randomly everywhere. Perpendicular to the Osterstrasse and in front of the Garrisonkirche (Garrison Church) is the Backerstrasse. Here in the Hochzeithau (Festive Hall) terrace, the permanent benches are set up for the Sunday noon presentation of the Pied Piper luring the children out of town.

The Dempterhaus was built for the Hamelin town mayor Tobias van Deventer (or Dempter) in 1607-08. A noteworthy feature of this house is that the ground floor and first story are built of sandstone, whereas the second story and attics are of a timber frame construction. Two coats of arms are situated above the Roman arched portal and the timbers of the upper stories have been richly decorated with wooden carvings. The elegant two storied bay window with its decorative roof increases the lively image of the sandstone facade.

After a full and satisfying day, for dinner that night I prepared Kaese spaetzle with Hameln ingredients since we didn't have it in Bavaria. The local cheeses and meats were fantastic!

Again, on Wednesday, we got an early start and headed for the Harz Mountains to the village of Goslar. The Harz Mountains are the setting for most of the Grimm Brothers' fairy tales. We hoped that we might see some of that influence.

Goslar is another city with diverse architecture. Romanesque, Gothic, Gothic-Renaissance, Renaissance, and Baroque styles are all represented. Although not far from Hamelin, and the history is congruent, this small city has a very different feeling to it.

The day we visited Goslar was either the beginning or the end of a festival with tents and booths partially set up in the town square (marktplatz), so we were not able to get many good photographs. The town is essentially built around its Romanesque church and the Kaiser Worth (once the guildhall of tailors and merchants). The front of the Kaiser Worth is adorned with colorful wooden effigies of emperors.

The history of Goslar is linked to the Holy Roman Empire. The grandeur of the medieval Imperial Diets are still evident in the Imperial Palace constructed between 1039 and 1056. Its nearby Rammelsberg silver mine led Goslar to become a powerful commercial center and founder-member of the Hanseatic League. The mine, which had been open for 1,000 years, closed in 1988.

The primary building material in Goslar is slate. Almost every building is sided and roofed with it. In many cases the slate is decoratively cut to create large, ornate patterns. The craftsmanship in these buildings is unsurpassed. It raises the wonder if this skill has been passed down to present craftsmen.

We had lunch on one of several squares, on the broad walkway outside the Butterhanne Tiffany Restaurant. The food was excellent and the local beer divine.

We spent a wonderful day walking throughout the town, each street more interesting than the one before. Although very much a medieval town, it was very different from Rothenburg or Augsburg (another Imperial Diet City).

When we left, we took the route south through the Harz Mountains, but saw nary a wolf nor a red cape, nor a house made of gingerbread. Actually, we found out much too late that there was a Brothers Grimm Museum in Alsfeld, north of Frankfurt… next trip.

Thursday morning was sunny as we headed for the Netherlands, but as we travelled the mist began and then the steady rain. We didn't seem to make the distance we had hoped in the time given, so we adjusted our decisions (but not our expectations) accordingly. We stayed on the highway, but didn't go all the way to Amsterdam. Instead, we chose to go to Zwolle, Amersfoort, Utrecht, and Apeldoorn. It took all day, and we didn't really get to see much. We did stop at a nursery, but couldn't buy bulbs – only cut flowers, so we bought some gifts to take home. We stopped to eat supper in a quaint hotel in Apeldoorn, then headed back to Germany.

The trip had started off enthusiastically enough, but as the day wore on, we realized we were mentally noting that a return trip someday was warranted.

On Friday, it was still a little gray around the edges, but we opted to head off on an adventure anyway. On the way back from the Netherlands, we had seen in the distance a huge monument of some sort. It became our mission to find it (not an easy task).

As we started our quest, we came across a canal which perpendicularly crossed the river Weser at Minden. We parked and walked a distance along the canal enjoying the engineering of it as well as the many camper canal boats moored there. (Another fun way to spend a vacation in Europe.)

Off in the distance we could still see the monument, so we continued our journey. It took a bit of navigating and map reading and following our noses, but we kept getting closer... and closer... and finally came upon it. It was HUGE! And very old. It was called the Kaiser-Wilhelm-Denkmal (Monument). Built between 1892-1896 as a tribute to the first Kaiser Wilhelm, it was really quite ornate and beautifully constructed. It sat high on a hill overlooking the Weser river, the city of Porta Westfalica, and miles and miles of open countryside. The view from there was spectacular!

Satisfied with our ability to search and navigate, we headed for the town of Buckeburg to see our final castle. This time we did go inside. To begin with, this was the first castle we had seen that sported an honest-to-goodness moat and, if that was not enough, it was filled with water. It looked like a shimmering, tranquil, private river. The castle was huge, comprising nine-tenths of a complete circle.

At the beginning of the 14th century Graf Adolf VI had the castle erected here. The building called "Buckeburg" was first mentioned in a chronicle in 1304. The castle consisted of a residential tower and the necessary kitchen, offices, and stables. During the following centuries the castle was extended and reinforced. From 1560 to 1563, Graf Ott IV had the old moated castle converted in to a four-winged castle in the style of the Weser Rennaissance. The current owner of the buff colored castle is Furst Philipp-Ernst. He and his family still live in a comfortably large part of the castle. We did not see that part.

We had to knock on a door or three before finding anyone to talk to. The woman we finally discovered was able to connect us to a tour already in progress. The tour was in German, but we picked up a bit. The castle houses significant works of art and artifacts as well as an important library. The history of the building spans 700 years, with the most important contributions stemming from the 16th, 17th, and 19th centuries. At the end of the tour, the tour guide returned to the beginning with us and spoke to us in English. It was a wonderful visit.

After nearly two hours, we retraced our entrance steps, down the walkway between the stables, through the ornate gates and into the square. While we were touring the castle, a fresh air market had been set up. We bought some sinful tasties to snack on and some fresh vegetables for supper.

At the end of the street was the most gorgeous church. It was under renovation so we could not go in. (Today one can "google" Buckeburg, Germany and see a photo of the Buckeburg Church. The architecture is indescribable.)

We returned to the chalet for supper and to get ready to visit with Renate at her home in Rinteln.

We found her garden condo easily from her directions. We also found that Rinteln was an interesting little city in its own right, and regretfully, one that we had missed.

Renate greeted us at the door and led us downstairs to the living room. The condo was on several levels. We had entered at a split foyer, the sleeping areas were up, the living areas were down. The lower level opened up to a lovely back garden. It was similar to our raised ranches, but tall and narrow... not more than two rooms wide, but four levels high.

Two of her aunts were visiting from Berlin. The five of us chatted, depending heavily on Renate to translate back and forth. She introduced us to some wonderful German treats and local German red wine. Renate had called her brother who lived close to Mannheim and had arranged for Jay to visit with him if there was time before leaving the country. We exchanged email addresses and hoped we could keep in touch, electronically. We had a grand time and left around 10 PM, tired, but exhilarated from the visit.

On Saturday we packed up, checked out, and headed back to Kaiserslautern. En route, we did have to make a stop in Frankfurt first. Jay needed to get his hair cut at the Ram Main Air Base before reporting to duty on Monday. It took a while to find things. With the downsizing of the base, many amenities were being moved to new locations. We also inquired about housing there for the night, but cutbacks had closed some of the facilities. So, we continued on to Kaiserslautern and Jay's apartment.

On Sunday he took me back to Frankfurt. On Monday, we would both be returning to the work world.

Sunday, April 30, 1995

I am sitting in my room in the National Hotel (a Best Western) right across the street from the hauptbahnhof in Frankfurt, Germany on the last day of a three week vacation with my son.

We just shared a wonderful late lunch at a great Italian restaurant in New Hausberg. He saw that I was comfortably settled and left to get back to his life with his military friends and to prepare to return to work at a new position.

I am settled in for the night. It is a good time to reflect.

Our weeks were filled with adventure, joy, fear, new friends, good food, some frustrations, and the sadness of the news of the bombing of a Federal building in Oklahoma City by an American.

Our travels took us to Paris, France; Innsbruck, Austria; Munich, Germany; Utrecht, Holland; and many delightful points in between. We bought beer with French Francs, Austrian Shillings, German Deutschmarks, and Dutch Guilders. We visited the Louvre, The Hapsburg Palace, a Nazi Concentration camp, several castles, and many Historische Alt Stadts. We were at Notre Dame on Easter Sunday; got locked out of Germany on the Zugspitz, slept within the walls of a medieval city, met a new friend in Hamelin, bought tulips in Holland, got absolutely lost in three Dutch cities, rode a cable car on the Rhine, located an elusive monument, and found a magnificent schloss in Buckeberg.

We tasted three kinds of Schnitzel, many kinds of pork, fresh Spargel, great salmon... we balanced smoked meat, aromatic cheese, and tasty rye bread as we drove through the countryside... and bought delectable, gooey sweets in the marktplatz.

I slept in a tower in Rothenberg, a closet in Paris, a chalet in Rott, in a spacious hotel room in Garmisch, and on the floor at Jay's apartment.

We did so much walking I had to buy real hiking boots – the 4K trek from the Zugspitz to Ehrwald, Austria clinched that purchase.

We rode on a tour bus, a double-decker bus, two subways, a taxi, a cog railway, a car, a large gondola, a small cable car, but no boats this time in spite of many rivers, lakes, and canals.

While in Holland we did <u>NOT</u> see windmills, fields of tulips, wooden shoes, or wheels of cheese – we did see a million bicycles, many ponies, canals, and the Zeider Zee.

The weather ranged from near blizzard on the Zugspitz to tropical (for 1 day in Hamelin) followed by a thunderstorm – rare for Germany.

We saw a Roman wall (not as grand as Hadrian's but impressive none the less), three Olympic sites, a number of churches ranging from Romanesque to Gothic to Roccoco to Italian Renaissance.

I climbed 500 steps (at least) to the castle at Heidelberg, and half as many to the castle at Marksburg.

Rothenburg, Hamelin, and Goslar are incredible walled medieval cities, and Heidelberg is grand, but sleeping spectacles are the Schloss and Church at Buckeburg.

Once again, I slept snugly under fluffy featherdeckers, keeping toasty regardless of the nippy nights. Tomorrow, after breakfast in the hotel, I will shoulder my memory-filled luggage and walk across the street to catch the Ubahn to the flughafen to return home. I am rested and tired at the same time. Although not ready to return to work, I am ready to go home. Jay and I had a good time for three weeks – just as Amy and I had last year – but,

I am sure he is ready to say good-bye to Mom and start making plans with his friends – many of whom will be moving to new posts in the next five months.

It will take me five months to get all the film developed, write the daily accounts and let time contribute the distance to properly focus on all that we experienced. It was good.

Monday morning I awoke early (eagerness had nothing to do with it), showered, shampooed, pampered, finished packing, and watched a little TV before going to the dining room for breakfast. Since I was going to be in the air for at least six hours and didn't know the exact moment of my next meal, I ate heartily of the scrumptious spread set in the breakfast room.

I guess I was the first person there and took full advantage of the time to explore all the goodies and make special choices. After tasting just about everything and drinking my umpteenth cup of coffee, I checked out at the desk, went back upstairs to reread the train schedule, and watched TV until it was time to go to the train station.

It was not that I felt like a pack mule with all my schtuff, but if a strong gust of wind had come along and knocked me over, I would not have been able to get up. I would have had to wait for some kind soul to help me regain my verticality. I picked my way across the fairly large intersection between the hotel and the Hauptbahnhof.

Once inside the train station, I found the right stairway to the right track and reached into the right pocket to get the right change for the ticket machine. (Jay and I had made a dry run the day before.) However, today was a holiday and the fare was different, so I had to shift the burdensome load, find more coins, and feed the machine more money to get the proper ticket for the trip to the airport. O. K. ... not too bad.

I arrived at the right platform just minutes before the scheduled train to the airport was due. Ten minutes later, I was still on the right platform for the scheduled train to the airport. After twenty minutes, I finally decided to sit down with my tonnage. I wasn't alone in being confused by the absence of the train. One after another, passengers would descend the stairs, look at the schedule board, check the clock, talk among themselves and then repeat the process when the scheduled train did not come. (They were listed to come every ten minutes.)

The platform was beginning to fill up, now, with families with small children, teens with bikes and backpacks, older people with luggage on wheels. I hoped there would be room for me and my bulging bags. Finally, one hour and twenty minutes after my eager arrival, a train came to a halt at the platform and immediately became saturated with travelers of every description. (The change in arrival schedules was due to the holiday. Who knew?)

I was tired from the early rising. I was tired from the anticipation. I was tired from carrying three weeks of souvenirs amid my soiled laundry. I was tired from the children crying. And, I was tired of waiting. Oh Well.

The train finally arrived at what I thought was the correct terminal and I departed along with the throngs. I looked for a luggage cart and finally found one just before reaching the escalator to take me up to another level on my journey to Terminal B and I had to give it up. (I was following the arrows as well as the crowd. It seems the train does not stop at Terminal B.) Up to the next level… no more luggage carts… stand in line to catch a shuttle to Terminal B.

Now, down the stairs to the ticket windows. Finally! Stand in line to report in and get rid of the bags. I was told all was on schedule, so I went to find all the wonderful shops. However, this was a new terminal, and I was told at one small booth that all the shops I had remembered were – you guessed it – back in Terminal A. So, I had a bottle of water, wrote some post cards, and finally decided to trundle toward the gate area. I would buy a book of some sort there, and wait.

As I went through the first checkpoint, I was told to go straight to the gate for loading. I zipped through all the other checkpoints, didn't stop for a minute to browse or buy, although I did see many interesting little booths. I got through the gate, got settled in with the other 200 or so people, read every pamphlet and poster available, then heard that there would be a slight delay. Not enough to leave everything to go shop, not even enough to carry everything to go shop, just a slight delay.

We left the airport almost two hours after scheduled time. Since we missed our original take off time, we had to wait for a new flight plan.

I slept a lot on the plane coming home. When I arrived in Boston, I had just missed the bus to Concord, so I went to Cheers (with all my schtuff), had a large beer and a big sandwich and waited the two hours until the next bus. (Didn't see Norm.)

I arrived home around midnight. Chris had left the car in the parking lot for me. Emily (the cat) was glad to see me. I was happy to be sleeping in my own bed. I don't remember much about the next few days. I must have been up, but not awake. As much as I had enjoyed every minute I had spent on vacation (minus the airport), I was glad to be home and I had such great memories to ponder.

A New Chapter -- 1997

When I was a child, I lived in a picturesque, little, bucolic town in northern Connecticut. Our school classes were small. Most of the students in each class became good friends over the length of years before graduation. There were several girls in my class who became my close friends. We shared common interests and our town was small enough that we could get together easily.

Some of us belonged to our 4-H horse club which had a mounted drill team. We practiced at least once a week and in the summer we were often the "half-time" activity at area horse shows. Many of us attended the same church and attended Sunday School, Teen Fellowship, and summer church conferences together. Our town also had a small public lake, and when we were not trail riding, we were hanging out at the lake.

The high school we all attended was not in our town. We were bussed twelve miles away to a regional high school which served five towns. Each of us was active in our personal interests and activities in high school and made new friends. We were the beginning of the baby-boomers. Our high school classes grew in size until we had outgrown the single building our mothers had attended, the elementary school building on the nearby corner, and the catholic elementary school building further up the hill. There was just no more room to accommodate the influx of the growing number of students from each town. So, for our last two years, we were to be put on split sessions. We all wondered how that would work, logistically.

Family decisions came into play. Janet's father was transferred to a new work territory. They moved to a small town in the mountains outside of Keene, New Hampshire. My mother had wanted me to attend Northfield School for Girls from the beginning of high school and I had balked. I did not want to be separated from the friends that I had known for so many years nor our mutual interests. But, that circle was soon to be broken anyway, so I agreed to go. (It turned out to be the best school years of my life.) Sandra stayed at home and weathered out the split sessions. (Our younger sisters attended new schools in our own town, four years later.)

We all graduated from our perspective high schools and got on with our lives. I went west to college; Janet became a nurse and moved to Phoenix; Sandra stayed in New England, began working and was the first to be married. I have to say, we lost touch with each other. Oh, Janet and I would send birthday cards with notes, and maybe a Christmas card. But, for the most part, we lost touch.

We gathered briefly at my wedding in our home town in Connecticut in 1960, but only briefly. My new home would be in Ohio.

In 1968, I attended Janet's wedding in Phoenix, Arizona. It was like old times. Her childhood family had been my childhood family and we picked up right where we had left off. But then, after all the nuptial festivities, I returned to my adult family of husband and two young children, now in Chicago, and it was back to Birthday cards and holiday phone calls.

When I returned to New England to care for my dad in 1990, I tried to reconnect with some of the old classmates. It turned out, that after all these years most of us really had very little in common to talk about for more than one long and reminiscing lunch.

It was at my dad's funeral that Sandra reappeared. I had tried to reach her on several occasions, but to no avail. (She worked in international trade and travelled a great deal.) Now, she was at the wake because she had seen the notice in the paper. I didn't recognize her at first. We had all changed during the thirty-some years since high school. But, as soon as I heard her voice, I knew.

After the funeral, my sister stayed with me for awhile, but she soon had to get back to her family in California. It was then that Sandra and I renewed our close friendship. She and I had lived fairly parallel lives and had much to talk about. She included me in her social activities and pulled me out of my grief.

Actually, this should not have been much of a surprise. We were friends almost by default. Our grandmothers had been friends in our small town. Our mothers had attended high school together. Our parents had double-dated before the Second World War. In the family photo album we had a picture of Sandra and me decked out in ruffle-topped sunsuits with matching sunbonnets playing in the wooden-slatted playpen in the side yard at Grandma's farm while the men were overseas.

Now, we were decked out in ski outfits and goggles and the photos showed us in front of several New England ski resort chalets and chair lifts. Life was good.

However, 1997 was another year of change. I had accepted a new position as Executive Director of an historic house museum in Marietta, Ohio. I would have to pack up everything one more time and, again, move cross-country.

I was to start on July 1. My grandson, Morgan (now nine years old) had been with me for history camp (at my New Hampshire historic house site) and my son Jay came home from his military base in Maryland. The house I had purchased in Marietta would not be ready until September, so I would board with a woman who lived close by. Morgan, Emily the cat, (another long story) and I travelled in one car, Jay in another. We stayed with Jay at Fort Ritchie, Maryland, one night and then Morgan, Emily the cat, and I travelled on to Marietta. The next day, Morgan was delivered back to his mom in Fort Wayne, Indiana. It was a busy week.

The house where I and the cat had a room was only two blocks from work. I enjoyed walking to and from the museum every day. Although it was July, the house was comfortable inside and a haven outside with its shaded garden with Koi pond and gazebo. It was in a lovely, quiet, Middle American neighborhood with tree-lined brick streets and graceful Victorian Era houses. (Although Marietta was settled in 1788, most of the earlier era homes have been burned or washed away by the many tumultuous floods inherent with settling at the confluence of two sizable rivers... The Ohio and The Muskingum.)

One evening, while keeping track of the elusive Koi, my cell phone rang and it was Janet calling from her home, now in Jacksonville, Florida. What a nice surprise! She said she had just finished her degree as a nurse practitioner and was planning to celebrate by going to London, England. Couldn't I go with her? I explained that that was the week that I would be moving into my new home in Marietta.

She said, "Well, then, I will come help you move."

I said, "Marietta is not London. It is a charming, historic city on a notable river, but it is not London."

She said she could go to London any time. So I gave her all the information on where I would be and thanked her. It would be good to see her again.

I boarded at Alice Pickerel's until late August when I returned to New Hampshire to retrieve my household. This time I filled the largest Ryder truck and had to pull the largest U-Haul trailer filled with even more. (I had all my belongings plus much more that I had inherited from my parents' home.) I could not in addition attach a dolley for the car. I would have to fly back to retrieve my car.

Sandra came to help me pack. She said that she had some time coming at work, so she was willing to drive with me and fly back home at the end of the week. So it was decided. I would drive the massive Ryder rig and Sandra would drive my '88 smoke-blue Camry. (The Corolla had lived a long and dutiful life, but was no longer with me.) We started out from Concord New Hampshire on Friday night, August 30, and stayed that night at Sandra's house in central Massachusetts. The next day, we hit the highway heading west. Now, I am close to being a train. (I am not sure of the overall length of this vehicle with trailer, but it was extensive.) I can only go forward. I can only use diesel fuel. And, the best speed I can get is about 45 MPH on the highway and even less going through the mountains. Sandra had walkie-talkies that she and her family used while skiing. She brought them along... one in the car, one in the truck. As I needed to refuel, I would check in with Sandra over the walkie-talkie. She would then shoot on ahead and scout out the best exit for me to use. Her information was invaluable. More than once, she saved me from a fate worse than death... a gas station that was not going to be easily accessible for me.

That night we made it to Bloomsburg, PA. It was August 31, 1997. When we turned on the TV that night we were stunned by the tragic news of the untimely death of Princess Diana. It cast a sad and sober tone upon the otherwise gladsome journey.

The next night we made it to Kent, Ohio, where we stayed the night with my daughter. On Monday, Labor Day, we drove the three hours south to Marietta, and when we pulled up in front of the house, there was Janet sitting on the front porch steps, reading a book. It had been thirty years since I had seen her and forty years since Sandra had seen her, but it was like yesterday.

After hugs and hellos and some catching up, we went to the boarding house and borrowed pillows and blankets and, that night, camped out on the floor of one of the upstairs bedrooms in my empty house. It was just like a high school sleep-over. In the morning, I complained that they had hogged all the covers, and I couldn't sleep -- but Sandra has a photograph of me fast asleep, all tangled up and cozily nestled in the quilts. Oh well!

It was Tuesday, and the movers were coming to unpack the vehicles. I had diagrams posted in every room for placement of the furniture. Janet took the second floor, Sandra took the third floor (renovated attic/guestroom) and I supervised the first floor. We had a plan.

That night we treated ourselves to dinner at The Becky Thatcher sternwheeler restaurant at the mouth of the Muskingum River as it flowed into the beautiful Ohio. It was like old times. We forgot just how tired we were. It was good to be together again. That night we each had a bed to sleep in and no one complained in the morning.

On Wednesday, we drove Sandra the 90 minutes south to Charleston, WV, where she caught her plane home to New England. Before she left, we agreed that we should not let another 30 years go by. We should get together each year for a week of fun and fellowship. And so we have.

For the first few years, they returned to Marietta for extended weekends. (Being the oldest organized settlement in the northwest territory, and a tourist destination, there is much to do here.) Then, we began reaching out. Having timeshare, it was easy to find places that were interesting and fun to spend a week once a year. We even talked old friend Margaret into joining us. All of us didn't make it every year. (Sandra was the only one who was retired as we began.) But, now and then we did.

Hilton Head, South Carolina -- 2004

October '04 was a special trip. All 4 of us were together. The location was Hilton Head, South Carolina. Hilton Head is about 95 miles south of Charleston. It is a barrier island shaped much like a high-top tennis shoe. We were to spend the week on the upper heel side of the island in the Port O' Call area of the Shipyards Plantation, one of the many gated communities. Our unit was a spacious, rare three bedroom – big enough to be a permanent residence. Janet and Sandra had one bedroom with twin beds. Margaret had her own bedroom (reward for all the vacations on the pull-out couch). I was on the other side of the unit in the master suite, with my own spa bathroom and my own screened-in balcony. (Since Sandra and I are early risers, we had many a morning coffee out there while Margaret and Janet slept in... and I shared my bathroom with Margaret... only fair.) In between the bedroom areas there were a large kitchen, a living room with dining area, and another screened porch... plenty of room for any of us to have personal space.

We also had two pools close by to enjoy for early morning laps, plus we were just a short walk to the beach... which we did each night just before sunset. Even in October the evening air was pleasant enough to walk barefoot through the surf. Sandra, Janet, and Margaret are all beach babies... they love the ocean. I was also raised with it, but being fair-skinned, I usually don't frequent the shore during the day. However, one afternoon, peer pressure was too much and we all headed for a swim in the Atlantic Ocean. Margaret was the first one out of the surf and acted as life guard and towel distributer for the rest of us. Great fun!

It was a time to relax and enjoy being together – we explored the island at length, but we also took some day trips elsewhere. On the route to leave

102

the island was a large Tanger Retail Outlet complex, so of course, we had to pay a call on Liz Claiborne. I actually found a shirt and ultrasuede jacket to match the raspberry jeans I had bought at St. Andrews, Scotland, in August. … Golf Colors, you know. Some days good things happen.

Of course, we had to go see the red and white Harbortown lighthouse at the Sea Pines resort and the Golf Course where The Heritage golf tournament is played every year. At the base of the lighthouse is The Café Europa. We had enjoyed lunch at Café Europa on St. Armand's Key in Sarasota on another trip. Although the food here was tasty, it was not nearly the same quality as the one in Florida.

After lunch, we lurked along the yacht basin a while secretly fantasizing of being invited aboard one of the sleek and glamorous vessels by a convivial crew member or a gracious and sun-tanned owner. But, when that didn't occur, we browsed the many boutique shops nearby.

Sandra took a break for a bit in an available rocking chair in the center of the garden, joining a whimsical bronze statue that sported a sign that said, "Out to Lunch." It makes a good photo.

Then it was on to new territory. At the South Beach Marina Village is The Salty Dog Restaurant. Folklore has it that fisherman John Braddocks and his big, black, dog Jake went out to sea one day on his boat, The Salty Dog. An unexpected storm roiled up 60 MPH winds and 20 foot waves and capsized the craft, tossing man and dog into the ocean. Swimming valiantly until exhausted, John firmly grasped Jake's collar. The intrepid pet swam for 3 days and 3 nights until he delivered his master on the beach of his home port. In his honor, the townspeople built a gathering place and called it, "The Salty Dog."

Lured by its legend, we agreed it would be a great spot for an afternoon libation, but, sadly, it was closed. However, outside its doors, among its levels of weathered board decks, were a couple of trees with the most beautiful birds sitting on its branches. Yup, these were indeed live Macaws. The older, larger bird entertained us by exhibiting his acrobatic prowess effortlessly gliding from tree to tree and swing to swing, a swirl of vibrant colors. Not to be outdone, the younger, smaller… yet just as colorful… bird tried to emulate his idol. Alas, the young one missed the swing and fell from the tree. As he lay there, limp and seemingly lifeless, we wondered if we should pound on doors in search of assistance. As we hesitated in decision, one of his keepers came from a nearby shop to see that he was reinstated upon his perch with grace and dignity. It turned out he wasn't hurt in the least… only embarrassed. Apparently, he does this regularly and is always in sight of those who know him.

Disappointed about the restaurant, but relieved about the bird, we agreed that we should try to return another time and set off for more adventures.

On the way back to the condo we saw a verrrry interrrresting hazard on the golf course. Right there, quite close to the road, on the grassy bank of the pond was a full-grown alligator sunning himself. I did secretly hope that he would stay on the golf course and not take the elevator up to our unit.

Wednesday, we went north to Beaufort. (Beaufort, South Carolina is pronounced Bew fert as opposed to Beaufort, North Carolina, which is pronounced Bow fort.) Established in 1711, and located on Port Royal Island, it is the second oldest city in South Carolina.

Being a quintessential, charming, southern coastal town, it is often the location for movies whose stories are set in the south. We set out on a quest to find the house where they had filmed "The Big Chill." Parts of "Forrest Gump" and "Something to Talk About" were also shot in this area. Although we did not find all the film locations, we did see the big white house with the tall columned porch and the broad front steps. It is every bit as alluring in person. (Will have to check "The Big Chill" out of the library when we get home.)

We visited the historical museum and several tempting Main Street shops, then, drove on to The Plantation restaurant on Lady's Island for lunch. The food here is extraordinary, but you can miss the turn. As you come off the bridge take the very first right. It doesn't look like much, and the sign is pretty obscured, so look fast. Otherwise, if you miss it, turn around at the traffic light and come back. It is well worth the search. A replica of a southern plantation, it is situated smack in the scenic lowcountry saltmarshes. Window walls allow one to watch indigenous wildlife amongst the Live Oaks and Spanish Moss while enjoying delicious southern fare.

On the way home we stopped at The Gay Fish Co where we watched the shrimp boats coming home for the evening. We bought fresh shrimp for supper... Yummm! There really isn't anything quite like shrimp right off the boat, delicately and swiftly cooked, and served with fresh lemons... oh yes, and Carolina rice... and don't forget the local white dinner wine.

We do enjoy a fine meal. Every trip we try to pamper ourselves with a dinner of especially fine cuisine at least once. Our upscale dinner this year was at the Red Fish on Archer. There are so many great restaurants on the island that it was almost like pulling a name out of a hat to choose one. The menu was creative, the food was delicious, the wine was full bodied, and the service was attentive.

Each year we plan for all four of us to be together, but it does not always work out. Sandra is the only one fully retired at this point. Margaret and

Janet are both working nurses and I am still managing a museum. Our schedules vary accordingly. Sandra arrived a day later this year and Janet had to leave early, but we had a great time while it lasted. We gave Janet a big send-off and then the rest of us partied on to the end of the week.

Sandra wanted to learn more about timeshare, so she went on her own tour of the facilities. Margaret and I went on a Gullah Tour. Not knowing what to expect initially, we found the Gullah tour to be most interesting. It took most of the morning. We rode completely around the island on a small bus with a man who was raised on Hilton Head before it became a golf community and a vacation phenomenon.

The Gullah culture has its roots in the West African rice growing region near Sierra Leone. Before our Revolutionary War, Africans with knowledge and experience in growing rice were brought to this area as slaves to the South Carolina rice plantation owners. They were very valuable property.

After the Civil War, this same South Carolina low country became a safe haven for the now freed Africans. They were able to celebrate their native culture here in unembellished obscurity until recent times. They own their property. They have their own communities. They continue to pass on their own Gullah histories even to modern day grandchildren.

When resort developers came to the area and purchased Gullah lands, those selling families migrated to the larger cities of the north... especially New York and Chicago. Many of them now send their children back during the summer months to experience their ancestral culture. Many who are now of retirement age are returning to the homeland to settle. They contribute to the present day Hilton Head visitor experience by sharing with them feasts and festivals of the Gullah culture. A most interesting history.

After the tour, Margaret and I had lunch at a hideaway spot on the intracoastal waterway... Hudson's... had the best shrimp and grits. They were called Charleston style, but, in my opinion, were better than I had eaten in Charleston. When I make them at home now, this is the recipe I use.

Of Course we had to spend a day in Savannah... and Tybee Island. They are only about twenty miles south of Hilton Head.

We didn't take the trolley tour of Savannah this time, but we did revisit River Street and the Pirates House and drove around the beautiful squares on our own.

Savannah is appealing on several levels. Historically, Savannah was founded in 1733 by General James Oglethorpe. It was originally the capital of colonial Georgia and its Royal Colony. It has two forts to visit – Fort Jackson, near the historic district; and Fort Pulasky which is on the way out to Tybee Island.

Savannah is the birthplace of Juliette Low, founder of the Girl Scouts of America. Her home is located on one of the 22 park/squares that are geometrically placed throughout the center of historic Savannah. It is one of many homes to tour in the area. Also worth visiting are the Green-Meldrim House (General Sherman's Headquarters), the Owens-Thomas House (located on Oglethorpe Square), the William Scarbrough House, and the Wormsloe plantation of Noble Jones. The Mercer-Williams House, the former home of Jim Williams, is the main location of Midnight in the Garden of Good and Evil and former home of composer, Johnny Mercer.

We are told that Savannah's formal city layout of squares and streets resembles the plat plan of Washington, D. C. because it, too, was laid out by noted designer Pierre l'Enfant.

The River walk is a shopper's paradise with shops, restaurants, pubs, and hotels built along the cobblestone passage in buildings that were once the cotton warehouses along the docks of the Savannah River. In addition to pleasure boats, on the river one might now see a Sternwheel tour boat, a HUGE container ship heading out to sea, or military ships based on Hutchinson Island on the opposite shore. It is not difficult to spend an entire day in this part of Savannah.

Savannah is also a hub for education boasting four colleges and universities. The Savannah College of Art and Design (SCAD) is probably one of the fastest growing schools anywhere. Once a small art school, it now permeates the downtown. As more room was needed for classrooms, labs, and studios, instead of erecting new, the school purchased and repurposed many historic buildings in downtown Savannah breathing dynamic life into the innercity.

Close to the river, but further into town, is the city market. Here are art galleries, more eateries, and shops. On the plazas are stations where one can catch a carriage ride or trolley tour. From here it is a short stroll to Paula Deen's famous Lady and Sons restaurant.

On the west side, housed in the Central of Georgia depot and trainsheds, are the tourist information center, city museum, and origins of the many trolley tours.

Not everything is near a square. The Pirates House is on the eastern edge of town, near the river. Reported to be the oldest building in Georgia, it was constructed in 1734. Fable has it that ship crews would come there for rest and recreation, as well as liquid nourishment. Too much liquid would find them down a trap door and out a tunnel, guests on a pirate ship on their way to Shanghai or some other untraceable destination. Their ghosts are said to frequent the premises. Costumed guides willingly escort you through the 15 rustic dining rooms. Oh, yes, and the food is great, also.

Continuing east, we drove out to Tybee Island. A barrier island for the state of Georgia, it was the place for Savannah residents to spend their summers. During the 19th century one could only arrive by boat, but in 1920, a road connected the resort to the mainland. It was a vacation Mecca during the 1940s. Today, the main commercial area at the end of the island has a decidedly nostalgic 1950s flair.

A must-see is the Tybee Island lighthouse. This statuesque black and white striped beacon is a result of several rebuilds... similar to Grandpa's straight razor with six new blades and three new handles. Nevertheless, it is regal having survived its share of hurricanes, and saved from disaster its share of ships. It has the distinction of being one of the few coastal lighthouses that is still in operation.

After enjoying Tybee Island, we stopped on the way back into town and had lunch at The Crab Shack... now there's an experience! Although it is possible to be served a meal inside a covered pavilion, most of the weathered tables are situated on outside decks overlooking the creeks and saltmarshes. Built around existing trees that provide shade from the hot southern sun, the wooden decks bear an assortment of table arrangements to comfortably accommodate any size party.

Not only did I find this environment whimsical, but it was also quite sensible. Each table was equipped with a sizable hole in its center with a raised lazy-Susan of condiments above and a family-sized trash container beneath... all refuse went down the hatch. Everything in one's order came with disposable materials and there was a HUGE roll of paper towels to be shared by all for any napkin needs. Very efficient. If any food remnant missed the container, there was a legion of well-mannered cats who waited patiently until the table was vacated and then, tucked their napkins around their furry necks and licked the area clean.

Having had our palates pleased and our funny bones tickled, we paid our tab and headed back to Hilton Head.

Margaret and I had driven to South Carolina this time, but Sandra had flown. She called to reserve transportation back to the Savannah airport. Then, we spent the evening getting packed and reliving the week's adventures.

It had been a beautiful week... full of interesting things to do, but restful as well. The walks on the beach at sunset were wonderfully relaxing. We looked forward to repeating this sometime soon.

Fort Lauderdale, Florida -- 2006

The phone call to RCI began when the answering voice said, "Hi, where can we send you for vacation?" What a great feeling! It was to be our annual girl's getaway trip. Where shall we go? The decision was Fort Lauderdale, Florida. One whole week in the sun, just the four of us... each getting our own separate vacation by being together... seven sun-filled, fun-filled days... it works for me.

I arrived at the airport in Fort Lauderdale a little early, but Janet was already waiting. She had had a good drive down from Jacksonville and had also arrived early, but walked around the airport to get some exercise after sitting for 6 hours in the car. I collected my luggage: one humongous red drag-along instead of the usual over-packed two small cases I normally take... one being the duffle I bought at Harrod's 12 years ago... an old friend by now... always take it. This year it stayed home, displaced by a newcomer who would hold all the contraband not allowed in carry-ons because of heightened security. The only other restriction was that it couldn't weigh more than 45 pounds... I told Sandra I could not lift 45 pounds, so all was safe.

Janet and I got out the maps and the written directions to Vacation Village at Bonaventure, our timeshare destination, and started out. We had no trouble finding I-595 west... you could stumble onto it blindfolded... it comes right out of the airport. Started reading the next directions and catching up on news. Look for Exit 1A... yatatata yatatata yatatata. 15 miles... yatatata yatatata yatatata.

Oops, here's I-75 splitting which do we take? Split second decision.... take the right... read the directions again... watch for Exit 1A. It is not yet 15 miles, so it should be coming up. Wow, look at the traffic on that side road! What is that? Exit 21 coming up???? ? Well, take it, we will get reorientated when we get off. Wait! The directions for the approach from the west say take Exit 22. We will go on to 22 and pretend we are approaching from the west. All is cool... It keeps mentioning State Route 84, but I do not see it on the map anywhere... Isn't that pretty... Oh, look there is Bonaventure Blvd... that is mentioned in the directions from the east. If we reverse them, we should be back on track. Turn right... Hmmmm... not looking right... There is a firehouse, they should be able to help us.

So we turn around (one more time) and go back to the firehouse... Do Not Enter... of course.... "You back the car in here so it looks like you're leaving and I will approach on foot".

"Hallloooo, Hallloooo, anybody home?" I hear a truck motor running... are they on their way out? Will they see me? These are huge trucks.... Halloo." Through the building to the other side, which turns out to be the front... who knew???? Tried the front door... locked... hmmmm... Pound, Pound, Pound... anybody home? The door opens and a VERY HANDSOME YOUNG firefighter appears. I didn't ask him what they all were afraid of... instead I so cutely said, "We need rescued!" Got a very blank look in return.

"We are SO lost... looking for Vacation Village at Bonaventure..."

"Don't know." he said. (Uh oh, a fireman who doesn't know his own village...) Another fireman, equally as handsome and equally as young appeared.

"She wants to know how to get to... where?"

"Vacation Village at Bonaventure..." I said with a GREAT BIG smile.

"Oh, yes, that is right up Bonaventure Boulevard, you can't miss it." he said...

I said, "We just did."

Seems we didn't go far enough...

Second question: "Is there a gas station between here and there? We need gas immediately." (thinking) "No, I don't think so... turn right at this intersection, then right at Weston, you will see one on the right... (with an afterthought) Then come back here to Bonaventure and turn right... go all the way to the end (State Route 84--AHA) and you will see Vacation Village."

Last question: "Where is your favorite place to eat?" (Who am I? Rachel Ray?)

First Fireman (very Italian looking) "McDonald's."

Second Fireman (very WASP looking) "I like everything."

Third Fireman (came to help the first two) "Over at Town Center they have everything, hamburgers, Italian, Cuban..." I like him.

So, I head back to the car with all my newfound information... What's this? The big doors through which I had entered are closed??? That door goes to the broom closet??? Let me out before they close the other big door behind me and I have to spend my vacation waiting for a 5- alarm fire and Janet thinks I have gotten a better offer.

So, now it is around the building on the lawn... but the grass is not short and thick and lush like a northern golf course, it is wide and coarse and sharp looking and I sink into it as if it were the everglades... now I am watching the perimeter of the yard looking for the alligators that surely are tying napkins around their chubby little necks by now... I quicken my pace toward the car.

We did not actually speed away... Turned right at the light, right again at Weston, found a gas station on the left??? Took it anyway. Filled up... washed windows... backtracked to Bonaventure Blvd. Turned right... About a mile up we saw a sign... Vacation Villages at Weston. Turned in to the parking lot... Nope. Next sign. Bonaventure Country club.... Turned in to the parking lot... Nope. Keep going... we are seeing a lot of lovely parking lots, though.

OH LOOK! Weston Tennis and Racquet Club... this must be it ... It is the end of the road! Racquet Club Road is on the directions (way at the bottom, and not approaching from the west.) Turn left, then right, then left and there you are... really.

Now to check in.... it was a long process... I will not bore you more. But, I did mention the difficulty with the directions to our greeter. She smiled... "We have been trying to get them corrected for years."

The name of our building was Ibis. We were on the fourth floor-- 9409 A & B. It was a double lock-off, 1500 square feet of living space. Quite lovely. We got settled, went out for dinner and a drink and stopped at Publix Market before coming home.

We went to dinner at Town Center at the corner of Royal Palm (Not in the directions, although it is the point at which the instructions stop when approaching from the west) and Bonaventure Blvd. It is a life-style center full of many interesting shops and such. We chose Draseros.... thought it was a Brazilian Restaurant, turned out to be Argentinean.... but good. (When so far from either, does it really matter much?) Ordered a Mojito... my first in Mojito country.... they don't serve them. (Do you see my smile beginning to curdle?) However, The Bombay Sapphire Martini was mahvalous, dahling.

The Chimichurri was red, not green. But the skirt steak was tender and juicy and tasty. And the Fried Plantain was a new experience.

Janet knows her way around Publix (thank goodness) and we purchased basics and schtuff for breakfast. Would shop again when Sandra and Margaret arrived. We found our way home to Ibis and 9409 A & B. Slept well.

On Sunday, I awoke early and headed for the pool for my laps. (Janet and I both belong to Curves and had packed travel passes and workout clothes. There was supposed to be one on Royal Palm, but we had not found it yet, and it didn't look as though we were going to spend time trying... swimming was just fine. Instead of Curves, we would do Waves.) It was 7:30 AM. The first gate was sort of encumbered with deck chairs, but I pushed them aside and moved on through the kiddie pool area to the adult pool... which, by the way, was huge -- long and lagoonish -- with a tropical waterfall in the center. There were still people with cleaning tools in the area... also a sign *inside* the fence that stated that the pool opened at 8:00 AM. I stated that we had plans for the day (didn't tell them we weren't sure what they were yet) and could I just swim my laps and be gone? Weak smiles were returned, which made me wonder if I was speaking the correct language... The tall man finally said, "I am through at that end... I am working at this end, now."

I asked, "If I swim just at that end will I be in your way?" He acknowledged that I wouldn't be... Swim, swim, swim, out... "Thank you." I was back upstairs by 7:45 AM. (The next morning the gates all had padlocks on them.)

Janet and I had breakfast on the balcony. We looked over all the literature we had picked up and calibrated the timing of the rest of the day. We should be at the airport at least by 4:00 in case Sandra is also early. We also wanted to go over the directions again, now that we had a local map that showed us where State Route 84 was. It actually was the frontage road that ran along on either side of I-595. (You know, the one that had SO much traffic yesterday.) Exit 1A was located BEFORE I-75 and ran for miles alongside. hmmmmm. Must tell Margaret. She is coming from the airport in a rented car.

We had a late lunch at Town Center... this time at a cheese shop... yummers. Poked around a while, then decided... in case of getting lost again... we should probably head for the airport. It was 3:00 PM. We followed the new directions, got on the highway at the proper place, arrived at the airport, parked and were in place to meet Sandra's plane by 3:30... That's a good thing..... she could be early. We checked the schedule board. It said: NW 252 ON TIME.

We walked from one end of the concourse to the other, sat for awhile and chatted, looked at the schedule board about 4:10 expecting to see that

NW252 was arriving. (Many planes were.) But, across from NW252 it now said... 5:10.??? ???? ?

All planes scheduled before hers were listed as ARRIVED. Later planes were ARRIVING. Where was NW252? Janet went for another walk. I decided to camp out near the schedule board and watch the many travelers who were arriving and collecting their luggage... and how dare they, anyway?

I talked with a woman who had just arrived from Newark.... they had run into a bit of weather. Maybe that was it... bad weather. I saw a LARGE, TALL woman dressed in a white strapless, elasticized top, squaw-skirted dress, white platform open shoes, and a LARGE white bow in her tussled hair, from which flowed a short white tulle bandana. (Not quite large enough to be a tablecloth.) She carried a bouquet of flowers. (My guess -- she was a bride – or Alec Bladwin in drag.) Saw no one, however, that resembled a groom... in any manner of dress. Was this really a woman, a transvestite, a cross dresser, a mistake???? ?

Time passed. Janet returned. The bride returned... still no groom, but this time she was carrying a bigger bouquet of colorful flowers and a satchel that stated... 'New Bride'. I wondered if she was still looking for the groom... maybe he took another plane... maybe not. Maybe she was hoping to meet one at the airport.

Other, later flights landed. No Sandra. At 5:10 as Janet was leaving for a closer look at the schedule board, my cell phone rang... it was Sandra... she was on the ground. I said, "We are headed your way. We will meet you at the end of the ramp."

She said, "I am heading for the luggage area."

I said, "That's where we are, we are on our way."

But, by the time Janet and I could get to the foot of the steps to leave the luggage area, Sandra was halfway down the escalator waving the arms of her splashy lime-green and coral Coldwater Creek jacket and calling, "Here I am!" We spun around on the stairs and all reached the bottom at the same time... no travelers were hurt in this process of connecting with an old friend.

We collected all her luggage (that which she had carried on and that which came off of the beltway) and left for the car.

By now we were feeling like natives when it came to knowing our way around. We popped onto I-595 west like old pros. We chattered and purred for 10 miles knowing that our exit was not 15. By then, the traffic was horrific. When we approached our exit 1A, it was at a standstill. In one voice, Janet and I said "Exit 21" and feeling very smug, we circumvented the tie-up and sailed on to I-75, exit 21, privately embracing the awareness of our secret passage. (Of course, we only knew about it because we had gotten lost, but who needed to know that?) At exit 21, we dropped down to State Route 84 (what power in knowledge) ducked under the highway, turned left and followed below I-595 right to the back entrance to our parking lot. Are we good or what?

We carried Sandra's many totes and duffles into the building and pressed for the elevator. Inside the elevator we were surrounded by a swarm of grumpy new arrivals. (conversation) "Did you get caught in that traffic?"

A collective "grrrrrr" arose.

Heady with success, we happily offered, "We will share a secret... go on to Exit 21, on I-75, come under the highway, turn left along I-595 and it comes out right back here."

The elevator door opened in a timely manner at floor 4. We exited briskly to comments such as, "Where were you two hours ago?"and"What room are you in so we can kill you?" The plan was to walk way past our doorway if anyone was following.

We got Sandra settled in and then, when we were sure the coast was clear, we left for dinner. One more time, we headed for Town Center (we knew where that was). This time it was Tarantella's Italian. Yummarino. Walked around the center a bit after dinner (couldn't fit in the car, you know, too much Spumoni). Went to Publix one more time for Sandra's choices. When we arrived back at Ibis, people were still arriving who had been in traffic all that time. On the elevator, this time, we were silent.

Monday morning, after a delightful 8:00 AM dip in the pool and a leisurely and resplendent breakfast on the balcony, we, once again, laid out all the sightseeing information on the massive coffee table in the common room.

Our unit was actually two units. Each had one bedroom, one bathroom, one kitchen, a balcony, and one living/dining room. The difference was the size. Unit B was smaller... its one bedroom had a queen-size bed, the bath had one sink and a tub with shower, the kitchen had a fridge, a sink, and microwave. The balcony was the size of a chessboard. The living/dining room was cozy with a sofa bed. We turned Unit B into two bedrooms with a fridge.

Unit A had a king-size bed, a spa tub, two sinks in the bathroom as well as a large shower, a large balcony, and a full kitchen. The living/dining room was HUGE with a 50" TV and a dining table large enough for an international reception. We called this room the common room.

We charted the week's activities. Since we had not heard Margaret's plans as yet, we decided to shop at the outlet mall on Monday -- it is way at the bottom of the list as Margaret's favorite pastime. We would take the bus tour of Miami on Tuesday as that was the only day it was offered. On Wednesday, we would visit Billie's Swamp Safari. On Thursday, we would go to Ft. Lauderdale, and on Friday, after a free breakfast with our friendly time share salesperson, we would go to the Keys. Saturday, of course, it would all be over and we would all head back to the airport... but I get WAY ahead of myself.

The outlet mall is described in the AAA travel book: "More than 400 outlet stores, including many upscale and high-fashion retailers, comprise Sawgrass Mills." We approached it tentatively... could we take in 400 stores on an empty stomach? Would we lose Sandra at store number 4 or 40? Would our credit cards melt before we could get to the other end? Would we ever find a place to park?

We chose to park near the entrance by the Rainforest Cafe. 1. We thought we could remember where the car was parked. 2. It was not the entrance near Nordstroms.

We parked among the Humvees and Range Rovers and, walking very proudly from our Chevy compact, found our way to the entrance. Before we could even get to the Rainforest Cafe to have lunch, we lost Sandra. We had been looking at belts on a kiosk... safe enough. Janet and I each bought one. I had been losing the weight that had steadily, surreptitiously, and insidiously appeared after the divorce and my giant economy size cargo shorts no longer had a tummy bulge on which to hook the waistband. A belt would keep them up when the pockets got full... avoiding embarrassment for all.

Janet wanted (actually, we both wanted) to go into a shoe store with an extra 50% off, but when we counted noses, we only found two that belonged to us. Where had Sandra gone? She had on a bright lime green top... easy to spot... except it was the couleur de anno and everyone had on bright lime green tops... even men. I stood watch while Janet entered the shoe store... would we ever see Janet again?

Soon, (maybe ten minutes) Sandra reappeared with a great big smile... "I told you I would be right back"... Janet bought some shoes... we all went to lunch.

If you have never been to a Rainforest Cafe (which I had not) you are in for a treat. There are animated jungle animals all about, waterfalls everywhere, and brightly colored birds in every tree. (I don't think any of them were real.) After we were seated, our server came to tell us about the specials of the day... as soon as she opened her mouth, the recording of all the jungle sounds began. We could see her mouth moving, but all we could hear were the trumpets of elephants and chirping of chimpanzees. Over her shoulder two large mechanical gorillas were having a great time terrorizing a live Children's birthday party. She smiled and left, we smiled and pretended we had heard her.

We discussed what we thought she had said and made decisions on what we hoped she had said. She returned to get our order. As soon as she opened her mouth, the recording of all the jungle sounds began, again. I must have smiled much too broadly, because she thought I was laughing at her... I quickly told her what had been happening and that I was amused at the circumstances and not at her... she joined us in our laughter. She was so used to the place she didn't even hear the elephants anymore. Lunch was ordered to everyone's satisfaction and she left.

We watched the animals and the people eating and the servers bringing fantastic looking trays past us... ours came in a timely manner and we ate it all amidst the shrills and the chirps and the birdcalls. Then we were on our way through the outer jungle of outlet shops.

By the time we were through... I think it was suppertime... we had walked more than 10,000 steps (according to Janet's pedometer). Janet had had her nails buffed, we all had had our glasses polished, we had dodged the incense salesgirl, and we had managed to stay together and not melt our credit cards! We were so proud. We found the right parking lot and the right car. We asked a lovely blonde yuppy as to the whereabouts of a common grocery store. She looked pained, but thought there was one at Sunrise and Flamingo(names of streets... really!) We decided not to follow her out of the complex... we could get lost.

We found Sunrise and Flamingo. There was a Publix there. We stocked up on good wine (2 bottles for $10. Bought 4 bottles -- you never have enough good wine) salad in a bag, and a roasted chicken. That would be supper tonight... we all decided we had already eaten too much and it was only Monday. Oh, yes, and ice cream.

When we walked in, the red message light on the phone was blinking. Margaret was not going to make it this year. We were all very disappointed.

Eating from the massive coffee table, we watched "My Big Fat Greek

Wedding" on the massive TV set. We all went to bed fairly early nursing our screaming calf muscles.

Actually, it was the only night that I spent some quality time in the spa tub. I slept well.

Tuesday, we awoke, not so early, went to the pool to limber up the walking parts of our bodies, had a lovely brunch. I had made the arrangements for the bus ride to Miami and had asked about food on the trip. Although we had had a very helpful concierge for the vis-a-vis visit, the concierge on the phone for later questions had been a bit vague. She wasn't sure about food.... didn't think they stopped for lunch, only supper, but there was food in the area... couldn't really say...

So, brunch it was, and we passed up Dollar Dogs poolside so we wouldn't be too sated in case there was to be food in our near future.

We arrived at the bus stop at the requested 11:45 AM. Boarded the bus at the scheduled 12:00, but didn't leave until almost 12:20... my brunch was beginning to wane.

The bus traveled I-595 toward Ft. Lauderdale. Our Tour Guide was very informative about what we were seeing along the way.... the older rural town of Davie, the newer upscale town of Plantation across the highway...

We stopped in Ft. Lauderdale to pick up more passengers and then it was on to A1A. Traveling south we learned about Hollywood and all the stars that came to visit or live there, Dania Beach, Hallendale, Bal Harbour. This entire stretch even into Miami proper was mostly under construction... some from Hurricane Wilma, some from planning for future events to be held there, and some from razing buildings built mid-century to make room for the highrise Trump towers style hotels of the 21st century.

Our first stop in Miami was at the Holocaust Memorial. It is a bronze sculpture of a giant hand stretching to the sky surrounded by gaunt, haunting figures pleading to be rescued. It activates vivid memories of the disturbing images seen at Dachau. It sits in the center of a reflecting pond where visitors can walk among the sculptures. It is powerful. Its street address, quite meaningfully, is 1933-1945 Meridian Ave. It is not far from the Jackie Gleason Theater for the Arts. Such a contrasting juxtaposition.

From there, we went around the corner to Lincoln Road, a walking mall of interesting bistros, boutiques, galleries, and beautiful Art Deco buildings... and characters... and we saw a few. Once the social center of Miami, it was turned into a pedestrian area in the early 1960s. In addition to a modern multi-plex, and stunning contemporary sculptures, it also is the home of the newly restored Colony Theater for the performing arts and a concert hall for the New World Symphony Orchestra. Off the bus for about 10 minutes there was too little time to absorb all that we were seeing. We only had time for a quick stretch and a nosh to tie us over. Janet had a California Roll... an upscale bag of chips.

Back on the bus, we took a slow ride down Ocean Drive in South Beach from Emeril's at The Loew's Hotel, past Versache's, past the club where The Birdcage was filmed... and Goodfellows... etc, etc, etc. It was great, but not enough time. I would like to go back there and absorb it better... walk it, even. I didn't get any photos, but Sandra did, I think. She was on the right side of the bus.

Then it was on to Coconut Grove, past Vizcaya--10 acre Italian Renaissance estate and winter residence of James Deering, of the Deering/McCormack, International Harvester dynasty... and Coral Gables, planned community of early developer George Merrick, and its Miracle Mile. We also saw the notable Biltmore hotel and the Venetian Pool--an old limestone quarry now a Spanish tiled public swimming pool.

The Biltmore Hotel was built in 1926 by George Merrick. It took ten months and ten million dollars to build. When completed, it was the tallest building in Florida. It was the place to see and to be seen. Movie stars, royalty, and socialites alike enjoyed its luxury. At one time, its pool was the largest pool in the world. Its attractiveness enhanced by its lifeguard, Johnny Weismuller ... later known in the movies as Tarzan. Johnny Weismuller and Esther Williams both swam here in public performances, and during the 20s and 30s, Sunday afternoon synchronized swimming extravaganzas drew people by the thousands.

During the Second World War, the grand hotel was turned into an Army hospital and remained such until 1968. In 1973 it was given to the City of Coral Gables in a condition far from its glory days. In 1983, the city decided to restore the, by now, historic building. It took nearly four years and Fifty-five million dollars to accomplish this feat. On New Year's Eve, 1987, 600 guests celebrated the new year and the new life of a first class hotel with a black tie gala. In 1996 this Grande Dame of hotels was designated as a National Historic Landmark.

Just a few blocks away is the Venetian Pool. Originally a quarrie from which limestone (some sources say coral) was harvested for use in building Coral Gables, it is now an 820 thousand gallon, daily spring-fed pool for the enjoyment of the neighborhood. Its overall motif and structural architecture are Venetian. The fresh water is crystal clear and refreshingly cool in pools ranging from two feet for the kiddy pool (children under 3 years old are not allowed admission) to eight feet deep. The picturesque pool also includes a café, waterfalls, caves and grottos to be explored. Admission ranges from a bit more than $6 for Coral Gables residents to $11 for non-residents.

We took off our sandals and paddled our piggies in the shallow end before taking photographs of each of us in front of the waterfall and then getting back on the motor coach.

It was time to sit back and relax and be driven back in to Miami to the section known as Little Havana and visit a small shop... a very small shop. I bought some very small Cuban cigars and a very small bag of Plantain Chips. The owner prepared Cuban coffee for us... served in very small cups... what a jolt that was, but by then a jolt was welcome. Outside the shop we watched Senors playing dominoes in a small park. From there we went on to Bayside Market where we had two whole hours on our own. Janet, Sandra and I headed for Los Ranchos... a Cuban restaurant with waiters and white tablecloths.

By now, my stomach was not only growling, it was barking, and hurting. I was eager to put something into it. Our waiter came hustling up to see what we wanted for drinks. We ordered a round of Mojitos... surely they would have them here... he disappeared. We had some questions about the menu... other waiters brought the drinks. He reappeared, we asked questions, he disappeared... where DID he go? He was talking with the other waiters... grrrrr... we ordered 3 appetizers.... a shrimp ceviche, a fish ceviche, and a quesadilla. Wait, wait, wait.... another waiter brings 2 appetizers... only one ceviche... grrrrr... we finally had to order the other ceviche.... grrrrrr and snort. Janet thought that I was being impatient. This was a Cuban restaurant, Cubans are slower, the food will come in time... I explained that my function in this restaurant was to eat, our waiter's function in this restaurant was to see that it happened. I was expecting better service... and I wanted my stomach to stop hurting.

After much more waiting, and another round of Mojitos, our food finally came. Sandra had Argentinean Beef. Janet had beef tips and peppers. I had ordered pork chops with chimichurri. (This time it was green.) We all had sides of red beans and rice, plantains, and asparagus. Everything was spectacular... and ample. We ordered to-go boxes and took half of everything home.... each carrying her own box.

We left the restaurant and headed back through the center of the marketplace observing the shops, dodging the hustlers and the fingernail buffers. About in the center of its length it became an open air market. On one side there was a man sitting with two gorgeous parrots or Macaws on a stand. We were intrigued with them. The object was to have your photo taken with one. Sandra was quite interested. I was engrossed in the whole scenario when another young man appeared from nowhere wearing a boa around his neck.... no, not the feather kind. He thrust the snake's head at me saying isn't he beautiful? I was so startled, I jumped backward uttering such a guttural sound as I have never heard come from my aged throat. I was shaking... he seemed surprised. Didn't I want my picture taken with a beautiful boa? NOT ON YOUR LIFE!... I called to Janet who was right next to him, but also unaware of the snake. When she turned, however, she had a much less dramatic reaction and ended up petting the snake. Sandra, who was on the opposite side of the kiosk with the birds, turned away telling the bird man that he had just lost a sale. She was not going to stand still in the same vicinity as a snake and she left...... Deep breath, deep breath...

Gathering our composure, we walked on. Janet had to go to the Ladies, Sandra popped in to an accessory boutique. I was outside waiting where both could see me and we would not lose each other.... a man of color came up to me and said, "I am not a crazy black man, I will not hurt you, don't be afraid." Having seen many people nearby and a policeman or two over the course of the evening, I said, "I am not afraid." He said, "I am starving. Can you give me a dollar or two to get something to eat?" I said, "No, but I can give you this food." and I eagerly offered my last porkchop with redbeans and rice in his direction. He took it.

Janet came from the Ladies, Sandra came from the boutique, and we all headed for the Gelato stand. Out of the corner of my eye, I could see that the man was now at the trash can. He didn't put any of the food in it, but seemed to rest the package on top. When he saw that we could see him, he picked it all up and went in to the men's room. I was hoping he was going to wash his hands and eat the food... we will never know.

They were damn good pork chops...

We bought our gelato and headed back to the bus. We left Miami. It was after dark. The city was beautiful in the dark... and busy. We arrived home about 9:30. What a convoluted day!

On Wednesday, we swam, ate breakfast, and dressed for the Everglades... long pants, closed shoes, hats, and sun block. We were going to Billie's Swamp Safari. It was not very far.... across I-75 to exit 49 and then 19 more miles into the Everglades to the Seminole Reservation. The trip itself was uneventful. We followed the well-placed signs right into the parking lot.

The first building we came to, of course, was the gift shop and admissions counter. Such a menu of things to see and do! Since we could not make a decision about which one or two we most wanted, we bought the day pass which included everything.

The first event on our itinerary was the air boat ride. Janet, Sandra, and I were fortunate to sit in the very first seat of the boat. We fastened down our hats, were warned that we could get wet, and prepared to have the time of our lives. I think there were nine of us on board altogether. While we were waiting to board the boat, we had seen movement nearby among the lily pads, but couldn't get a close-up look. Now, we were able to see that It was a very large alligator. It must have been his favorite spot to lurk and wait for food. It is against the law to feed the alligators, but people feed dry dog food to the fish and the alligators are not far away.

On the way to the boat we had passed by several exhibit areas.... one had Caimans, one had crocodiles, one had several alligators... we thought that was all that we would see. it was quite a number, really. However, out in the swamp area we saw a great many more. They were very abundant.... shall we say, "everywhere."

The boat stopped near a grassy plain. On the plain were a herd of water buffalo, a herd of American Bison, and a herd of Indian Blue Cows. A flock of black tipped Storks flew in. On the bank was one rather large Alligator, sunning himself with his mouth open to release the excess heat. As the boat came close, out of the swamp growth on the right came another Alligator, two more popped up from underwater, another one came from upstream... before it was all done, there were about eight Alligators all in the same proximity to the boat.

Later, inside the mangrove forest, the boat was stopped again. Two more alligators came close by, one right up to the side of the boat... keep those fingers and toes inside. We saw many turtles and fish swimming just beneath the surface of the clear water. It was an exciting experience.

When we came back in to dock, it was time for lunch. We walked down the sandy path to the eating Chickee (palm frond-roofed building) to order "Indian" food. From the menu, I ordered an Indian Hamburger.... crumbled ground beef with some tasty seasonings all wrapped in Indian Frybread and deep fried. Yummy. Janet ordered an Indian Hot Dog... a very large hot dog wrapped in Indian Frybread and deep fried... it looked tasty. Sandra ordered an Indian Taco... the base again was frybread, which was then piled high with all the ingredients found in a Taco Salad. Large serving... it looked good. We had invited a lady from Los Angeles, who was traveling alone, to join us at table, she too had an Indian Taco. Neither she nor Sandra finished, there was so much food.

After lunch, we went on the Swamp Buggy Ride... an hour in an open swamp buggy tooling through the Everglades amongst the overgrowth and the wildlife. In addition to all the animals we had seen on the airboat ride, we also saw Elands and Ostriches. Although not indigenous to the area, the Ostriches had come from a farm which had gone bankrupt and the Seminoles took them in. (Note to those who want to do this... Ostriches are huge and ill-tempered... keep your hands inside the vehicle.)

In the center of the forest, there was a Seminole Indian encampment set up... the sleeping Chickees and a cooking Chickee. All were built up off the ground among the forest of scrub trees for protection from the natural wildlife with which they cohabitate. How anyone ever found the Seminoles to chase them from the Everglade area is beyond me.

The most uncanny thing we saw occurred almost at the end of the ride... the driver stopped the buggy and dismounted to the road. She threw some Cheezits into the water and crinkled the bag while making barking sounds... pretty soon, out of the darkness of the mangrove swamp came the largest Alligator I think I have ever seen. He came right up to the edge of the bank... she said she had hoped he would come up **on** the bank, but he didn't... at least not this time. He was huge! When she got back up into the buggy she called him a "Nuisance Alligator"... one who has lost his fear of humans and so cannot be allowed to be in any vicinity where humans might be.... a park or a lagoon.... a golf course, etc. They have taken him in to the reserve and he will, by choice, stay there.... his life is good... Cheezits every day. It was a bit disconcerting to me to see an Alligator come when called.

When the Swamp Buggy Ride was over, we had just enough time to find a privy and buy new bottles of water before we went to see the "Critter Show." A naturalist took about 40 minutes introducing us to the critters and the reptiles indigenous to the Everglades from skunks to possums to cockatoos to alligators. It was very informative and Janet got to handle another snake.

It was now 3:00 PM and we still wanted to stop at one more attraction down the road, so we left Billie's Swamp Safari and went on to the Seminole Museum. It was very well done with diaromas showing different aspects of Seminole life. There was also an outside nature walk that went back to a living history village, but it was too late in the day to go there. They were short on volunteers, also, so it was open fewer hours. Perhaps if we are back another time we will see that part of their presentation. The museum also housed an exhibit gallery displaying paintings, crafts, and sculpture by contemporary Seminole artists. Well worth a revisit. I must say, we were the last to leave.

Wednesday night we finished all the leftovers for supper and watched the movie "Calendar Girls." It took a bit of doing to get a DVD player and get it hooked up to the big screen TV and running, but a call to the maintenance department solved all our problems and we had a lovely evening at home.

Thursday, was the day we decided to go to the Keys... Friday was beginning to sound too tight for time. We left by 10:00 AM and arrived at Islamorada just before noon. The trip was an easy one down I-75 and the Florida Turnpike to Route 1 and on to the Keys.

We stopped at Holiday Isle for lunch at the Sports Bar. Sandra and Janet both had Shrimp. I had a Cuban sandwich which was a lovely ham and cheese on a crunchy baguette. For dessert Sandra and I had the very best Key Lime Pie... Janet had scrumptious Carrot Cake.

While we were waiting for the food to come, Sandra spotted a policeman finishing his lunch and went over to ask some directions. She told him what we had hoped to see and do and he told her the best places to go to get this accomplished.

After lunch, we went to the beach to see how it was set up. Then we went down the road to scout out a couple of restaurants for supper and the sunset. When we were happy with plans for the evening, we went to the Theater of the Sea for the rest of the afternoon.

The Theater of The Sea is an interesting place. It is not very large, but it houses many species of ocean wildlife as well as colorful tropical birds. We only had a few hours there, but we went on a bottomless boat ride, a nature walk (where we saw a 500 pound sea turtle), saw a Parrot Show, a Dolphin Show, and a Sea Lion Show... his name was Seth. Very charming. The shows were all very well done. Located right on Highway 1, this stop is recommended if you are ever in the area.

At 5:00 we just had time to return to the Holiday Isle for a swim (or float) in the ocean... long enough to get the body temp back down to normal... it felt terrific. The beach was very south sea islands in motif... set up for hundreds of swimmers, but since this was October, we had the place to ourselves. It was delightful. After about thirty minutes of leisurely paddling about in the ocean, we showered under the palm trees, redressed, and headed for the Lorelei Restaurant for dinner.

The Lorelei was on the Bay side of the keys. There was a building for dining, but most of the tables were on the beach. Sandra picked out a large glider swing with a table in the middle and took claim. From the white chairs on the water's edge, a man shouted, "That's our table. We were here first!"

Undaunted, Sandra said, "Well, we are here now. You lose."

I held my breath for the knock-down, drag-out fight which surely must be coming... Janet, the peacemaker said, "There is another one right there you can have."

The man began to laugh... he had been teasing us. His party was down from northern Florida for his wife's 40th birthday (they looked like children). Had to give us a hard time. Sandra went down to their spot on the beach and took pictures of their party for them. Before they left, they invited us to stay the night with them, if we didn't want to drive back home.

We ordered drinks and several hors d'ouerves... tapas.... for supper. Everything we sampled was scrumptious, and the servings were generous. We took home half of the coconut shrimp for Friday's lunch.

The day had been overcast. The cloud formations had been interesting. Nothing threatening, but we were skeptical of seeing a sunset. What we did see were some interesting partings of the clouds and backlighting of a retreating sun. It turned out to be a pretty evening.

By 7:30 it was quite dark... we were on the road by 8:00 and home by 10:00. It had been a full and satisfying day.

Friday morning, we met with our Timeshare person for a bountiful breakfast at the Bonaventure Country Club (we mentioned we had seen the parking lot before). By noon, we had been thoroughly informed of the benefits of owning timeshare and had firmly assured our man -- John-- that none of us was in the market at this time. I did, however, compliment him on his presentation of facts and his never-failing good humor and professional attitude even after he knew he would not have a sale today. It was most important to us. After nearly twenty years of ownership, I learned several new facts about timeshare from him that no one else had ever explained as clearly. I thanked him for that.

We went back to the condo to have a lunch of leftovers and plan our last afternoon in Florida. It was decided that we would go back to Fort Lauderdale for a few things. It was too late in the day for the Bonnet House, but we could catch the Stranahan House if we hurried. We could be the last tour of the day (you know how attractive that is when you are in the historic house business). It closed at 3:00. We also could see Las Olas Blvd and its shops as well as cruise the ocean drive and see all the beautiful homes and beautiful yachts of the beautiful people one more time... and so we set out.

Maps and the signs are not always what they should be. We found Las

Olas Blvd without any trouble, but then it took several passes before we decided that our instructions to the Stranahan House must be erroneous. We found new street signs that pointed the way to the Stranahan House, but still had trouble. We inquired of a cab driver... he didn't know. We asked a hotel concierge... he smiled and pointed. "It's right there." Oops... so it was. In all its early Victorian majesty, it was over shadowed and nearly hidden by the highrises that surrounded it. We turned into its parking lot... it was 3:00 PM. Jumping from the car, we inquired of the nearest person, "Are we too late? Where is the entrance?"

The caretaker said, "No. Just there around the corner." Again, not a sign in sight. I was already at the front door... my heart sank... it was locked.

Janet said, "He said to pound on the door."

So, obediently, I pounded on the door... it sounded like thunder. Would I break the door? The door opened and a lovely lady said, "Come in." We apologized for being so late, blamed it on a late start and the inadequate signage. I tried to cover up my discomfort for arriving so close to closing time and being the person who keeps them from going home.

She was very gracious. She said we would be the last tour of the day and it would be a good one because she was ready to sit down for a while and talk to us about the people who lived in the house. And so, she took an electric moment and turned it in to a soothing hour-long tour.

The Stranahan House was built in 1902 by the founder of Fort Lauderdale, Frank Stranahan, as a trading post, town hall and post office. It was situated right on the New River, the avenue that the Native Americans and others could travel from the interior to the coast. He built a ferry to take people across the river where they would access one of the first roads in the area. In 1906, he added a second story to the building and it became the residence for him and his wife, Ivy Julia.

Ivy Julia was an educator. When the interior families came to the trading post, they brought their children with them. Ivy Julia would spend time with the children, introducing them to new experiences such as reading, geography, and arithmetic, without calling it teaching. Knowledge of the outside world was not sought after by the natives. But, Ivy was resolute. In time, Ivy Julia Stranahan officially became Fort Lauderdale's first teacher.

The house is a comfortable size for the early 1900s, but today is dwarfed by the hotels and condominiums nearby.

As we were leaving, we were able to briefly meet the Executive Director. We spent even more time asking questions of the caretaker who was quite eager to share his tour information with us as well.

Since it was approaching dinnertime, we asked for directions to the River Walk from the house... and a good thing, too. We would have headed in the wrong direction. So much for the information from our vague concierge.

Following their advice, we found our way to the River Walk. Now, granted, it was off-season, but in its best time it is no San Antonio. We walked from one end to the other in less than 10 minutes. One thing it does have is a number of interesting places to eat. We ended up at Ugly Joe's for supper. And a good supper it was.

Feeling fully fed, we walked back to the car past more shops which were not very busy. In the car, we found our way once more to Las Olas Blvd and headed for the ocean. Now, that is where the action is. At a time of year when the tourist population is barely enough to cover costs, all the tourists (except us) were on Las Olas Blvd. Shop after shop, restaurant after restaurant were bustling with business.

It was getting dark. We kept driving... one last look... mansions, yachts, (ships, really) waterways, long cars, we inhaled it all. Now the ocean... and darkness was upon us. We traveled down 1A until it bent west and we were headed home.

Friday night we packed and organized and turned in early. Sandra had to be at the airport by 9:00 AM.

When we arrived at the airport, Sandra checked in at curbside. I went to the ticket counter. A lovely young lady greeted me. I said that I was booked on the 5:47 PM, but the rest of my party was leaving this morning and so I had to come to the airport. Did she have anything earlier that I could change to?

She put me on the same flight as Sandra. I could go "Stand-by" or, for $25, I could confirm a seat. I said that I had all day. If I didn't make this one, there would be another. She agreed that the risk was slight. I was first on the list and the plane was not crowded. And so, we said good-by to Janet who headed up the highway to Jacksonville and Sandra and I went to the gate.

First to come was a pilot... flying seat-available. Next it was a soldier in uniform. Then it was a family of 5... probably an airline employee. I was beginning to squirm. However, I had checked in as soon as an attendant had appeared. He had said for me just to sit where he could see me and he would call my name as soon as he had everyone else accounted for... I did as I was told.

As I sat there waiting and people watching, thoughts returned of the buxom bride and her bright bouquet of a week ago. I wondered if she ever found her groom.

The flight was called. First class and families with children or aged were boarded first... then the rest... then... the pilot, the soldier... so much for being first on the list... and then the family of five. He called for people to exchange their assigned seats for seats in Exit aisles (more leg room, but carried some responsibility in case of crashing). Several came forward... that left their seats available. Finally, he called my name... YAY! I was on. Sandra was in 15C, I was in 25C. She had the Turkey wrap sandwich we were to share for lunch.

We were 30 minutes behind schedule landing in Detroit. That cut down considerably on Sandra's transfer time. I still had an hour. By the time I exited the plane, she had the instructions for our next gates... she was headed back to Hartford, CT., I to Columbus, OH. We were able to take the monorail together for two stops before she was gone. Hugs and promises to call when we got home... the doors closed.

I had no trouble getting passage on the plane to Columbus... it was only half-filled. We landed at 4:27 PM... 6 whole hours earlier than my original flight plan. I caught the shuttle to the hotel, popped my luggage in the trunk of the car, cancelled my reservation for the night, and headed home. After stopping for the scheduled necessities... gas, Sam's for groceries, supper, and such... I arrived in Marietta about 9:00 PM. Sandra actually called as I was rounding the corner by the hospital. I asked for 15 minutes to get in to the house.... she called back.

Janet had made it home about 4:00 PM. Sandra had landed about 4:30. We all had gone out to supper and now were all safe and sound in our own abodes, rested and refreshed after a wonderful week. We are already talking about next year......

Durango, Colorado -- 2008

Fifty years since high school. Janet, Sandra, and I had been friends since grade school – and, although we now live all over the United States, we would be together again this year.

You remember, Sandra and I go back to the playpen – in fact, our mother's were friends in high school and later double-dated with our fathers – they are all gone now – SO, it was good that we were still friends.

Janet came to town in third grade. We were together in school, in Scouts, in church, and in our 4-H Horse Club – now there's another whole story – until the end of our sophomore year.

Our high school – the same one our mothers had attended – would be going on double sessions because of the baby boomers. A regional high school for five towns, it just plain had no more room. Each town was building its own new schools, but they would not be ready until long after our class had graduated.

Janet's father was transferred and the family moved to Munsonville, New Hampshire, where she graduated from Keene High School. I followed my mother's deepest dreams and wishes and finished my high school years at Northfield School for Girls in East Northfield, Massachusetts – about midway between Janet and Sandra. We stayed close until after graduation when the tide of life swept us in different directions for almost forty years.

Here we were, fifty years later, still compatible, still enjoying the same interests. Our childhood roots are long and strong.

I arrived in Durango first on Saturday. Janet was to arrive on Sunday and Sandra was coming in on Monday.

Our timeshare was in a small, converted upscale hotel, so we had two adjoining suites – one became the girls' dorm, the other the common space as we had done in other years. It was right downtown, so although we rented a car for the week, we could walk all over central Durango and did – often.

But, I get ahead of myself.

I flew out of Columbus, Ohio, on an early morning flight –VERY EARLY! SO early that they said the computers weren't up and running yet. Uh huh. They put a hand-written tag on my only checked bag instead of a bar coded tag – I had two stops, one in Minneapolis, one in Denver.

You guessed it, by the time I made all those changes, my luggage didn't arrive with me.

Luckily enough, the stores on Main Street were open on Sunday. After a FANTASTIC breakfast at Jean Pierre's Bakery and Tearoom, I walked very slowly back to the hotel. My walk took me past many interesting stores including Ralph Lauren's Polo and The Timberhaus Co. Sports Shop.

Polo had turtlenecks on sale (it was October). The only white one in my size – giant economy – was soiled from falling on the floor. I asked the clerk if they had another one. He was fantastic…

"No, unfortunately", but he would knock off more dollars assuring me that it would wash up nicely. I paid $6. 00 for a $40 shirt. (I did think about walking by the kiosk and knocking more on the floor.)

At Timberhaus Co. I found a very stylish fleece – could that be an oxymoron? But it was sharp – and it fit—also on sale. ☺And so went the walk back home.

Janet was due in at 4:00 PM. I returned to the hotel, showered, donned my new clothes, used the new tooth brush, and turned on my cell phone. New message: Janet was rerouted – will be in at 10:00 PM.

Well now, rethink dinner. I had had a lovely dinner on Saturday night at Ariano's, right around the corner. But, this time I decided to walk further north until I found something else interesting. I ended up having dinner at the Irish Embassy Pub – Guinness Pie, and a pint. Really tasty stuff. Had no trouble walking off all those delicious calories on the return.

When I got back to the hotel, there was another message… Janet would be in at midnight. WOW! Oh well, I could go to the airport early and check on my wayward luggage as well.

Janet did arrive at midnight, but for a moment, it looked as if her luggage had not. We went to the desk to inquire and it turned out her bag had come in on one of her earlier scheduled flights. Mine was still among the missing. (Sears has good underwear.)

Janet and I had a lovely visit on Monday. Sandra came in on time – with her luggage. It is purple, how can it get lost? I checked once more on mine

– nothing. I mentioned that my meds were in my luggage and Tuesday would be the fourth day without them.

After getting Sandra settled, we toured the driving part of town. Following signs up to Fort Lewis College, we found ourselves on the top of the world overlooking the town of Durango far below in a lovely river valley. Across the valley rose a range of rugged mountains. It was quintessential southwest scenery.

On Tuesday morning, before we were headed out for the day, a call came through from the airline saying that my bag had arrived and would be delivered before long. It had been found way back in Minneapolis and flown in on the first morning flight. Woo Hoo! We were back on track with the wardrobe and meds and headed for Mesa Verde.

Now, it was not only 50 years since high school, it was 53 years since Mesa Verde took on a special meaning for me. My mother worked with a new friend, Maggie Wetherill. Maggie's husband was military – a Marine recruiter—and my dad was retired military. They all became good and long time friends. Bill's grandfather and great uncle were the discoverers of the Cliff Palace at Mesa Verde in 1888. To a teenager, that was pretty impressive. I vowed then that one day I would go to Mesa Verde. I didn't think it would take 53 years.

Mesa Verde is not too far from Durango, but you can see it for miles. Its majestic and memorable shape is an awesome sight.

After being welcomed at the main gate, there are still many miles of twisting, rising roads before you get to the first information station.

In peak season there are several cliff dwelling areas of the National Park to explore, but by October most are shut down in readiness for early snows. We only had three choices open to us… 1. Cliff Palace, 2. Spruce Tree House, and 3. Balcony House. It all depended upon whether we were ready to scale the side of a cliff. We opted for Cliff Palace. It was the right choice.

We drove to the proper parking area, prepared ourselves for the unknown, and met the rest of our tour group on an outcropping which was fashioned into a platform with steps, railings, and walls.

From there you could look down into a very deep valley (the valley in which the Wetherills searched for their cattle and discovered the Cliff Palace) and on the far sides could see other carved out dwellings. You could also look down into Cliff Palace itself.

We followed our guide down and down on steep, narrow paths, then up a short ladder to another level of stone, then down some more to a not-quite-spacious resting place.

Ultimately, we reached our destination... the base of Cliff Palace. We picked our way among the uncovered kivas and peered into rooms of the long ago. It was exciting – a spiritual experience—to walk the sandy ledges and peer into the empty, echoing chambers of The Ancient Ones. While satisfying the sense of quest from childhood, it also enhanced the curiosity to know more about this prehistoric culture.

Reality returned when we faced the double set of ladders we had to climb – straight up—to get back up to ground level. (No elevators, here.)

Now, if I had been smart, I would have left my purse in the trunk of the car. It is quite uncomely (did I tell you we were all 68 years old) not to mention awkward, to climb a ladder while balancing a purse the size of a small steamer trunk on your shoulder. SO, I would toss the purse up to the next ledge – climb past it, reach down, pull it up, toss it ahead, climb up, reach down, and so on, until we were both back on the surface... a lot like "Hit the ball and drag Charlie." If I ever get back there, things will be done quite differently.

Back in the car, biology took over – we were all in need of finding a ladies room and our stomachs were rumbling the 1812 Overture in unison. We followed the signs to the complex of buildings which included restaurant, bathroom, and museum. Oh yes, and the path to one more cliff dwelling ... The Spruce Tree House.

We tinkled, we ate, we museumed, we watched the video, and we shopped, but in the end, we decided not to visit the Spruce Tree House. It wasn't the moderate descending grade to the dwelling, it was the thought of the long, steady climb back up to the car that stopped us.

We agreed it might be more prudent to find our way back to the entrance and the highway before darkness set in. On the way home, we watched two things... the amazing, grand scale scenery along each mile and the gas gauge. We had driven many more miles than expected and saw not one gas station. Making it on fumes to the nearest town, we eagerly filled up. Now, we could relax and enjoy the rolling countryside watching for herds of Elk and Bison.

That night we had a great Mexican dinner in downtown Durango. I must admit, we took home no doggy bags.

On Wednesday, We awoke a bit stiff from our cavalier cliff climbing and decided it would be a great day to go to Pagosa Springs and experience the spa – a collection of hot springs of different heat levels all more than 100 degrees.

The drive from Durango was scenic and one hour long. We had hoped to cruise through the Chimney Rock anthropological site, but it was closed for the season. Shucks, but then more time to spend at the spa.

I had been able to spend time at Chimney Rock on my previous visit to Pagosa Springs. It fed my fascination with the Anasazi period of the southwest and prompted my return this year. I was disappointed that it was closed, but it may take another full vacation to explore the ancient ruins in the area from Salmon Ruins and Aztec Ruins just south of Durango to Chaco Canyon in the center of New Mexico where the largest collection of ancient pueblos is to be explored.

We continued travelling east. We stopped at The Choke Cherry Tree for jams and dips and candies, and other homemade goodies; and the Fred Harman, Red Ryder museum before having a scrumptious lunch in town at Victoria's Parlor.

The Choke Cherry Tree was opened in 1999 featuring forbidden edible spreadables homemade from local fruits and berries. With culinary success, the store outgrew its first location and is now housed on the west side of town right on the highway... cannot miss it... do not want to. We tasted all their samples, bought a few gifts to ship back home, and stocked up on condiments we thought we just could not live without this week.

Everyone remembers Red Ryder and Little Beaver. They lived in comic books and Saturday matinee movies. We loved their adventures. Well, this is where they were originated... in Fred Harman's home and studio. Red Ryder came late to Harman's life. After many false starts at a variety of careers... one involved an early partnership with Walt Disney before either knew success... Harman's artwork was noticed by publishers in New York City. Harman, born in 1902, was in his thirties when he created Red Ryder and Little Beaver and they were the center of his life for thirty more years.

He retired them in 1963 to paint evocative southwestern scenes of his youth. His nearby neighbors in the Pagosa Springs area were the Utes, the Apaches, and the Navajo. (They still are.) Harman was proud to be only one of 75 Caucasian men to be adopted into the Navajo Nation. The revered cowboy artist died in 1982.

The Pagosa Springs newspaper still runs the Red Ryder comic strip in its Sunday edition. Harman's home and museum is located on the west side of this small resort village on the San Juan River. If you loved Red Ryder, you will love this visit.

Victoria's parlor Cafe is located downtown in one of the largest, oldest, and most colorful Victorian homes. There are several small dining rooms scattered throughout inside the building as well as casual tables out on the lawn. (We chose inside.)

The menu includes homemade soups, Her Majesty's Salads, His Lord's Sandwiches, Lady Caroline's Quiches, (all with global ingredients) and melt-in-your-mouth Decadent Desserts, as well as homemade breads and muffins. One may also experience High Tea by appointment. There is something tasty for the royal in each of us.

They have a custom here of providing a wall of hats of great and amusing variety to patrons for their commemorative photographs. We chose personality specific hats and the waiter took our photos (one for each camera).

From there, we went straight to the spa, rented bathing suits, and hit the pools. The waters were warm and relaxing, but the October air was cold. I found I was most comfortable in water between 101 and 104 degrees. Janet and Sandra could stand higher temps... but then, they were hot-tubbers and beach-babies at heart. Some brave souls even went from the hot pools to the cold San Juan river – very Scandinavian, but not my cup of Kirschwasser.

The hot springs are a natural phenomenon and have existed there since the beginning of time. The name Pagosa comes from the ancient Ute language for "boiling water." During its early history the springs were coveted for control by the indigenous tribes of Ute, Apache, and Navajo. There were several skirmishes over ownership. However, dominance by one tribe did not last very long.

In more recent times, a resort spa has emerged and the springs have become a destination of healing for those with health and body issues. The warm/hot sulfuric baths were thought to be therapeutic. They certainly are a relaxing way to spend the day.

We were there all afternoon. All the aches and kinks in our aging, creaking bodies disappeared, but we didn't melt any fat or shrink any lumpy areas. Our leisure was shortened as we watched dark storm clouds approaching from the west. Wrapped in the large, thick, soft, warm towels provided by the spa, we headed inside. We showered, shampooed, and dressed, spun dry and handed in our suits. (You want to rent your swimwear, no matter how unflattering. The water has a high sulfur content and the acrid odor permeates and lasts – an aroma not longed for on the eastern seaboard beaches.)

Feeling relaxed and refreshed, we were aware that it was time to think about dinner. We drove out of town toward Wolf Creek Pass hoping to go to the top of the continental divide to see the fantastic view, but the storm now came in from the west and we thought better of it. We ate at The Ole Miner's Steakhouse. Not much to look at from the outside, the inside is very rustic, very cozy... and the food was outstanding! It offered entrees such as pheasant, venison, quail and other Colorado game. Yum and well done!

After a satisfying dinner, it was time for the hour-long return to Durango and beckoning beds. We all slept well that night.

Durango was originated as a railroad town. The Denver & Rio Grande railroad company founded the town in 1880 as a base for operations in southwest Colorado for their long awaited 45-mile push into the mountain silver-mining town of Silverton.

When we walked out of our unit on the second floor of the hotel, we faced an open common area game room which was lined on its exterior by a wall of windows. Through those windows could be seen the rail yard for the steam train which still travels daily to Silverton. Only, now it carries tourists and elk hunters instead of ore.

The simple Victorian train depot is a focal point of Downtown Durango. The sound of the steam whistle can be heard with each departure and arrival. The coal dust from the smoke is palpable and omnipresent. The history is there to be experienced. We had to ride that train!

The morning we chose, the train left the station at 8:15 AM. We had to be there 30 minutes before. I prepared breakfast sandwiches and coffee to eat on the train. (O. J. for Janet.) We were up, but not necessarily awake, and aboard, when – with a long, plaintive wail of the whistle-- the train pulled out of the station.

This train was basic. The seats in our unsophisticated car were not known for comfort. The wooden windows could be easily opened to accommodate a camera. There was no heat – not even a warm brick for your feet. But the scenery was astounding.

Somewhere, while the intrepid train clung to the side of a mountain above the Animas River, we ate our picnic basket breakfast.

The trip was spectacular. It was October. The Aspens were golden and there was snow already covering the mountain tops.

The shimmering river was far below at first, but in time, as we got closer to its origin in the mountains, it came closer... sometimes on the left, sometimes on the right. Always beautiful.

About half way, the train rolled to a stop... in the middle of nowhere and on a high trestle. Fearing an Indian attack – or pack of outlaws -- or such—we were relieved to learn we were only stopping to refill the empty belly of the water tank – steam, you know.

A bit further on, we passed a hunting resort reached exclusively by this steam train. If you are a hunter of elk, this vacation sounds intriguing. Oh, yes, the resort offered one more amenity… right there in the middle of the thicket… a zip line. Yup! Fascinating!

The approach to Silverton was interesting. After climbing into the mountains for more than three hours, we had come to a high plateau. The river and the train were now on the same plane. In the distance – rather in the middle of nowhere –could be seen a community encircled by still more mountains.

We watched the buildings grow larger as we approached until we were in the middle of town – literally—the train track ran right down the middle of the street… then stopped… right there. No depot, no platform – no sidewalk -- just get off the train onto the dirt street.

On the far side of the train there waited pickup trucks pulling horse trailers. They were here to meet those adventurous elk hunters and take them, by horseback, into the wilderness.

Our stay in town was about 2 ½ hours– just enough time to walk about. Oh, yes, find a ladies, shop a bit (I needed sunglasses), and have lunch.

After scouting the many restaurants, we ate at Grumpy's at the Grand Imperial Hotel. Yup, another bright blue Second Empire Victorian… where we had THE BEST Bison Burger and sweet potato fries. Ate the whole thing… wouldn't need dinner.

The shop next to the hotel was resplendent with Indian turquoise jewelry. I bought a pair of lovely turquoise teardrop earrings with my timeshare credit card. The proprietor said they were Hopi… it didn't matter to me, they matched the color of my new turquoise suede jacket. Bingo!

After a quick-paced trip around the shopping block, we made it back to the train by departure time.

The return trip in the late afternoon was every bit as awesome as the morning trip. Although the sun was different, the river still sparkled and the golden trees were backlighted. I must say, though, the seats did not get any softer.

When we got back to Durango, we were happy to have one more delicious supper at a lovely restaurant within walking distance of the hotel. Although not famished, no one wanted to cook or do the dishes that night.

We went to bed with tummys full and memories happy.

This year I was the one who had to leave a day early to get back to work for the weekend– Big October children's event at The Castle. Janet and Sandra would stay one more day. In the morning, they escorted me to the airport. While having a cup of coffee in the airport café, we met a family of men who had been elk hunting up in the Silverton mountains. The retired father and four adult sons hadn't bagged any game, but said it was one of the most rewarding trips they had experienced.

After hugs and goodbyes and last thoughts for next year, Janet and Sandra departed to rediscover Main Street and all its retail glory. On their last night, they had dinner downtown at the historic Hotel Strator.

It was hard to leave early. I must return to that part of the country… before another fifty years.

Park City, Utah -- - 2009

NAME	Carrier	Flight#	From	ARRTime	Depart
Sandra	United	6075	Chicago	12:29PM	Thurs11:00 AM
Janet	Delta	4784	Reno	6:17PM	Sat. 11:15 AM
Margaret	United	6449	Chicago	7:54PM	Didn't make it
Lynne	Northwest	541	Detroit	9:00PM	Sat 2:10 PM

Saturday, July 25.

As you can see from the itinerary, there were some alterations. It all started when I called Margaret in Fort Wayne Saturday morning to give her a wake up call and she said she wasn't going to be able to fly that day. She would try to reschedule.

I drove to Columbus, left the car at the Ramada and caught the next shuttle to the airport. Arrived there a bit early, checked in, had lunch at Max and Erma's and then went to my gate to read and wait.

There were two plane loads already in the area waiting for their delayed flights from Detroit. Much explanation from the desk, nothing satisfying. Apparently, somewhere in the schedule, the planes lost time and never recovered. Since they are essentially shuttles that fly across Lake Erie between Columbus and Detroit and back and forth, there was to be no solution.

In time, both planes landed, refilled, refueled, and left. When the attendant came around to tag my carry-on for luggage check, (small plane) I asked if my flight would be on time... "We hope so" was the smiling answer.

Well, it did come in on time and we left on time, arriving in Detroit with only 30 minutes to board my next flight. When I deplaned I asked the desk attendant the location of my next gate. She pointed and said, "About a mile."

"Are there carts?" I asked.

"No carts." She told me.

So I headed for the first moving walkway and geared up for the journey. (Good thing I wore my best walking shoes.)

I arrived at the gate, a bit red in the face and moist around the edges, and got in line to check in only to find that *that* flight was to be delayed one and one-half hours. Apparently, the crew had used up its time back and forthing and a new crew had to be put together. The soonest the pilot could get to Detroit was 10:10 PM. We were to leave at 10:30. I asked the desk whether Northwest (now owned by Delta) would pay for the change in my rental car contract and they just looked at me in disbelief. "You shouldn't have to pay more, it isn't your fault."

"Right, but it is a change in the contract and they will charge." So, I went to a seat, took out my paperwork and cell phone and started the process of notifying Salt Lake Avis about the delay. I talked to Max.

I called a Salt Lake number, but he sounded more like he was in Pakistan. After MUCH confusion and EMPHATIC conversation, Max assured me that there would be a car waiting in Salt Lake City at 10:30 PM. He had tried to give me a car in Detroit... NO! !!! I am in Detroit—delayed—I need the car in Salt Lake City! He had tried to raise the price on the car.... NO!!!! That is not acceptable! This contract was locked in in April. The delay in planes is nothing I can control!

As I put away the paperwork and the cell phone, I became aware of an entire group of people across from me wearing black tee shirts with Utah in white lettering.

"Was I shouting? I bet I was shouting. I'm sorry. I am not usually this loud." They were very polite. The only indication was the way they rolled their eyes skyward in answer. It turns out that they were part of a group of chorus members from 72 high schools in Utah (and their adults) who had sung their way across Europe in a 3-week swing through 6 countries and were now on their way home. Nice People.

And so... I board the plane and who are my two seat mates? Two people from the Utah group who had listened to my phone battle with Max. I smiled and said again, "I am not usually that rude or that loud, he didn't seem to hear me or understand what I wanted. I think he was Pakistani."

They smiled and said, "If he sounded Pakistani, he was probably in Pakistan and doesn't even know where Salt Lake City is." I thanked them for their graciousness and sat down.

We had a lovely flight. They told me all about their European trip and what we should see while we were in Utah.

The plane landed on time at 10:30 PM.. I met Janet, who had arrived earlier (Sandra, who had arrived at noon, was already at the condo with refreshments waiting) picked up the waiting car (upgraded to a Pontiac G6) and left the building.

It was a 30 minute drive on I-80 East to Jeremy Ranch. Following the reservation directions, I had no trouble finding the complex, but couldn't find Unit D16... finally called Sandra on the cell phone and she came down and stood on the curb to flag us in. It was after 11:30 PM. We talked until about 4 AM.

Sunday, July 26

We took our time getting collected on Sunday morning. About 11:00 we headed for Park City to see what was happening. Parking was interesting, but while searching we learned that it was "Silly Sunday." Every Sunday, the two bottom blocks of Main Street are a bazaar. Stalls and tents fill the uphill street, goodies of every description and size fill the stalls and tents. I bought a straw hat for the omnipresent sun.

I had skied Park City about 30 years ago. We had gone to the peak of the mountain in a closed gondola and had eaten lunch in a restaurant at the top of the snowy world. I had said then that if, when I died, "heaven did not look this beautiful, I would not be staying." I vowed, this trip, to show the girls what heaven looked like. But, alas, upon inquiry, we learned that the gondola was no more and the restaurant had been closed. We were told that there were plans to rebuild the gondola and reopen the restaurant, but, with the economy in decline, it would not happen this year. Nowhere in the area did such a thing of beauty exist.

So, we strolled the first block and then had lunch at a quintessential western mining town ski resort sports bar, sitting out on the covered sidewalk under the gallery railing... great food, tasty microbrew, ginormous servings. Tucked half of everybody's lunch into boxes to tote home for supper.

After walking the rest of the street of stalls... and back... we found the car and headed to explore Deer Valley. Deer Valley was the venue for some of the 2002 Salt Lake City Olympic events. It was an interesting site, not too large, pretty much straight up. They were currently installing a finicular. The car for which had just arrived that week. They planned to have it up and running for the coming ski season.

We found our way back to Kimball Junction and Redstone lifestyle village. Shopped at Smith's market for accoutrements for supper leftovers and headed back to the condo. Everyone turned in early.

Monday, July 27

Sandra had wanted to visit the Olympic Park, just long enough to take some photos and then we could move on. We were there for 6 hours. The Olympic Park (just around the corner from us) was where the ski jumping, the aerial, the bob-sled, and the luge competitions had taken place. It was enormous. It had a great museum, several short movies about different aspects of the 2002 Winter Olympics, a bus tour of the area, a school, a summer aerial practice area, and much more that we vowed to return to enjoy.

We started with a 30 minute bus tour. Our guide was retired bobsled professional, Carl Repke. He had been the commentator for the luge and bobsled for the 2006 Winter Olympics in Turino, Italy and would be again in 2010 in Vancouver. He took us first to the bottom of the ski jumps. Then we drove to the top of the luge run. Spent some time there. Watched the bobsled... on wheels... in the next run... summer fun... for younger people.

Emily Cook came by. She is an Olympic athlete in women's aerials. Sandra had her photo taken with her. Then we went to the top of the ski jumps. My, it looks different from up here. Now, back to base. As we were getting off the bus Carl said we should be sure to watch the students from Australia, who were attending the on-site school, practice their aerials. So, after finishing the family-focused museum, we went next door.

The practicing skiers are fully dressed in ski garb and skis and boots and helmets. They climb to the top of the ski jump, prepare themselves mentally, soar down the chute, vault into the air, twist, twirl, tumble, and land in the biggest pool of water I have ever seen. As they are tumbling, an operator turns on the bubble machine. Now, we all assumed that it was to aerate the water to offer a soft landing, but, in fact, when the skiers are in the air, they cannot tell the difference between the blue of the sky and the blue of the water. The white bubbles let them gauge which end is up so they land on their feet. We watched this from the provided bleachers for a couple of fascinating hours. Had a hot dog and drink, from the concession inside the building, then headed back to Park City.

We walked the rest of Main Street... no stalls today... just great shops and galleries, and then headed back to Redstone Village for dinner at The Red Rock Grill. We were so hungry and the food was so tasty that we ate the whole gargantuan thing... and suffered all night long. : -(After dinner, we cruised several interesting art galleries. While enjoying one, Margaret called to say she had tried to reschedule, but it was not going to work out for this year. We were all disappointed for her.

Tuesday, July 28.

Sandra had shipped a TV transmission tower installation to Provo before she retired and was interested in seeing it. There was also a Mormon temple in Provo that she wanted to see... so we headed for Provo... the back way. It took us through beautiful country... big, open, high, large lakes or reservoirs here and there full of people playing with water toys and making waves. It took us through Heber City, which proved interesting on several levels, one of which was inexpensive gasoline. It took us beside the still waters and into the lush, cool mountains. About 11:15 we were turning into a narrow canyon and up a grade that would require chains in the wintertime. The twisting road ran along a winding brook. At the end of the road was a sign that said simply, "Sundance."

The front parking lot was small... intimate. Just beyond was a rustic building that is the Inn. To the left was an Alpine meadow at the base of a glacier and a small chair lift up. To the right was a path to another small parking lot. Across the stream was a building marked "Rehearsal Hall." Beyond the parking lot was another path to another rustic building tucked back among the Aspens. This one housed a general store... very upscale general store... a deli, a formal dining room, a gathering room, a hallway with plaques of written history and photos of notables, and a patio for dining. We chose the patio. It was tucked between the formal dining room and the pub... Apres Ski... both buildings were new, but of rough hewn logs with chinking... not the round Lincoln Logs, but square cut and massive. The stone patio was covered with a pergola laced with strips of sailcloth for shade. Behind us was a small, babbling waterfall and a trickling brook. To the right was a short stone wall adorned with Columbine and other wild flowers among the birch trees. It was totally comfortable.

We had seen posters announcing the Saturday night opening of the play The Fantastiks and asked our waiter where it would be held. He told us of an amphitheater up beyond the chairlift. It held about 250 people, but more were able to sit on the hillside beyond it. Sundance partners with the theater department of the University of Utah Valley in Provo who provides the casting and producing of the show. We were sorry we would not be in town to see it.

Lunch was lovely. I had an Ahi Salad Nicoise. Delicious. Left some of the baby bib lettuce behind, but ate all the Ahi... seared just right... and the avocado and such. The waiter took our pictures by the waterfall. We gave him a healthy tip and went to read the hallway. We learned that up beyond this building there were Brazilian glassblowers (but they were not in today) and a gift shop of their wares. We also learned that a film workshop was in session... that is probably where Bobby was. The film workshop runs all summer for those budding film makers who later bring their work to the Sundance Film Festival. So much creativity going on! I love it!

Reluctantly, we said good bye to Sundance, vowing to return... if only in our dreams. We drove to Provo. Sandra saw her installation and temple and we came back north on the interstate. We went downtown to Temple Square for some orientation and preparation for Thursday's return to listen to the rehearsal of the Tabernacle choir, but Sandra would be gone by then. We spent an hour or more in the visitors' center and then headed back to Jeremy Ranch. Again, after so much food, we went to Whole Foods and picked up soups and such for dinner. After which, we happily put our feet up and relaxed for the evening.

Wednesday, July 29.

We had been told somewhere that there would be an open air market on Wednesday in Heber City. So Wednesday morning... we are doing better getting out of the house now... we drove the highway south to Heber City... if nothing else, by now we needed that affordable gas. Found the gas station and then searched for the train depot. (There was a steam train ride in the afternoon.) At the depot, they said the market was on Thursday night.... hmmmm.... we had other plans for Thursday night. What else could we do in town? We were told that just to the west was Midway, and Soldier's Hollow, venues for cross country and biathlon in 2002. Then, if we went up the mountain, there was the Huber homestead and beautiful views and good places to eat. So off we went.

We drove and drove, up and up, until we were at the gate of the national forest. (Learned later that Brighton and Solitude ski areas were on the other side of the same mountain.) Then we started back down. Found the Huber homestead... small, stone, very Swiss... and decided we were hungry. Not far away we found the Blue Boar Inn for lunch. Now, here we were in the middle of Utah and we could have sworn we were in a Swiss village. Mr. Huber (undoubtedly with an oomlout) had settled here and brought his family, friends, and fellow villagers to settle with him. But the Blue Boar Inn looked more Austrian or Bavarian than Swiss. It had the frescoed paintings on the outside walls as well as on the inside. (Perhaps they had come from northern Switzerland.)

We went in, found some people to ask directions, and ended up out on the picturesque stone patio for lunch. Had great food... roasted chicken on a ciabotta bun with avocado and red onion. Yum. Iced Tea.

Lovely breeze. Later went in to explore the interior and visit the fraulein's zimmer. The hallway walls were lined with pins and postage stamps from the many winter Olympics throughout the world, as well as photos of the local Schutzenfests. The waitress took us into one of the lodge rooms to see how lovely it was... hmmmm like being in Europe, right here in the old U. S. of A.

We found our way back to the train depot in time to board for a 90 minute ride around the reservoir. The train ride was very relaxing. We did ask when the steam engine ran (we had a diesel). They said one more weekend and then it had to go in to have its boiler cleaned. It would be back next year. The cars were open to allow full view of the scenery and to let the welcome breeze waft through. By the time we returned to the depot it was late afternoon and rather warm.

We drove the short distance back to the condo. Got home just in time to eat a small bite and head for the spa... massages R us... for an evening of relaxation. Oh yea! Just a little to the left. : -)

Went home, finished supper and enjoyed our vegetative state for the rest of the evening.

Thursday, July 30

I got up early to take Sandra into Salt Lake City to catch her flight. Although retired, she has a dog-sitting business and is quite busy on the weekends.

We left the house at 8:30, dropped her off at 9:00 and I returned at 9:30 just in time to catch Janet coming down the stairs. Had a leisurely morning enjoying drinking coffee and talking girl talk. We were planning to head back into the city for the afternoon and evening.

We had lunch that day in Redstone Village at Bajio, a Mexican restaurant to die for... buffet, build a meal. I had a salad as big as a grocery.

We arrived in Salt Lake about 2:30. We had been told the best free parking was under the conference center. So we boldly went down the ramp only to meet a sign at the bottom that said, "$10." Oops... no backing out now. We asked the attendant about the "free" parking... Hmmmm... There were lots of ways to get free parking... if you were Mormon. After much conversation about taking the tour and attending the rehearsal of the Mormon Tabernacle choir, he said, "go on and park," and lifted the gate. When I made a motion to back up to get a ticket from the machine, he said, "It's alright, you won't need a ticket." So, we shrugged our shoulders, parked, and went on a tour of the buildings. We asked our guides about the best way to get to Trolley Square (without driving-- without moving the car).

In Salt Lake City, they have a land train called the Trax. It is free. Woo Hoo! We were able to get a Trax all the way out to 600 W and 400 S. That left only a short walk to get to Trolley Square. We were winded and warm upon arrival so we found a restaurant to get a cold beverage. The restaurant was Brazilian, the beverage was a lime smoothie... yummers! Janet had a Papaya smoothie... or Passion Fruit.... but either way it was good.

Being refreshed, we cruised Trolley Square... many upscale stores... many also closed... and went in to a small shop called "The Silk Road." They had many antique items from Central West Africa, Burma, and Thailand. I was talking with the proprietress about my son's Egyptian room. She said she had something Egyptian and took me to the jewelry. On a T stand were several necklaces... they were small pieces of something chalky and gray. She told me, "These are Egyptian trade beads. They are from Mali. From 1000 BC to 1000 AD the Egyptians traded with Mali." I didn't think they were too exciting, except for the provenance. I could put them in a shadow box, just for the story. Then she said, "I have been wearing some for a while. Come see how they change color." The necklace she had been wearing was all bright, shiny blue and green and turquoise stones. Hmmmmm.... So, I bought one strand.

Then she said, "I had some Egyptian art in a portfolio, but I am not sure where I put it." We said we were going back upstairs for dinner, but could stop back before we left for the Trax.

145

So, it was back to Rodizio's, the restaurant of smoothies. They had an ENORMOUS salad bar... a hot bar with pasta, rice, etc... 2 cold fruit soups. Then, the waiters, dressed as Gauchos, came around to the tables with skewers of meats and sliced them off for your plate. They had 17 kinds of meat and fish and fresh pineapple... all roasted on the spit with yummy glazes... Mmmmm good. (We didn't consume all 17.) Did have a cup of creamy, cold Mango soup, though. : -)

We ate until we thought we were going have to be rolled out on a furniture dolley, then went back down to The Silk Road. The owner had found the portfolio of Egyptian Art. OOOhhh. OOOOhhhh. They were all exquisite. It was difficult to choose just one... so I bought 4. They were on papyrus... modern papyrus, but nevertheless, papyrus. They would look SO good in my son's guest room. I will find frames and such in Columbus. So, they packaged them in a flat box/envelope so I could put them in my carry-on to get them home.

A note about my son's Egyptian room: My son, Jay, had recently retired from twenty-three years in military service and had purchased his first home. It was his wish to decorate each room for a part of the world to which he had been deployed during his service career. His living areas were classic continental with cordovan leather and brass and rich dark woods... with a stein or three here and there. And, of course his commemorative chunk of the Berlin Wall. His dining area and guest bath were Asian... colorful, yet artfully minimalistic. Egypt was one of the countries where his unit had trained in preparation for going to Iraq. He had brought home a few items from Egypt, but still needed a few more to give the room a broader definition. I couldn't pass up this opportunity to get him these authentic gifts.

After all the preparations, explanations, and "Thank yous", Janet and I fled for the Trax and arrived at the Conference Hall on time.

The Conference Hall is new since I was last in Salt Lake City. In fact, there is much that is new in Salt Lake City. The city continues to grow as does the Mormon complex. The conference hall is north of the temple (on North Temple Street and West Temple Street. There is also a South Temple Street. I imagine them growing to the east until there is also an East Temple Street... now the eastern border is at State Street.) The Conference Hall was built to seat 21,000 people in a building with an unsupported dome. It is magnificent. The Tabernacle choir rehearses and performs there in the summer months. The old tabernacle only seats about 2,500, but, it is still in use for smaller events.

The choir was truly awesome in person. How many times have we seen them on TV or heard them on Christmas recordings, but to hear them in person is beyond imagination. Having said that, there was much rehearsing, but little actual singing of complete pieces. Much detail of phrasing was emphasized by the conductor. The choir usually sang from 8:00 - 9:30, but tonight, about 8:45, they broke. About 75 people from the center of the chorus got up and left. It turns out they were members of a class of music students majoring in conducting from one of the nearby colleges. They were here to learn technique from the conductor of the chorus and were also substituting for a chorus from Great Britain who would be filling those seats on Sunday for service... another exchange program.

Upon leaving, I had to go to the Ladies Room before our journey home... can you imagine a ladies room to service 21,000 people? Or even 10,000. It was immense and splendid... lots of marble and granite and corridors and banks of stalls. Bigger than any airport restroom I have seen. Impressive. And had paper, too.

Taking the elevator down to the parking garage, we found the car at D9 and plotted our exit. We knew we wanted to exit on West Temple Street to go south to I-80, so we turned left and followed the long line of cars out the same tunnel we had entered so many hours before. Lo! And Behold! The gate went up and stayed up! We didn't have to pay the $10. 00 !!!! God is good... or, at least the attendant we had talked to upon entering finally had a heart and knew if we stayed until the rehearsal was over, there would be no need for a ticket... hmmmm. Anyway, we smiled at each other, put away our money, and headed for the highway and home.

Friday, July 31

Lazy morning. No plans... Janet talked about heading for Wyoming, just because. So, we cleaned out the fridge except for last meals and headed east. Sandra had left an ice pack belt in the freezer, so we had to look for a way to return it to her. We went trekking up the road toward Wyoming. At Coalville, Utah, we exited the highway to find a post office. Now, this was a small town (no traffic lights), but it had an inviting look to it, and a wide Main Street. We found the post office, mailed the "if it fits, it ships" package and asked the friendly postmistress if there might be anything in her town that a tourist might enjoy.

She mentioned a few things, but we were most interested in a "small museum under the court house." We were invited to leave our car there and walk the block to the Richardsonian structure. We entered the side door, climbed the moderately broad staircase to the main floor and found the sign that said simply, "Museum" over the doorway of the basement stairway. Not finding anyone to ask about protocol, we ventured below into the coolness, turning on our own lights as we went.

Well! Who'd 'a' thunk it! Such a big museum in such a small place! It had everything! It was immaculately clean for all its openly displayed dust- catchers. Each tiny room was set as a well done theme. The room we enjoyed most, however, was the kitchen. Every utensil, every gadget ever used was on display. There were notes of information everywhere. But the ruler of the room was the big, black wood stove... a Majestic... an iron and chrome Victorian beauty. Back east, these monsters, which dominated every kitchen, burned wood. I suspect in Coalville, Utah, it heated the home and cooked the meals with coal.

From Coalville we continued east across the Wyoming border to Evanston at Exit 5. The sign said "River Walk" so we searched for that. Found a parking lot and a path... lovely foot bridge over a swiftly moving river with a swimming hole hosting some teens having a splashing good time. Two more teens came toward us on the path. We asked about restaurants... had seen a sign for The Olde Mill. "Out of business." They said. We were directed to J. B. 's, a family owned, home cooking restaurant through town, up by exit 3. We thanked them and went through the center of town, up the hill, to the right and sure enough there on the left was J. B. 's.

Had a lovely lunch... turkey and the trimmings for me... pulled pork sandwich for Janet. Pretty tasty stuff, too. We talked about the rough, chalky Egyptian necklace and wondered if mine would turn bright and shiny the same way the other one had turned. I still had it with me in my purse, so I put it on. It was about 1.30. PM.

We asked about things to see in town... decided we had already seen them on the drive through, so we headed back to the roost. Now, you have heard of Big Sky???? Well, this is the country for big sky... big everything in fact. You can see for miles. The sky is big, the mountains are big, the rolling prairies are big... and beautiful.

That evening we made one last trip to Whole Foods for soup and back home for the rest of the evening. When I took off the necklace, about 9:30, it had already begun to change color.

Saturday, Aug. 1

Janet and I left for the Salt Lake airport about 8:30 AM I dropped her at the airline departures level a little after 9:00 and went to turn in the car. After the dust-up with Max over changing my pickup time because of flight delays, I was happy to see the final amount was the original amount agreed upon. Then, I checked in at the kiosk for my own flight... this is getting easier all the time... and headed to concourse D to find Janet. The place was packed. There was hardly room to navigate. This was a busy time at a busy airport. And, of course, her gate was located all the way out at the end of the concourse, but I finally found her. We talked until about 10:45 when it was time for her to board her plane. I wished her well until next we talked, and watched her disappear down the "Breezeway."

Then, I headed back up the concourse to find a place to have lunch before going to my gate in concourse C to catch my plane. The return to Columbus was uneventful. The plane actually arrived a bit early. I took the shuttle to the motel and had no trouble at all sleeping that night.

I spent the next day cruising Columbus looking for frames for my son's Egyptian art and for a shadow box for the Egyptian necklace. The next time Jay gets home, together we will frame the artwork and the necklace. After wearing it for only two days, the necklace is already surprisingly much brighter. The greens and blues are bright and the yellows are coming out... didn't even know it had yellow in it. The reds, for which I bought it, are not yet changing. Hmmmm.... What an adventure this week turned out to be.

Taos, New Mexico -- 2011

Well, the day has come. This destination has been number one on my Bucket List for awhile. I have been wanting to go to Santa Fe/Taos for years, but it has been very difficult to get time share there. This year the opportunity came and came quickly. There was space one week in early May. The resort was rather new to RCI. Wyndham had just recently purchased the Fechin Inn, remodeled it to fit time share use, and named it WorldMark, Taos. The unit was small, a one bedroom, sleep 4 (Murphy bed in the living room) kitchenette with no stove (microwave only). BUT, it was Taos, so I grabbed it.

Janet jumped on the opportunity after checking with her husband, who was travelling in South America, and Margaret tried to make it work, but her 100 year old mother was not in the best of health. It would have to be a last minute decision for her. And, this wasn't Sandra's cup of tea. She was getting reorganized from a long ski season.

It was Mother's Day weekend and Jay stopped on his way to Fort Wayne for a week's rest between semesters. (He was retired from the service now ... after twenty-three years... and finishing his college education.) We both left Marietta on Friday morning. The forecast had been rain, but the only precipitation I encountered was within the I-270 loop around Columbus... and that was a deluge, (scratch off car wash) but it didn't last long.

I stopped at Trader Joe's to pick up Muesli for breakfast and headed for the Baymont Hotel at the airport. After checking in, I skirted rush-hour traffic by going out the back gate to Hamilton Road and found a Bob Evans for supper... spinach salad with apples, cranberries, nuts, hot dressing, and a cup of Tomato Basil Soup... all 5 star! Had a good night's sleep, woke early ... all bright-eyed and bushy-tailed... and caught the shuttle for the airport for the start of such an adventure.

I was flying Southwest Airlines for the first time and had to become acquainted with their open (unassigned) seating system. Since I only had 30 minutes between landing and taking off again in Chicago, I was concerned about being in the back of the plane and not having enough time to disembark. I was in boarding group B (not the first group.) As I boarded, I quickly realized that all the window and aisle seats had been taken. I headed for the first middle seat I saw... near the front, between two young men. One was from Utah, near Salt Lake City. He had been in Ohio for a family funeral. The other was from Chicago. He was a member of the chorus of the Chicago Opera Company. He had just been accepted by the Met in NYC. He had only until July to find a place to live in NYC, decide whether to keep or sell his condo in Chicago, rent, buy, or co-habitate in New York. He was quite excited about the opportunity. We talked about it the entire trip to Chicago.

We landed on time at Midway Airport. That airport had changed quite a lot since we had lived in Chicagoland, forty years ago. My fears of missing my connection vanished, though, when I deplaned from Gate 15 and found I would depart from Gate 19... two doors down. It should have been time for this plane to board, except it had been a little late landing and was still emptying. Group after group of cammy-clad military men and women kept appearing from the jetway. As they came in to view, the entire gathering of waiting travelers broke into extended and appreciative applause.

The next leg of my flight found me seated between two older women (yup, older than I.) The one near the window was returning from a wedding in Michigan. She was a new resident of New Mexico... loved it, so far. The woman in the aisle seat was a longtime resident of New Mexico and had been an anthropologist, teaching in the state universities. She and I had great conversation about the Anasazies, Chimney Rock, Aztec Ruins, Chaco Canyon, etc. until the baby in the row in front of us began to cough. It caught her attention... "It sounds like croupe." She said. And later, "That mother should check with a doctor, it could be strep." By now the baby was coughing so hard, he was vomiting. The mother was frantically trying to keep up with everything. We handed her our vomit bags.

At breakfast, in the airport, I had placed the extra crispy bacon between the toast pieces and wrapped the sandwich in a napkin to have for lunch (no time between flights). I wrapped the whole thing in yards of paper toweling from the ladies room so the bacon fat would not get on my purse. The toweling was still fine. (The napkin was not.) I took some of my water, moistened the paper toweling, and offered it to the harried mother. I don't know where the flight attendant was, and the father in the row further front was useless. The woman next to me was quite agitated. I reached for the "help needed" light.

Finally the flight attendant appeared, offered the mother whatever help he could give and things began to settle down. Only then did the woman in the aisle seat reveal that before she went into anthropology, she had been a pediatric nurse. Aha! She admitted it was difficult to sit there and not take responsibility for the situation.

She and I talked a bit more about ruins and ancient civilizations, but she soon succumbed to a restful nap.

The plane landed about a half hour early. I had been apprehensive about my bag arriving with me... since we had so little time between flights... but there it was on the carousel. I rescued it from the stack of similar bags and moved on to wait for Janet to arrive. (Margaret didn't make it.)

I stopped at the Visitor Center to pick up guide books and brochures about the area. The receptionist was very helpful. Stuffing all the reading materials and maps into my new home-made, brand name knock-off, quilted carry-on, I positioned myself at the base of the escalator. Janet had called on her cell phone to say they were on the ground and she was on her way.

Before her arrival, I spent the few minutes watching the feet and legs of passengers descending the escalator trying to guess what their upper torso looked like and what their occupation might be. That was fun...

Janet appeared... I didn't guess her shoes correctly. We found her carousel of luggage, gathered her goods, and headed for the rental car. We had to take a bus out to the newly built rental car center... all car rental companies were conveniently located in one off-site building. It came to pass that our car this trip was to be a Chevy HHR. Woo Hoo! (It turned out to be a really comfortable car... got 30 MPG, rode nicely, handled well, was easy to get in and out of... so important at our age. I liked it -- even though I am not in love with the exterior design.) After making all the adjustments of seats, mirrors, etc., we were heading north on I-25 in no time.

About an hour or so out... I think somewhere on the outskirts of Santa Fe... we realized we were getting hungry. The first sign we saw mentioning food said Encantado Restaurant, this exit. So, we took the exit and followed the signs that said **Food** with an arrow. We turned right, then left, as indicated, but all we saw was scrub brush and sand. The road was paved, so we took that as a good sign. About 3 miles later, there was a simple sign at a stone gate that said *Encantado – An Auberge Resort*. Uh oh. Upscale. But we were hungry, and had not seen any other signs for food.

We drove the circular drive and explained to the young men in starched white shirts that we had seen a sign that there was a restaurant on site.

"Oh Yes." They said with welcoming smiles. I asked how we went about finding it. They answered, "The restaurant is here," he said, pointing to large, glass, double doors behind him. "We can park your car for you, or there is a parking lot over there where you can park it yourself." I chose the latter.

Upon entering we found not one, but two restaurants… or rather, dining rooms… one with white table cloths and one with a bar. We were greeted by two lovely young ladies who assured us that the menu was the same in either room, so we chose the more sedate dining room. (We were ready for the quiet.) The waiters, the bus boys, the table cloths, the menus, the wine lists, the huge glass walls looking out on water features juxtaposed with the rock and cactus dotted desert countryside, all indicated this was, indeed, a 5-star restaurant.

We were offered water, sparkling or local (still), and of course, the wine list. We declined the wine since we were still at least an hour from our destination and hoped to arrive before dark and sober.

I ordered the Quail appetizer as an entrée and the cream of artichoke soup garnished with a lobster claw. Janet ordered the Market Selection plate and the soup. While we waited we were served a basket of mixed breads, including a roasted red pepper lavosh (to die for) and an amuse bouche of local goat cheese coated in crushed pistachios on a bed of strawberry couli in a little white china spoon in the middle of a BIG, white, china plate.

It took a while (I think they had to hunt the quail) but it was delicious. The Quail was on a bed of Anasazi black beans and roasted sweet corn with a puree of Utah truffles. Janet had Mac and Cheese (very tasty local cheese) asparagus and yellow beets with hollandaise, and Quinoa salad. We shared tastes… unbelievably good.

Declining dessert because of time, we promised to return someday, paid our $110 bill and were on our way… wondering if this was what we were in for on a daily basis… if so, we were surely to lose weight.

It took another hour and a half to reach Taos, but it was still daylight. The approach was spectacular… narrow, curving mountain roads beside a sparkling river (The Rio Grande not yet Grande.) We watched the passing road signs… Paseo del Pueblo Sur… for a long time. Then, in the center of everything it quickly turned to Paseo del Pueblo Norte… our destination. (Nearly missed it.) Now we had to watch very closely… saw the sign for the art museum, but missed the WorldMark gate just beyond. Executed a quick turn-around at the intersection and drove back through the adobe gates, past the art museum, and followed the signs to the hotel located behind. It was incredible! Pueblo Revival in design with much glass and hand-carved wood and grandeur. (Not to mention the blazing fire in the massive adobe fireplace in the public greatroom.) We loved it immediately!

We checked in, but went back to Smith's Grocery to buy food for breakfast, water, and wine... the essentials. Then we moved in. Our unit was on the second floor, very near the balcony overlooking the gorgeous great room. Janet took the living room with the Murphy bed, I took the bedroom. We each had our own full bathrooms. The kitchenette was serviceable, but no cooking appliance except a microwave. We did have a small refrigerator. We would count on muesli, fresh fruit and yogurt for breakfast and leftovers for supper. We were rarely disappointed.

We toasted our arrival with glasses of wine and turned in early.

Sunday was Mother's Day. With the time difference (Mt. Time) I awoke early. Janet slept in a while. (I was used to Eastern Daylight Time, Janet was used to Pacific Time.) When we were all collected and breakfasted, we headed out to see the world. Taos is a walking town. Almost everything is within walking distance. We were only two traffic lights from the Plaza, which is the center of town (and where sur becomes norte).

It was too early for the art museum, so we saved that for another day. (Rain was forecast for Wednesday... a good museum day.) We walked across the street to a series of art galleries and shops. One gallery was holding an opening reception that evening from 5:00 – 7:00 to which we were invited to return. We went on to check out Michael's Kitchen and Bakery. The line was out the door. Mental note... another day, come early.

Then, we turned and headed south. About two properties away was Kit Carson Park where there was an arts and crafts fair set up. We cruised the booths enjoying the beautiful paintings, jewelry, clothing, and sampling the local products. The temperature was in the low 70s, but the sun was hot. Because we are both redheads, we wore hats and tried to travel in the shade... there wasn't much shade.

We walked on south. It was getting hungry time, so we thought we would try Graham's Grille on the corner, only to be told there was a 45 minute wait... it was, after all, Mother's Day. So, we back-tracked to a delightful little hole in the wall café called La Dolce Vita. It was situated at the back of a little garden plaza. The small room had two tables and a counter for ordering. The atmosphere and the menu were very 60s. I ordered a Taos special sandwich – smoked turkey, aged white cheddar, avocado, bacon, tomato, onion, sprouts, and green chillies... panini style. It was delicious. Washed it down with a Mango iced tea.

After lunch, we crossed the intersection and window shopped all the way to the Kit Carson home and museum, which was free to Mothers today. I was aware of Kit Carson, mostly from the old Saturday morning TV show, but can't say I really knew much about him. We talked with the curator while we waited for the video to restart. He told us some very interesting things about the area and about the family.

The house itself was only three rooms. The closest room had had a dirt floor until the grown son lived there with his family. It was spartan living. The home had a full length front porch with a boardwalk floor, and roof... very saloon-ish. The rear courtyard held a horno, or adobe bake oven, just outside the back door. There was another wing across the back of the courtyard that probably had been the stable... it was still in its original condition.

On the opposite side of the courtyard from the house was the gift shop. It was full of beautiful things -- and all on sale. I had intended to purchase some artwork by the end of the vacation, but couldn't pass up a signed and numbered print by Taos artist Valerie Graves of a pueblo garden wall with a blue wooden gate ... it was just the thing for the wallspace I had in mind at home.

We went on to other galleries... each as fine as the next... and then went back across the street and down to the plaza ... the central focal point of the town.

On the low adobe walls of the plaza are signs that tell of the history of Taos. The first wall told of ancient Taos: "Captain Hernan Alvarado and his conquistadors from the famous Francisco Vasquez de Coronado expedition arrived in Taos on August 29, 1540. It is estimated that the Tiwa Indians settled in this valley around 1350 A. D. The name Taos is believed to be an adaptation of the Tewa Indian word Towih, meaning red willows. It is first recorded in history by Juan Belarde, secretary to Don Juan de Onate in 1598. Taos was first colonized by Spain in 1615."

The opposite wall told of more modern Taos: "The town of Taos was originally established on May 1, 1796 when 63 families who had petitioned Governor Don Fernando Chacon were placed in possession of the Don Fernando de Taos land grant by the Alcalde of the Pueblo of Taos, Antonio Jose Ortiz. The town has existed as a village under the Spanish Crown, then Mexico, and later when New Mexico became a Territory of the United States in 1846. On May 7, 1934 Taos was incorporated as a municipality under New Mexico state law."

The plaza was delightful. We sat on a cool, concrete bench enjoying the breeze and the scenery for quite awhile. Then, we treated ourselves to an ice cream cone and walked the perimeter of the plaza, window-shopping. We wanted to find the Alley Cantina – a restaurant that had been recommended for its food and its entertainment.

We finally found it… tucked away at the back corner of the plaza. Some of its tables were, in fact, in the alley. That evening their entertainment would be a jazz trio. We decided to walk back to the hotel, rest our wearies, and later, drive back for dinner and jazz at the Alley Cantina.

I had brisket … delicious, but WAY too much… took half home for another evening. The jazz trio was made up of a female vocalist from England (great voice), a man on bongos… Yup, three large and one small… and a man on guitar. They made good noise.

We went home happy and satisfied, watched one episode of West Wing (Janet had brought the CD set) and went to bed.

Taos abounds with the unexpected. We were aware of the history and the art community, but we were not prepared for the extent of the diversity we found. On our approach on Saturday, we could see in the distance an elongated disturbance in the earth's surface. It was simply called The Gorge.

Now, I have seen gorges before… Queechee Gorge in Vermont is quite breathtaking, and The New River Gorge in West Virginia is spectacular… but this is more like a gigantic nasty gash in the level landscape of the high plateau. It is long (many miles) and it is deep (no clue – actually, one account says 800 feet straight down at one point). The Rio Grande is not large here, but it is difficult to judge just how wide and just how deep it might be in ratio to the size of the gorge. It looks like only a narrow trickle way down at the bottom of the cavernous chasm.

There is a small state park here for parking and restrooms, but nothing else. One is free to walk to the edge at one's own risk. I have a slight case of acrophobia – can't get too close to the edge of high things… ran into it at Hoover Dam, as well. So, I just extend my arm and camera, zoom in, and hope for the best. The sun shining on the screen is no help at all in seeing the content of the camera shot.

I had thought I had read that there was a restaurant there. No such luck. One man visiting the gorge thought it might be further out route 64. There was a silly community out there that built their houses out of old recycled bottles and rubber tires. They might have a place to eat.

We went to inquire. And guess what! ? This silly community made out of old bottles and rubber tires is the Earthship Corporation! Yeah! Right out there in the middle of nothing. Of course, that is just where they want to be. They are self-sustaining. They run on solar and wind power and recycle whatever water comes their way. The tour was $10 and 90 minutes long and we were hungry, so we bought some home baked (solar?) chocolate chip cookies and talked about returning another day. When we said we were looking for The Gorge Restaurant, they knew where it was! It turns out The Gorge Restaurant is downtown on the plaza in the center of Taos... not anywhere near the gorge. Go figure.

So, back we went to the Plaza, found a parking space, scrapped the plans to go to the Taos Pueblo until another day and settled in for a great lunch! (Life has its moments.)

After lunch we began to systematically move through the many lovely shops surrounding the Plaza. The first one came before we even left the building. It was an artist's co-op with many media. We oohed and aahed as we enjoyed the artwork and made our way to the room with the person on duty. He was a photographer. His work was remarkable. One image especially caught my eye. It was a series of open doors in an ancient pueblo. The setting turned out to be Pueblo Bonito at Chaco Canyon. The light was fantastic. I knew I had to have it. Even though it was a photograph, I would never be standing at that spot at the moment that the light was that perfect to get that image. I bought it... with no second thoughts.

He had been to Chaco Canyon many times... camped there, just to get the right light. Since we would be going there at the end of the week, we talked about the best route to take. He looked it up on the internet and wrote down some names and phone numbers for us. I put it away until we needed it later in the week.

We thanked him for all his help and continued on our way to enjoy more plaza shops. Janet found the most beautiful pair of chocolate turquoise earrings... never saw such a rich color.

We finally made our way back to the car just before the meter ran out. Back at the condo we hit the hot tub and pool to massage our weary muscles. For supper we finished our leftovers from lunch, enjoyed the West Wing and some wine and went to bed. What a day!

We decided to start the next day at the Taos Pueblo and stay as long as it took to see everything. We had called to check on food availability and had been told they only cooked for bus tours. Hmmm... and no electricity, as well... hmmm. SO, we went across the street to experience Michael's Kitchen. It was packed, but our wait was very short. I had corned beef hash with poached eggs, wheat toast, and GOOD coffee. Janet had waffles and thick sliced bacon and eggs. We were carbo loading for the day. The owner came around with complimentary glazed doughnut holes just to tempt us. They were delicious, but we left buying some cookies from the bakery, instead.

Taos Pueblo is a National Historic Landmark and a World Heritage Site. The approach to the pueblo was similar to the approach to San Ildefonso pueblo… small, unassuming. We bought our admission tickets and inquired about guided tours. Their tour guides were college students, who, of course, were still in school. We were on our own. We consulted the printed sheet with map and info and entered the ancient pueblo proper.

The buildings were old looking and small. Adobe takes a lot of maintenance, but these walls were in questionable condition. The Pueblo is over 1000 years old… maintenance, maybe 45 or 50. We walked the perimeter until encountering a sign that said "No Admittance", and then cut between buildings toward the center of the north plaza. To our right was a small building with art for sale. We went in.

A young man and a young woman (30s) were behind a case which held beautiful pottery. All the walls of the room were lined with artwork and shelves of pottery from a number of other pueblos… Santa Clara, Santa Ana, Zuni… but there was only one San Ildefonso pot. On the same table were some figurines fashioned from a sparkly clay. We were told that this clay was indigenous to the Tiwa area and these figurines were made by members of Taos pueblo. It was a clay laced with Mica. Janet bought a family of bears and I bought a smaller version.

We enjoyed more discussion of the pueblos… Tiwa (Red Willow) … of Taos… was pronounced Tea wah. They were distantly related (from Chaco Canyon?) to the Tewa … pronounced Tay wah… of San Ildefonso. It was also mentioned that we should be sure to visit the Millicent Rogers Museum. It had the largest collection of San Ildefonso pottery of anyone… many of Maria's bowls as well as the pottery of her descendants. Hmmm.

Let me digress for a moment and explain my interest in San Ildefonso, Black-on-Black pottery.

For about ten years I have been in awe of the story of Maria Montoya Martinez — Tewa girl of the San Ildefonso Pueblo who created the beautiful little black-on-black bowl we have at The Castle Historic House Museum in Marietta, Ohio. It is part of Dr. Bertlyn Bosley's collection from her time spent working in the 1960s as a nutritionist with the Native Americans in our southwest.

Maria's story is a long story — a most-of-her-life story -- so I recommend reading the books which hold these tales so well. But Maria was one of those special women who move forward with their lives, taking their community with them — in this case her pueblo, her tribe, her family. Her life is full of stories where she seized an opportunity and all those around her benefitted from her personal decisions.

Maria is long gone — having lived from 1880 or so (no birth date was recorded) until 1980. Her husband Julian, sons Adam, Felipe, Popovi Da and Juan Diego are also gone, but her spirit and the pueblo's pottery industry live on. Her grandchildren and great grandchildren, as well as other members of the pueblo, continue to make Black-on-Black pottery. The pots today are still made with the same process that Maria used. It is a primitive process, but it produces beautiful artwork.

I had had the spiritual pleasure of visiting the San Ildefonso Pueblo in 2007. I had trod the sod of Maria Montoya Martinez and had touched the gnarled, statuesque Cottonwood tree that had been her shadetree throughout her life. I could only fantasize that my life was anywhere close to hers creatively.

When we walked back out to the plaza, I explained to Janet that the one small San Ildefonso, Black-on-black bowl was a good price… in town, at the galleries, it would be a great deal more… this artist was not a relative of Maria's, but still, it **was** her style… OK. Enough talk. I went back in and bought it. It will go on its own shelf next to my rosy-brown bowl from my San Ildefonso visit. I felt very good.

The north plaza of Taos Pueblo held the largest building… quintessential, sand-colored, soft-cornered adobe with multiple levels and primitive ladders. It is the building most associated with the Taos Pueblo and the most photographed. However, in the expansive open plaza, I did not see a Kiva.

A Kiva is a circular, ceremonial room or structure. In ancient times they were totally underground and not very large… perhaps 10 to 15 feet in diameter. The Kiva was a chamber sacred to the beliefs of the Puebloans, and for centuries, no women were allowed inside. Religious rituals as well as Pueblo communal or council activities are held in these quarters.

There are Kiva ruins and modern structures that are also partially above ground. Aztec Ruins National Monument in northern New Mexico and present day San Ildefonso Pueblo outside of Santa Fe both have above ground Kivas… at least the entrances and roofs are above ground. More of the structure may be subterranean. These Kivas are also much larger and would indicate that many male tribal participants would enter at one time.

The reconstructed Kiva at Aztec Ruins, a National Historic Site, can now be entered and appreciated by men and women alike.

We walked across a footbridge over a small, and rapidly moving, stream to the south plaza. Aptly named, Rio Pueblo, this stream was the main source of water for the residents of the pueblo. Small footbridges across the sparkly, swiftly moving stream connected the north plaza with the south plaza. More multileveled homes and tiny walkways made up the south plaza. Adobe hornos were abundant. One woman was advertising fry bread. It sounded tasty (it was about lunchtime). She didn't bake it in a horno, however. She had a small Coleman camp stove set up with a pan of hot oil at the ready. She took a small piece of yeast dough from a container, rolled it out on the table to the size of a dinner plate and dropped it into the hot oil. It only took a few minutes. When it came out, she laced it with honey, cinnamon, and powdered sugar and cut it in half. It was a treat for the palate. We often received Sopapillas with our New Mexican lunches, but nothing was as good as this Indian Fry Bread. Yummy!

As we ate, we ambled back across another stone bridge to the north plaza, picking up a few friends along the way... no, not the couple from The Netherlands, who were tasting fry bread for the first time... these friends were the dogs of the neighborhood. They were sure that we would share our tasty treat with them. They stayed with us until the last bite... which, of course, we reluctantly, but obligingly, shared.

We were now in front of the small Catholic adobe church. It was very much the same style and architecture as all the other adobe Catholic churches we had seen... it was just quite small. Built in 1850, it was not the first church of the pueblo. The original church, built in 1619 and rebuilt in 1680 had been destroyed in the War with Mexico by the U. S. Army in 1847. Its ruins are still present on the west side of the village.

On the way out of the pueblo, I talked with a native vender about the church. Although small, it was able to seat a full congregation of tribespeople... those who lived at the pueblo and those who lived outside it, but on the reservation. I said I had not seen a kiva. He assured me there was one... it was under ground, behind the largest buildings and out of sight of visitors. (Most likely where we had encountered the No Admission sign.) It was large enough for all the private tribal kiva activities. He sat on the kiva counsel which means he had contribution status for making community decisions.

Feeling quite fulfilled, we walked the short distance back to the car. It had been an enlightening visit.

From the Pueblo, we decided to go directly to the Millicent Rogers Museum. It wasn't very far. The Millicent Rogers Museum is housed in the former home of Claude Anderson and his wife, Elizabeth. Anderson built it without formal architectural plans. The lore is that he walked the plot, marking the rooms in the dirt with the heel of his boot and telling the builder that is what he wanted… the living room here, the kitchen there, the bedrooms here, the library there… all around a spacious inner courtyard. From the original photos, it was a beautiful home. It has been changed somewhat to house the collections of Millicent Rogers. Many windows have been removed to create exhibit walls. The garage and workshop are now the gift shop, and a front entrance with public restrooms has been added. It is still a beautiful building, but not so homey.

Millicent Rogers, Standard Oil Heiress, was an eastern high society personality who loved to travel and to collect beautiful things. After three marriages and three sons, she settled in Taos and now her collections have become a museum. She does have many outstanding examples of art and artifacts from around the world… paintings, sculptures, turquoise jewelry, etc. but I especially wanted to see her collection of San Ildefonso pottery. It is said to be the largest in the world donated from Maria's family. The exhibit was amazing. Besides the pottery, they also had photographs of Maria, Julian, her children and sisters. (These, of course, were from the 1930s and 40s---Julian died in 1943.) They also had a pictorial history of the black-on-black pottery-making process as well as a family tree of Maria's extensive family. It was inspirational to see.

At San Ildefonso pueblo, outside of Santa Fe, most of the current residents still make pottery, so no one individual is singled out for praise. When I visited there, I was disappointed that such an exhibit as this did not exist. Now, I am happier. It would be interesting to know how the family came to the decision to contribute these pieces to this specific museum in Taos. Certainly the museums in Santa Fe or Washington D. C. would covet this collection.

We were told that only about one-tenth of the collection is displayed at any given time. It keeps enthusiasts coming back.

When we were through enjoying the museum, we sat for awhile on the patio enjoying the brisk, but pleasant breeze… just sat… and enjoyed. It was wonderful.

On the way home, we found Cid's Market… a small, organic food store. We shopped for incidentals and treats, but took notice of prepared foods that we could buy and take to our oven-less kitchen for dinner some night.

From there, we stopped at Guadalajara... A Mexican restaurant that had been recommended as a "Must Eat." They were right! I had a chicken Aztec Quesadilla and a Dos Equis. I thought there would never be a Chicken enchilada or burrito as good as Fort Wayne's El Azteca, but here it was. Hmmmm good... muy delicioso!

Feeling fat and happy, we went looking for Kit Carson's grave. The location had been described to us by several people... in vague terms. We had walked from one direction and driven from another, but were not able to find it. This time, we drove to the street that dead-ended into the cemetery... couldn't miss it. Janet got out and walked the small area and found the graves. I stayed with the car in the no-parking zone, in case I needed to relocate.

It was a modest grave, by historic celebrity standards, but well maintained. We paid due homage to the frontiersman, explorer, trapper, soldier, scout, and many more vocations in the early southwest territory. At his home and museum, we had learned he was so much more than our textbooks or TV mention.

At the end of the day, we headed home for wine and West Wing for the evening.

Wednesday was the day that had been forecast as inclement and had been designated as Museum Day. We walked to the Art Museum located just in front of the hotel, past the freshly sprouted toadstools next to the sidewalk. (Took many pictures, just because they were so artistically cute.)

The Taos Art Museum is housed in the Nicolai Fechin house. Its entrance is through the sunroom, off of the rear courtyard. This home has not been altered to house exhibits. It is spectacular in its own right. For me, the current art exhibit took a back seat to the splendor of the house itself.

Nicolai Fechin was a Russian artist who had been brought to the area by Mabel Dodge Lujan (another transplanted eastern heiress socialite. She was a fascinating, albeit enigmatic woman—you might say a genuine character.) He and his family were her guests, staying in one of her many cottages for several months, but rumor has it Fechin didn't get along with Mrs. Lujan, so he soon purchased his own 7 acres of land adjacent to hers, and began to restructure the existing small house. The layout of his finished home is gorgeous! The front half is multileveled. The living room is raised in front of a huge adobe fireplace adorned with hand carved wood; the library/study is to the south, down a short flight of stairs and with its own entrance to the rear garden; the music room to the north is an open extension of the living room but sunken a few steps ... with enormous windows letting in great light.

The rear half of the house is mostly dining room, entered through hand-carved doors. The very back is the 1920s kitchen, storage, and sunporch/ breakfast room.

The upstairs is delightful. South of the landing (and in the front) is a large solarium, completely encompassed with large windows on three sides. The back of the house holds two ample bedrooms with a bathroom between... again, multileveled. The front north of the house is the master bedroom as large as the music room beneath. It had its own kiva corner fireplace and entrance to the main bathroom in the front, center hall.

So many details... hand carved wood throughout... niches for artwork... cedar-lined closets in every bedroom... windows to let in the sun. Very homey... except the kitchen... state of the art for 1927, but a bit tight and bare-bones for today's standards.

From the house, we went out to the studio... now a gift shop. The studio itself is another masterpiece... huge open room with majestic fireplace... entire north wall and roof are glass for great light. Over the minimalist bathroom is a shallow loft... hmmmm.

We poked about and wondered, until we pushed open a door that was ajar and stumbled into the office of the Museum's Executive Director (the former kitchen). She was at her desk and happy to be interrupted. We spent the next 45 minutes with her learning about the artist, the buildings, the organization and its long-range plans and programming. They have begun an out-reach summer program which brings in art students from universities throughout the U. S. It is ambitious, creative, and successful.

The loft turns out to be where Nicolai slept when he came back for the summers to work in his studio... long story about divorcing his wife, Alexandra, in Taos in 1933 and taking their 19 year-old daughter, Eya, with him to New York and then back to L. A. This story raised many more questions.

In later years... after Nicolai had died and Alexandra was in her 80s and in frail health, daughter Eya returned to take charge of the property. The buildings were in great disrepair. Alexandra had moved into the studio, since she was left no money at the time of the divorce to care for the property. Eya sold the back 5 acres to a hotel company with the understanding that the hotel would reflect the architecture and design style of the house. The Fechin Inn was built with its Pueblo Revival look and hand carved wooden surfaces to match the Fechin home. Gorgeous! Eya used the money from the sale for the much needed renovations and repairs of the main house and grounds.

We enjoyed every minute spent with Director, Erion Simpson. Exiting through the gift shop, Janet bought a T-Rex hand puppet for her grandson,

Joe. (She had been looking for one for him for a couple of years.) It turns out, the manager of the gift shop, Vickie Snyder, had fairly recently moved to Taos from Marietta, Ohio. She had lived right across the street from The Castle in Marietta's own national artist A. James Weber's house! What a small world!

Yup, I have to return to Taos!

When we left the studio, it was precipitating... not just raining... It was SNOWING! Yup, mid-May, mid-day, it was snowing. We walked back to the condo, freshened up a bit and headed out for lunch... it was now about 1:30 PM... hoped people were still serving.

We chose to go to another recommended dining room. I will refrain from naming it, since I hope this experience was an aberration. It turned out to be our only negative experience the entire week. It didn't spoil our day, but it did surprise us.

We stopped at the front desk for directions and options for lunch. The receptionists were lovely and helpful. Again, the bar and the dining room had the same menu. The dining room was less noisy. We went in that direction. We stood for several minutes waiting to be seated. No one came, but there was a waiter (we thought) talking with some people at a table. We waited for someone to notice we were waiting... nothing... just more talking. After more minutes, I decided to inquire.

I approached the table and said, "Excuse me, we are waiting to be seated, but no one is coming. Is there something else we should be doing?"

The young man (who turned out to be the maitre'd/host) immediately became defensive... and on the edge of rude. He then tried to put us at a tiny table in a cramped corner on the lower level, out of the way. We asked for something else and pointed to several larger tables.

"Those tables are set for dinner." He said.

I replied, "But, it is lunchtime."

There was a table for two near the window that seemed to be available. "It will have to be cleaned." He offered.

We said, "OK. That would be fine."

I swear he snorted -- cleaned the table and seated us, then stormed off. When our waiter came, he looked as if he was about to run into a buzz saw... we smiled and hopefully put him at ease... never too sure about that. We had good service, and great food. Maitre'd/Host did succeed in seating a single person at the tiny table in the corner, and seated another group at a table "set for dinner."

As we were leaving, Maitre'd/Host was approaching from the front, did a BIG left turn to go the other way, and avoided us entirely. I had the suspicion that he had been out at the desk giving his version of the story... oh well. Probably will not go back to that address... there are many other good restaurants in Taos. Wouldn't want to upset him, again.

After lunch, we drove to the south end of town to see the St. Francis church that Georgia O'Keefe had painted. When I saw her painting, I thought it was her impression of the church... almost cubistic... but, it is in fact the way the church looks from the rear. When you walk around to the front, it looks like any other adobe Catholic Church, with the spires and the crosses, etc. But, what an unusual structure from the back!

On the way back, we took a winding by-pass around town and stumbled on to a street with a sign that said, "Mabel Dodge Luhan House". So, we turned right onto the narrow road and went to explore. The street was a dead end with interesting houses along the way... all pueblo revival, but all different.

We parked in the designated parking lot and walked to take photos. I was interested in the large house at the end of the cul-de-sac. Janet started up the weathered wooden steps to see the multi-storied adobe house at the top of the hill. (The parking lot had no signs to indicate which house was which.)

I followed a bit behind. At the top of the long flight of steps was a dog to greet me... a great, brown dog of indiscriminate lineage, wearing a red cowboy bandana tied around her neck. She didn't bark, or wag her tail, she simply sat on the stairs, bottom and tail on one step, front paws on the lower step, tacitly greeting those who came to visit.

It turned out that the hilltop house was Mabel Luhan's home, but some of those on the lower level had belonged to her, also. The large compatible house at the end of the road was more recently built by the current owners to house their overflow guests when cultural conferences are held on site.

The inside is interesting... small rooms for the most part, except, again, for the sunken dining room, which was huge and reached by several half-rounded steps. The kitchen was beyond and we were invited to visit. The people in the kitchen were preparing dinner for a large group, so we didn't stay long. Great kitchen, though. Although vintage, it looked organized and easy to work in.

Although encouraged to do so, we didn't go upstairs to see the rooms, but were told that Mabel's bedroom, on the second floor, is the largest, has its own fireplace, and is surrounded by huge windows that look out to the mountains. Pretty nice vista. On the third floor is an equally large conservatory with equally stunning views.

Through the years, Mabel had many famous guests stay at this house... D. H. Lawrence (they didn't see eye to eye either), Georgia O'Keefe, Ansel Adams, Dennis Hopper, and many more. Her website shows many of the rooms in the house as well as the adjacent guest cottages. This site is surely going back on my bucket list.

That evening we snacked for supper on hummus, cheese and crackers, had some wine and finished the first season of The West Wing.

Thursday was our day to visit Santa Fe. We got off to a fairly early start, and arrived at the old Plaza just before lunch time. The visitor map indicated a public parking garage right in the center of downtown. From the garage it was a short walk to the plaza and the action. We took a few minutes to peruse the wares of the Native Americans displaying their talents on colorful blankets along the walkway in front of the Palace of the Governors and the New Mexico History Museum. I purchased a lovely, simple pair of silver tear drop earrings for $20. Not a bad price for very pretty handmade earrings.

We made our way across the plaza to The Fonda Hotel... mostly because they were the only loo in town... also to see where Alexandra stayed when Nicolai came back to spend his summers in Taos. After the comfort station, we decided to remain right there and enjoy the ample southwest lunch buffet for $9. 95. You can't beat the prices in this town, so far.

After lunch we walked up the block to the St. Francis of Assisi Basilica. The churches are all similar in architectural style, but vary greatly in size. They range from chapel size to cathedral size, but on the inside they are quite individual. This one looked every bit like a European Cathedral... French Romanesque arches, flying buttresses, rose windows. The difference was the color... instead of the aged natural wood and stone tones, the interiors of the churches in this area are brightly painted. Whether it is the tile work, or icons, or columns, primary colors prevail. This Basilica was particularly colorful. Tours of the premises are given by dedicated volunteers.

Across the street from the Basilica was the Institute of American Indian Arts Museum... beautiful building. We didn't go in, this time. Instead, we walked around the block and back toward the plaza and then decided it was time to find the Georgia O'Keefe museum. Consulting the map in our visitor's guide we walked the few blocks to the location indicated... but the museum wasn't there. There was an interesting house on site, and it was an art gallery, but not Georgia O'Keefe's.

We went inside to inquire. It turns out, the map was incorrect… if we had looked further in the guide to find the written street address, we would have been better informed and found it. Oh well. We had a lovely conversation with the woman in the gallery. She gave us the correct directions and we headed off to the next block. When we got there, we found that the O'Keefe museum was closed to allow for the mounting of the new exhibit. So, after spending a few minutes in the gift shop we returned to the previous gallery. They had room after room of lovely artwork.

Janet likes to collect pins of state flags when she visits a new state. We backtracked looking in shop after shop and although we saw many beautiful things, no one had a state flag pin. It was finally suggested that she might find what she wanted at the 5 & 10.

Just across the plaza was an honest to goodness "Five and Dime" and they did have the state pin that she was looking for. Who knew? Right next door was an ice cream parlor… oh yes, Hagen Daz. Just what the doctor ordered on a hot day in Santa Fe.

We window shopped a bit more before heading for the car and the trip back to Taos. In this last mall we found one more potty, and Janet found the silver chain she had been looking for to hold a brooch/pendant she had purchased in Crete. The brooch was a copy of a museum piece from ancient Greece representing two honey bees on a flower. It was just begging for a matching silver chain.

We left Santa Fe just before rush hour and, still satisfied from the large lunch, agreed we would wait to have dinner in Taos. Arriving in Taos, we went to Cid's market to buy sushi and dolmades (Greek grapeleaves) and wine for supper. (Are we international, or what?)

Very satisfied, we turned in early. It had been an abundant day.

When we first arrived at the hotel and looked about the rooms, we found, through French doors off of the living room, we had a balcony. It was small… only large enough for the petite patio table and two chairs provided. To the left of the balcony was a large conifer tree. While we were enjoying the view of the back parking lot… and the mountains beyond… from the balcony, we became aware of two black and white birds flying close-by in a rather agitated state. Hmmm… could there be a nest in this tree? Is it theirs? Could there be young in it?

We examined the tree quite closely and found that there, indeed, was a nest… a rather large, deep nest near the top of the tree… quite well hidden. We retreated into the unit and agreed that we would not frequent the balcony... even for wine on a lovely evening... so we would not stress the parents.

We weren't sure just what kind of birds they were. I mentioned that Magpies were that color, but I thought they were a tropical bird and not found this far north. We asked about and found that, in fact, they were Magpies and they were abundant in the area. Pretty birds.

Every morning, we watched the nest from my bedroom window... good view through the slats of the wooden blinds. They never knew we were watching. Yes, there were young. Couldn't ascertain how many. The parents made many trips to the nest with food. We were sure there must be at least two.

One morning, I saw a black and white, fluffy, chick on the edge of the nest waiting for mom to bring food. It was a rather large bird for a baby. Janet thought it must be a fledgling about to make its maiden flight.

The chicks were elusive, yet curious about the world beyond the nest. We watched them every morning, yet still couldn't tell how many there were. The nest was quite deep. As the week went on, we saw the chicks more often. They became an integral interest in our vacation week.

Friday morning I awoke at my usual early EDT hour. Janet was still asleep in the next room. I made coffee, and checked the nest. One of the chicks was poised on the edge of the nest looking about. Janet had mentioned that they looked ready to fly... maybe this was to be the day.

I poured a cup of coffee and settled in to watch the current golf tournament (remember, a two hour time difference.) About fifteen minutes went by when I became aware of a cacophony of bird screams outside my window. I went to investigate.

On the branch closest to me was a crow. On the branches beyond him were the screaming parents. On the rim of the nest was the limp body of the baby bird. The parents were trying their best to chase away the crow, but were having no luck. I watched for a minute or two trying to wrap my foggy mind around what I thought I was seeing... watching the limp, feathery lump hoping it would move... and then, said, rather loudly, "NO! NO! NO!"

I ran to Janet's room. "Janet! Are you awake? You must come see this!" (I clearly wanted someone else to share this tragedy with me.) "I think we are watching a murder."

Well, you can imagine! She was out of that bed and into my room before I could tell her it did not involve humans. It was, nevertheless, still very heartbreaking. I was angry and sad at the same time.

The parents finally flew at the crow enough that he moved on. They, then, set about the task of assessing the situation at the nest. One adult (I would guess it was the mother) lifted the lifeless body and flew with it to the ground. It was a heavy burden. It took her at least three attempts to carry the fallen fledgling to the far side of the parking lot and out of harm's way.

She then returned to the tree and began coaxing the next chick to the edge of the nest. It popped up, looked around, and at the mother's insistence, hopped out of the nest onto the tree branch. My, that's a long way down!

Mother then flew across the parking lot to a tree on the far side. She called to the fledgling from the far branches. Father encouraged it from the tree. In, what seemed to be a very short time for a bird who had never been out of the nest, it flexed its feathers and stepped off into the air. It flew almost to the far side and landed upright on the edge of the parking lot.

Now, the next fledgling appeared on the side of the nest... hmmmm, there were three. Mother flew in, gave words of instruction and encouragement, flew back and beckoned. Father stayed close and cheered it on. Soon, that chick also ventured out onto the limb, tried its wings, found them to be in good working order and took the leap of faith into the world. This one, too, made it almost to the far side, but it landed with a face plant on the dirt surface of the parking lot.

Mother, now happy that her chicks were with her, flew to the fallen chick. She tried frantically to revive it. She moved it to higher ground. Father flew from the tree to supervise the two chicks who were practicing this new ability called "flight".

Then, surprise! One more chick appeared at the edge of the nest. This one was smaller than the others. It did not seem as confident. Perhaps it had hatched a day later. Mother flew to its side. She gave it the same pep talk she had given the others, but this one was in no hurry to leave the nest. He stayed close to the trunk of the tree.

Father flew in. Mother flew away... "Like this. It is easy. Just flap your wings like this." She seemed to say. Father flew away... "We all fly. You can, too. Like this."

Mother and Father flew to the tree and flew away... several times in several directions, so the chick could see that it worked every time. The mother returned to stand next to the chick and chatter words of encouragement, if not insistence. Again, she flew to the far side. The chick moved away from the treetrunk to the branch. It worked its way out to the edge... here we go... nope. It turned its back to the world and carefully walked all the way back to the tree trunk.

Mother returned – chattering all the way... "You must fly! We must leave this place! It is no longer safe! Come with me!" But the baby bird did not budge.

We watched this for about an hour. Our fear was that the crow would return.

The two older chicks were having a grand time flying up to the fence top, then down to the surface of the parking lot. While I had been concentrating on the baby bird in the tree from my window, Janet had been watching the older two from her French Door. "There is a problem." She said.

The little birds had gotten themselves into the backyard next door, behind a wooden structure and didn't seem to be able to figure out how to get free.

"The problem is" said Janet "there is a cat in that yard watching with great interest."

OH NO! I don't think I can take any more deaths. Father and mother still took turns trying to revive the first chick. They had four to start with. One has been killed by a predator bird. One is refusing to leave the tree... will the crow get that one, too? Now, a curious cat has entered the picture.

Father is trying to tutor the frightened chicks in the yard behind the wooden well. Mother is still returning to the tree for the last reluctant chick. Such angst! Such ado! Such drama!

I needed more coffee. Then, of course, I needed a bathroom. When I came out, I saw that the final fledgling in the tree was gone. Now, for the chicks incarcerated in the yard with the cat...

Janet said the man who lived in the house with the wooden well in his yard, heard the frantic fussing and came outside. Quickly assessing the situation, he lifted the interned chicks, one by one, from behind the structure and put them on the top of the fence where they were safe and could fly away. Then, he took the inscrutable cat into the house. Whew!

The feathered family flew away. ... somewhere safe, we hope. Mother came back to the tree one more time... I am sure to count noses... she was missing one. We never saw them again. She put the fallen fledgling somewhere out of sight. The last and littlest chick in the tree was with the family... we think and we hope... we both missed that part. Soberly, we went forth into the day wanting the best for them.

I was still angry and grieving over the murder of Malcolm Magpie. (In his untimely death, he needed to be named.) Whenever we saw a black bird... crow, raven, or whatever... I said, "I am not happy with black birds, today. Don't mention black birds to me, today."

Janet has worked more with animals and volunteered at zoos. She took this much better than I did. I felt a closeness to that feathered family outside my window and I was sad and angry at nature.

We took the rest of the morning to do laundry and get semi-ready to leave the next day. Just before noon, we hopped into the HHR and headed across the mountain for Angel Fire for lunch. I was looking forward to thinking about something less mournful.

Angel Fire is a town with a ski resort located on the Enchanted Circle. The Enchanted Circle is a route that loops south to east to north to west through and across the Sangre de Cristo Mountains past several ski resort towns and back south to Taos. It is unquestionably picturesque country. Each area has its own beauty and personality. When we return, we will have to spend more time in each town to fully appreciate its character.

The leg to Angel Fire is about an hour's drive through the Carson National Forest. Winding mountain roads twist along babbling brooks and rugged ridges. Just about the time you wonder if you are ever going to see civilization again, it opens up on a high plateau. Turn right on the open plain and you are in the town of Angel Fire.

"Hutch's" restaurant had been recommended by hotel staff who live in Angel Fire. Hatcha's restaurant was the first one we came to and we decided it was close enough... lot's of cars in the parking lot meant good food... AND... we could see no other restaurant signs closeby.

Well, the food was scrumptious... home cooked goodness. I had a t'riffic chicken burrito and a vegetable dish with a Spanish name that turned out to be corn and black beans and zucchini... very tasty. Will have to try that recipe at home. (Still haven't had black beans as good as the Anasazi black beans at Encantado, though.) AND sopapillas for dessert... with honey. ☺

After lunch we poked about the ski resort just to see what it was like... small, by western standards, but had a Zugspitz-sized tram to carry skiers to the top, which might indicate that there was much more on the back side of the mountain... hmmmm.

After a few commemorative photos, we continued the circle journey -- past Eagle's nest, on to Red River. Now that ski mountain rises up from the center of town... no wide open spaces, here. I would like to go back to Red River just to see all the secrets that lie in this tiny tourist town. Then it was west to Questa and back south to Taos to complete the circle.

Friday night, we finished cleaning out the fridge... interesting supper of leftovers... hummus, chips, Chex Mix, and wine. Took last minute inventory in preparation to travel the next day and got a good night's sleep.

Saturday morning, we were up and out by 8:30. ... a surprise to both of us. Our next destination was Albuquerque and the revered Chaco Canyon. We decided to take the "High Road to Taos" south... after all, we had all day. It was pretty. It took us to the small towns beyond the main routes. Almost to Chimayo, we took state route 503. It was a marked state route, but it was small... and kept getting smaller. I said,"if this turns into a dirt road, I think we should go back". The yellow line disappeared, but the road stayed paved. We twisted and turned and saw some very private scenery. The road finally went between someone's house and barn (just like in Europe) and then widened out and the yellow line reappeared. Hmmm. Interesting route... and it is on the map.

At Espaniola, we caught the main route south and then 599 (the relief road) around Santa Fe. I never did see the sign to Encantado, again... I think it was our Brigadoon.

We arrived in Albuquerque about 11:30... just in time to park in Olde Towne and catch lunch at La Hacienda (first restaurant on the plaza). Another great chicken burrito... but, this time we had to eat the whole thing since we weren't sure the hotel room had a fridge. Oh, evil indigestion.

After lunch, we walked the old plaza square in Albuquerque. It had very interesting buildings, shops, and more restaurants, live music on the plaza... and, of course, a church. About 2:00 we bought tall, cool, homemade lemonades and climbed aboard the trolley for a tour of the city.

The Trolley Tour was owned and run by two young men who had graduated from the University of NM in Albuquerque. They had it together. They knew the history of their town and of their state... and they had a great sense of humor.

The tour lasted 75 fun-filled minutes (but who's counting?) and took us throughout the town... Country Club, Nob Hill, Downtown, University, the zoo... very interesting town. Much of the original Route 66 is still intact and being used... the vintage buildings along the way are amazing.

Albuquerque is often being used as a set for many modern movies... much less expensive than NYC or LA., but has all the amenities. We also went past the home of "Outrageous Architect" Bart Prince... ultra modern to say the least. It looks more like the set for the Jetson's, or a UFO that missed Las Alamos. No Pueblo Revival, here.

Full circle brought us back to the Olde Towne Plaza. When we left the trolley, we made two calls... one to our hotel to get directions, and one to Chaco Canyon to learn the best approach from Albuquerque for our trip on Sunday. One more potty stop, one more gift shop, through the church on the plaza (very quick stop—vespers were in session), one small detour to the smallest church in town... two tiny rooms, located in an intimate inner courtyard... and we were on our way to the hotel.

We checked in, found our room (the toilet was still running since ? ? ?) called the front desk to report it, made sure it had stopped, and then went to dinner. We had seen an Applebees and a Fuddruckers both within walking distance. We opted for Fuddruckers. Janet had a Bison Burger and I had my first Dogzilla... a ginormous hot dog smothered in chili and cheese and beaucoup goodies from the garnish bar. Oh yes, and a Sam Adams to wash it down. Life is definitely good.

After eating all that food, it was beneficial to our health that we were walking. When we got back to the hotel, the front desk said they had checked the toilet and it was alright. We unpacked and turned in. Tomorrow was going to be such a day!

How do you define rapture? The day has finally arrived for me to go to Chaco Canyon. I have been looking forward to this since visiting Chimney Rock... located between Durango and Pagosa Springs, Colorado... in 2007. According to accounts presented from Chimney Rock and Mesa Verde (2008), Chaco Canyon was where it all began, more than 1500 years ago. Many of the modern Puebloan tribes are descended from those who were active in Chaco Canyon.

I say, "active" because they are still exploring and debating whether these Ancient Ones lived there, or governed there, or worshiped there, or marketed there, or celebrated there, or all of the above. As more study is done and more data is interpreted, opinions change on this topic.

I was drawn by the astronomical connection (archeoastronomy) between Chimney Rock, Mesa Verde, Aztec Ruins, Salmon Ruins, and other "outlier" pueblos. This was, perhaps, my only disappointment in this year's visit. Although scholars acknowledge the existence of coinciding practices, they are reluctant to say that the astronomical alignment and lunar and solar-friendly constructions between sites was any more than that – coincidence-- and not a purposeful or meaningful, interrelated plan.

The trip was, nevertheless, fulfilling for me and I will plan to return for more virtual connection to our own pre-Colombian civilization.

But, I get WAY ahead of myself. We arose early enough, had a substantial breakfast at the hotel, grabbed a couple of oranges to go and were on our way 8-ish. We wore sun hats, sun screen, long pants, and hiking boots. We packed snacks and the remaining bottles of water and headed out for the 3 hour trip to Chaco Canyon.

We had been advised to travel up Rte 550 (which, by the way, goes all the way to Durango and north), past Cuba (the town, not the island) and between Lybrook and Nageezi we would see a large sign directing us to the site.

The topography was breathtaking... very prehistoric looking... whole areas of geological epics if we only knew how to read the signs and striae. Cuba was a small town two hours out, but it had public bathrooms so we stopped. It was not far from Cuba that the map indicated the existence of the smaller town of Counselor, then, just a few more miles on, Lybrook. If there are actual towns of that name, we did not see them from the highway. But then, shortly, sure enough a large sign with a big arrow pointing to the west indicated that Chaco Canyon, in fact, did exist.

We turned left from the smooth 4-lane highway to a small two lane road with little shoulder and much open space—Route 7900. We saw scattered horses and cows grazing on the open range... now and then a residence. The circular buildings raised the question... were these Hogans? Navajo homes?

We kept driving. Soon enough, we came to the road sign Route 7990. We turned right. Except for the direction, nothing else changed. The road was still narrow, the countryside still open... wait... we just left the paved road. So, this will be the 16 miles of unimproved road that was mentioned in the literature.

Now, I was raised with unimproved roads. When my parents built our home on the back acreage of my grandfather's farm, it was on a small, dirt, farm road. When, as teenagers, we rode our horses up over the mountain to the next town and circled back to be home for supper, it was all on unimproved state forest roads. As adults, we visited New England byways accessible only by unimproved roads ... but, I cannot say I had ever seen roads such as these. They were actually pretty wide, and pretty hard surfaced (except, I am told, when it rained... occasionally), and pretty well scraped. BUT, for a stretch of about 5 miles it was the roughest washboard surface I think I have ever encountered. It shook the car enough to shake lose the fillings in our teeth and the change in our watch pockets and challenge the most intrepid shock absorbers. I was sure we would lose, at the very least, the hubcaps. (And how would we explain that to the rental car agency?) We had to slow down to about 5 mph or plane sideways — and, not wanting to land in a rose-dusty ditch, we slowed down. So, *that* is the last hour of travel time — not the distance, but the speed.

Then, in the middle of nowhere, there was the sign... **Chaco Culture**

National Historical Park. We reencountered a paved surface and traveled forward for another few miles… nothing in view except a huge butte to the left and a related mesa to the right. We drove the hem of the mesa until we had passed between them. Only then did we see any signs of humankind. The first area we passed was called the Campground. It looked pretty primitive, but the sign indicated it had no vacancies. A few vehicles could be seen, but we guessed that most folks were somewhere else in the canyon and would return by nightfall.

Further down the road we saw more vehicles… they seemed to be grouped together… perhaps in a parking area? A small sign indicated that we should turn in here, park, and register.

Now, at most National Park sites there is an entrance gate with a ranger in the gate house collecting admissions and giving directions… not here. We parked in the paved area and followed the signs (and the other folks) to what looked, for all intents and purposes, like a Tibetan Yert. We climbed the wide wooden steps to the wooden deck that surrounded the small round building. Inside was one large, open room with a counter on the right, behind which stood the ranger that collected admissions and gave directions.

We asked if there was food on site. He didn't laugh, but did point out the vending machines and the granola treats amongst the souvenirs in the gift shop area… just in front of the book department. We quickly got the message… no cheeseburgers, here. We bought granola bars, new bottles of room temperature water, and a couple of books that, we hoped, would serve us well as tomes of information about the day we were about to experience.

We learned we were to meet at the parking area of Pueblo Bonito at 2:00 PM for the 90 minute tour; there were rest rooms here at the center; there was also one small great house just up the path from the rest rooms, if we wanted to go there.

We put everything in the car, grabbed our sunhats, and headed for the restrooms… the next time might be a mesquite bush. These were actually permanent structures… with running water, TP and hand towel dispensers. We were grateful.

When we left the loo, we followed the signs to Una Vida, the first of many great houses in Chaco Canyon. A great house (according to *The Chaco Handbook – and Encyclopedic Guide* by R. Gwinn Vivian and Bruce Hilpert … great reading, by the way) is the replacement of an ancient word that means "Town". It is calculated that Una Vida was built circa 850 AD, which makes it among the first in time as well as proximity. Our journey had begun.

It was only a short distance to the first ruin. We enjoyed it with all the fervor of Columbus discovering America.

We took pictures, climbed the paths, followed the signs obediently. The sun was hot. It was almost noon, so there were no shadows or shade near the age-old walls. Just past the first Kiva ruin, there was a sign that said PETROGLYPHS. We looked up at the long, rising path to the high mesa wall of sandstone… "Where?" Janet decided she would explore. I decided to decline. I found 12 inches of shade beside a 10 foot wall and retreated from the sun and the heat… camera at the ready.

An older man and his daughter came down from the cliffs and stood with me in the shade for a few minutes.

"How are they?" I asked, meaning the petroglyphs.

"Hard to see." He said. "They are faint and in the shade. I hope the pictures I took come out."

Secretly, I was reaffirmed that I had made the right decision to stay behind. At first, we thought they were only halfway up the steep, rocky climb, but this man told Janet that they were clear at the top. Ooof.

I watched as she followed her commitment to reach the prize. When she reached the top she turned and waved. I returned the wave, but she looked like a speck against the vastness of the sandstone wall. It was then that I learned that my camera will zoom in, and then zoom in again, and then zoom in one more time. The photos I took of Janet are probably at least one quarter mile away. She stayed what seemed to be quite a while (the sun was getting hotter). Then she started down.

When you were a kid, did you ever climb way high in a tall tree… just because. It wasn't the climb up… reaching the next branch, first with your hands and then with your feet following… it was the getting down. Where did I put my feet coming up? Where can I get a good hold with my hands? Janet was on her way down. I watched each step as she picked her way down among the rocks and pebbles… testing to be sure they would not slip from under her. I thought for a while, she might even sit down and scoot her way to the bottom… but champion that she is, she stayed upright.

I thought, if she fell, what should I do first? We had left purses and cell phones in the car. I would run as fast as I could back to the Yert to alert the ranger. Would he do anything? Are we entirely at our own risk here?

Thankfully, she did not fall. She made it all the way back without even a slip of the foot on the loose stones. She joined me in the shrinking shade.

"Well, how are they?" I asked.

"Hard to see." She said. "They are faint and in the shade. I hope my pictures come out."

We finished the tour and headed back to the restrooms and the car to prepare for the next part of the day. (Do we visit restrooms a lot? We are both 70 years old. It is allowed.)

In the car, we continued on the route to the next parking area. This ruin was larger than the first. The sign said, HUNGO PAVI. We had time, so we went to explore ruin number II.

It is the construction that is so fascinating. I had seen it (and photographed it) at Salmon Ruins in '07. The inner core is quite wide and quite crude... larger stones held together with a clay mortar. The outsides are more refined... a veneer of smaller, fashioned stones and rocks placed together very tightly with no mortar. Over all of this was a coating of stucco or adobe which has disappeared over time. All of these buildings had, at one time, looked just like the adobe structures we see today in Pueblo Revival architecture.

We moved on. When we arrived at the parking lot for Pueblo Bonito it was about 1:20. To the right was another, fairly large great house, Chetro Ketl. Did we want to see this one, too? How long would it take? How large was it, really? We opted for lunch in the cool car and rest before the long, hot tour of Pueblo Bonito. The oranges that I had overlooked at breakfast tasted really good at lunch. Our Chex Mix was tasty and the granola bars were filling. We drank more water from the new bottles and felt fortified for the afternoon.

Just before the tour at 2:00, I visited the nearby convenience stop... no running water... just a "long drop" and hand sanitizer... but, it was a permanent building... with shade.

The crowd gathered in the parking area. The Ranger arrived. We were ready for the tour.

What can I tell you about Pueblo Bonito? Entire libraries have been written about the assorted significances of this place... this ancient village. For me, it was the ability to trod the sod of those who created an intelligent, talented, hardy civilization here on our soil before the western written word. That was enough. It was 90 minutes of touching another world... an earlier world from which we have all descended... whether native American or import.

I learned many things that I did not know before coming, and I will still have unanswered questions after leaving, but that is the stuff that keeps us searching. I did see the sign that said "Wetherill Cemetery." When I asked which Wetherill? I was told it was Richard and his wife, Marietta. Hmmmm... more research. Was this Bill's Grandfather? Great Uncle? I had thought they were from Arizona. Didn't know about this tie to Chaco Canyon... only Mesa Verde. Oh, well... that all took place way before state lines.

At the end of the tour, I asked our ranger about the astronomical interconnectedness of the canyon with its outlying communities. Although his background was astronomy, he, also would not make any conclusive statements... my only disappointment. I will keep reading and searching and when I return, I will ask the question again, if it is still relevant.

Although each of these separate pueblos is made up of many buildings and apartments and kivas, and often are enclosed within a high wall, in the historic vernacular they are now collectively called "Great Houses."

Across the wash on the south side of the canyon are a series of "Small Houses" a group of individual houses or buildings not connected within a wall.

When we were through with our tour, we were too spent to explore any more houses today—great or small.

We were sunburned, tired, hungry, and still had a three hour drive back to Albuquerque over some very crude roads. We slowly walked to the car way back in the parking lot... our hearts really wanted to stay longer, but reason moved our feet. We reached the car, started the motor for the AC, drank the rest of the water (rather warm by now), changed from our hiking boots to sandals (feet said, "Ah, yes. Thank you.") threw the sunhats in the back seat, fluffed our sweat-dampened hair and started out. There was a long line at the nearest "Long Drop" so we drove to the other side of the canyon where one had no lines.

Refreshed, we wound our way back to the beginning... the visitor's center, then the majestic Fajada Butte, (on the way out, we know its name) then the washboard road, then the route 7900 and finally the main route 550. We decided to stop at the first restaurant, wherever it was and whatever it served. We surmised that it probably would be in Cuba... about an hour away.

As we rounded the curve into Cuba, I turned into the first parking lot of the first restaurant we came to... El Bruno's. We were hoping for a hot dog stand, or a mom and pop café. Tacos... anything. Instead, we encountered a delightful surprise!

It was a rambling layout with many hacienda style rooms. The floors were cool stone tiles, the furniture was large and sturdy and comfortable.

The waiter wore a very large smile, spoke with a Spanish accent, and was eager to please. He was disappointed when we turned down his offer of their signature Margueritas, but we explained that we were traveling. (I also wanted all my faculties when we turned in the car at the airport tonight... some seemed to be missing already.)

I finally selected trout, encrusted with pinon nuts, and fried spinach... yup. Who knew spinach could be fried... and a tall water with ice and lemon. The food was delicioso! The spinach must have been flash fried... it was still bright green and crisp and dissolved on the tongue. The fish tasted right out of the nearby stream. So Fresh! So Sweet! So Good!

Although fully sated, we had to finish this excellent meal with Flan. It was superb! It came with a drizzle of butterscotch couli decorating the dish, and then another lacing of aged, thick, Balsamic vinegar... OMG! I could feel all my faculties contentedly returning. ☺

The best part was the tab... no $110 here. We left an appreciative tip and headed for Albuquerque.

When we picked up the car, I had agreed to let them fill the tank at $3. 26 per gallon... on the street, the best we ever found was $3. 64 in Taos. The price was $58 for a full tank... no credit for gas in the tank when it was turned in. We calculated that we got 30 miles to the gallon and had plenty to reach the rental car return. (What we forgot, was that we were now using the AC... Didn't know how that fit into the equation.) Well, we watched the tank and the miles. As we got quite close, but still on the highway, the bell dinged a warning at us. The arrow was on the red, *empty* indicator. As we exited the highway at Gibson, the readout on the dash said LOW FUEL. Now, I was new to this car, so I had no idea what all this meant, quantitatively... did we have enough fumes to coast into the lot?

Well, we made it. I parked and turned off the motor. The check-in girl appeared with her hand held computer... our calculations for cost were only $7. 50 off. (She said it must be taxes.) I reluctantly, but quickly, accepted her numbers, handed her the keys, got on the shuttle to the airport and hoped we would soon be long gone, in case the car did not restart for her.

At the airport, we went to the transportation counter and made arrangements to be taken to the hotel. We had great plans to soak our aged muscles in the hot tub and swim a few laps before collapsing for the night. I had a very early flight in the morning.

When we got to the hotel, we were greeted with a great big smile and the news... "We will have to move you to another room. The toilet in your room broke. None of your belongings got wet." Oh Joy!!

So, we didn't get to the pool. We didn't get to the hot tub. We packed up all our schtuff and moved one room down and while we were at it, packed for the next morning. We took hot showers, polished off the last of the wine, cranked up the AC and settled in. Ironically enough, the movie for the evening was "The Bucket List." What could be more appropriate? We enjoyed watching what must become a classic before turning off the lights.

For early Monday morning, I had left a 5:45 AM wake-up call, but I was up before it rang. I was to catch the 6:30 AM shuttle from the hotel for an 8:30 flight. Janet did not have to fly until almost noon. I tippy-toed around the room and made it out the door without waking her. After a breakfast of scrambled eggs and toast and coffee, I was ready to face the day.

All went smoothly getting to the airport and checking in. Again, it was open seating on the Southwest flight. Again, I was not in group A. (Have to learn how to do that.) I did get a middle seat fairly close to the front. The woman near the window was already asleep (how do they do that?) The woman on the aisle looked friendly. As it turned out, she lived in Albuquerque, worked for the state, and was going to Phoenix for a week-long conference. (Why was I going west to go east, you ask? – You've got me.)

She was delightful. We talked the entire 50 minutes in the air. She asked me where we had been and what I had liked. When I mentioned El Bruno in Cuba, she said many people who live in Albuquerque make the two hour trip just to eat there. YAHOO! We picked a good one!

Had a nice layover in Phoenix... did have another bite to eat, just because it would be suppertime by the time I landed in Columbus... time differences, you know... and I get snarly when I am hungry.

The second leg was uneventful. I don't even remember the details, anymore. Landed in Columbus on time, caught the shuttle to the hotel, picked up my car, and headed home. After a few stops for essentials at Sam's and a wonderful dinner of lamb chops at Feta Greek Kuzina, I arrived in Marietta about 10 PM. Yellow Tiger cat, Miffin was happy to see me. (Matronly Emily had left us in '07.) We spent some wind down time together and then headed for bed... my bed... snore. I am, once again, a happy camper and grateful for my timeshare.

Lynne Bodry Shuman Biography

Lynne Bodry Shuman was raised in New England. Her youngest years were spent relocating among Army bases with her parents, probably accounting for her love of travel. She now lives in Marietta, Ohio, an historic town on the Ohio River. Her grown children do not live close by. Her daughter, a theater professional, lives in Cleveland, Ohio, and her son, retired from the military, lives in New Port Richey, Florida… more reasons to travel.

After thirty years as a Not For Profit administrator, Lynne recently retired. Although she loved her work, she thought, at seventy years of age, it was time to play. After years of writing publications, brochures, commemorative programs, quarterly newsletters, and two award winning videos, she wanted to concentrate on gathering together some of the more interesting chapters of her life.

This book will take you on that journey.